SUPERCHURCH

- *Eisenhower's War of Words: Rhetoric and Leadership*, Martin J. Medhurst, editor
- *The Nuclear Freeze Campaign: Rhetoric and Foreign Policy in the Telepolitical Age*, J. Michael Hogan
- *Mansfield and Vietnam: A Study in Rhetorical Adaptation*, Gregory A. Olson
- *Truman and the Hiroshima Cult*, Robert P. Newman
- *Post-Realism: The Rhetorical Turn in International Relations*, Francis A. Beer and Robert Hariman, editors
- *Rhetoric and Political Culture in Nineteenth-Century America*, Thomas W. Benson, editor
- *Frederick Douglass: Freedom's Voice, 1818–1845*, Gregory P. Lampe
- *Angelina Grimké: Rhetoric, Identity, and the Radical Imagination*, Stephen Howard Browne
- *Strategic Deception: Rhetoric, Science, and Politics in Missile Defense Advocacy*, Gordon R. Mitchell
- *Rostow, Kennedy, and the Rhetoric of Foreign Aid*, Kimber Charles Pearce
- *Visions of Poverty: Welfare Policy and Political Imagination*, Robert Asen
- *General Eisenhower: Ideology and Discourse*, Ira Chernus
- *The Reconstruction Desegregation Debate: The Politics of Equality and the Rhetoric of Place, 1870–1875*, Kirt H. Wilson
- *Shared Land/Conflicting Identity: Trajectories of Israeli and Palestinian Symbol Use*, Robert C. Rowland and David A. Frank
- *Darwinism, Design, and Public Education*, John Angus Campbell and Stephen C. Meyer, editors
- *Religious Expression and the American Constitution*, Franklyn S. Haiman
- *Christianity and the Mass Media in America: Toward a Democratic Accommodation*, Quentin J. Schultze
- *Bending Spines: The Propagandas of Nazi Germany and the German Democratic Republic*, Randall L. Bytwerk
- *Malcolm X: Inventing Radical Judgment*, Robert E. Terrill
- *Metaphorical World Politics*, Francis A. Beer and Christ'l De Landtsheer, editors
- *The Lyceum and Public Culture in the Nineteenth-Century United States*, Angela G. Ray
- *The Political Style of Conspiracy: Chase, Sumner, and Lincoln*, Michael William Pfau
- *The Character of Justice: Rhetoric, Law, and Politics in the Supreme Court Confirmation Process*, Trevor Parry-Giles
- *Rhetorical Vectors of Memory in National and International Holocaust Trials*, Marouf A. Hasian Jr.
- *Judging the Supreme Court: Constructions of Motives in* Bush *v.* Gore, Clarke Rountree
- *Everyday Subversion: From Joking to Revolting in the German Democratic Republic*, Kerry Kathleen Riley
- *In the Wake of Violence: Image and Social Reform*, Cheryl R. Jorgensen-Earp
- *Rhetoric and Democracy: Pedagogical and Political Practices*, Todd F. McDorman and David M. Timmerman, editors
- *Invoking the Invisible Hand: Social Security and the Privatization Debates*, Robert Asen
- *With Faith in the Works of Words: The Beginnings of Reconciliation in South Africa, 1985–1995*, Erik Doxtader
- *Public Address and Moral Judgment: Critical Studies in Ethical Tensions*, Shawn J. Parry-Giles and Trevor Parry-Giles, editors
- *Executing Democracy: Capital Punishment and the Making of America, 1683–1807*, Stephen John Hartnett
- *Enemyship: Democracy and Counter-Revolution in the Early Republic*, Jeremy Engels
- *Spirits of the Cold War: Contesting Worldviews in the Classical Age of American Security Strategy*, Ned O'Gorman
- *Making the Case: Advocacy and Judgment in Public Argument*, Kathryn M. Olson, Michael William Pfau, Benjamin Ponder, and Kirt H. Wilson, editors
- *Executing Democracy: Capital Punishment and the Making of America, 1835–1843*, Stephen John Hartnett
- *William James and the Art of Popular Statement*, Paul Stob
- *On the Frontier of Science: An American Rhetoric of Exploration and Exploitation*, Leah Ceccarelli
- *The Good Neighbor: Franklin D. Roosevelt and the Rhetoric of American Power*, Mary E. Stuckey
- *Creating Conservatism: Postwar Words That Made an American Movement*, Michael J. Lee
- *Superchurch: The Rhetoric and Politics of American Fundamentalism*, Jonathan J. Edwards

Superchurch

The Rhetoric and Politics of American Fundamentalism

Jonathan J. Edwards

Michigan State University Press • East Lansing

♾ The paper used in this publication meets the minimum requirements of ANSI/NISO Z39.48-1992 (R 1997) (Permanence of Paper).

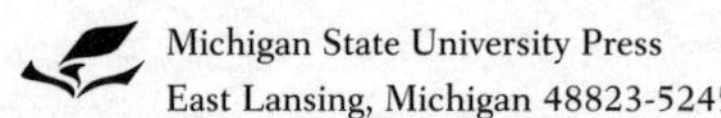
Michigan State University Press
East Lansing, Michigan 48823-5245

Printed and bound in the United States of America.

21 20 19 18 17 16 15 1 2 3 4 5 6 7 8 9 10

Library of Congress Control Number: 2014949057

ISBN: 978-1-61186-159-4 (cloth)
ISBN: 978-1-60917-447-7 (ebook: PDF)
ISBN: 978-1-62895-170-7 (ebook: ePub)
ISBN: 978-1-62896-170-6 (Kindle)

Book design by Charlie Sharp, Sharp Des!gns, Lansing, Michigan
Cover design by Erin Kirk New
Cover image is ©Jennifer Pitiquen, Dreamstime.com

green press INITIATIVE Michigan State University Press is a member of the Green Press Initiative and is committed to developing and encouraging ecologically responsible publishing practices. For more information about the Green Press Initiative and the use of recycled paper in book publishing, please visit www.greenpressinitiative.org.

Visit Michigan State University Press at www.msupress.org

Contents

⌘

Acknowledgments

⌘

I must begin by thanking the faculty and students at Northwestern University and the University of South Carolina for helping to make the last decade of my life wonderfully rich and full. I have been privileged to be part of such amazing intellectual communities. This book began as a dissertation, and my first thanks go to the members of my dissertation committee. The late Ernesto Laclau expanded my intellectual vision and my perceptions of what generosity, humor, and scholarship can and should be. Dilip Gaonkar has consistently pushed me to ask bigger questions. David Zarefsky opened the doors of rhetorical history and public address scholarship. Finally, Robert Hariman offered insightful critiques throughout the evolution of this project, and he has consistently motivated me to take my research and my writing to the next level. Among my fellow graduate students at Northwestern University, special thanks must go to Tim Barouch, Randy Iden, Brandon Inabinet, Kate Johnston, Kim Singletary, and Sara VanderHaagen who have all read and responded to various portions of the text. At the University of South Carolina, Erik Doxtader has been a thoughtful colleague and mentor, and I am grateful for his advice, suggestions, and support.

At Michigan State University Press, series editor Martin J. Medhurst has been instrumental in guiding the manuscript through the review and acquisitions process. I want to thank Kristine M. Blakeslee, Bonnie Cobb, Travis Kimbel, Julie Loehr, Annette Tanner, Anastasia Wraight, and everyone else at the press who worked to bring this book to publication. Frank Beckwith, Denise M. Bostdorff, and G. Thomas Goodnight offered critical and insightful reviews of the manuscript. Sherry L. Smith provided indexing services. Finally, a portion of chapter 3 was previously published in the journal *Rhetoric and Public Affairs*, and I am grateful to the Michigan State University Press journals division for allowing it to be reprinted here.

This book could not exist without the generous assistance of many librarians, archivists, and support staff. In particular, I want to acknowledge the staff of the Northwestern University Library, the United Library at Garrett-Evangelical Theological Seminary, and the Thomas Cooper Library at the University of South Carolina who graciously tolerated my continual questions and requests for obscure Fundamentalist books and pamphlets. The Billy Graham Center at Wheaton College provided critical texts from William Bell Riley and other early twentieth-century Fundamentalists, and the third chapter of this volume owes much to the generosity of their archivists and staff. Finally, thanks are owed to the churches that I visited during my time working on this project, including the Moody Church, the First United Methodist Church in the Chicago Temple Building, the First Baptist Church of Hammond, Indiana, and the Willow Creek Community Church campuses at South Barrington and the North Shore.

Without the support of my family, none of this would have been possible. My parents, Phil and Barb Edwards, have consistently modeled a humbling work ethic and encouraged me to ask questions. Perhaps most importantly, they created a home full of books and offered me regular trips to the public library to get more. I want to thank my siblings—David, Joel, and Ellen—for their encouragement and for not taking any of this too seriously. Finally, I am deeply grateful to my wife, Tiffany Beverly, who devoted hours of her own time to reading drafts, kept me going when I most needed the encouragement, and kept believing that I would publish when I believed she was crazy. She is my home, my best friend, and my partner, and to her this work is dedicated.

Introduction

⌘

Christian Fundamentalism is an undeniable facet of public and political life in the United States.[1] Yet its status within the public sphere remains an ongoing source of confusion and frustration for political theorists, pundits, and ordinary citizens. Seemingly out of nowhere, Fundamentalist believers rose up in the late 1970s to transform the American political and social landscape. Pastors have joined with media personalities and conservative politicians to advocate against defense-spending cuts, gun-control legislation, abortion, and feminism. Fundamentalist perspectives dominate debates over welfare reform, rights for same-sex couples, and education standards in the public schools. Questions abound: What motivates Fundamentalist politics? How is political engagement justified in the face of apocalyptic narratives that seem to negate the efficacy of human action? What exactly are they fighting, and what are they fighting for?

These questions cannot be adequately answered unless we take seriously that Fundamentalism is, at its essence, a church movement. By this I mean not that Fundamentalism is wholly contained within a particular institution or denomination, but that Fundamentalist political concerns are intimately intertwined with concerns about the survival and status of the Fundamentalist church. Conversely, the church is the center of the Fundamentalist political landscape. Any responsible attempt to understand the political reasoning of Fundamentalist believers cannot ignore their ecclesiastical commitments. Aside from the call to personal conversion, no demand is more significant upon believers than that of joining, contributing to, and participating in a local, "Bible-believing" church. No religious or political activity receives more time and dedication. No institution has more influence. The church addresses believers as a public community, calling them to speak and act as members of "the body of Christ" in the world, enforcing the bonds between sacred and secular demands.

In this book, I explore the tensions between these demands within Fundamentalist rhetoric. I demonstrate how rhetorical discourse about the church influences political identity and public action among Fundamentalist communities. By rhetoric, I mean simply the use of language and symbols to persuade popular audiences. Studies of rhetoric and of Christian speech have a long and complex association with one another. From Augustine to Luther, Jonathan Edwards to Jerry Falwell, a rhetorical perspective has been critical to the extension of doctrine and the constitution of Christian communities.[2] In the chapters that follow, rhetorical analysis functions as a diagnostic tool for exploring the relationship between Fundamentalist language, identity, and politics. Expanding on previous work that situates Fundamentalism within broad historical and social movements, I closely consider a representative series of Fundamentalist sermons, films, and other narratives in order to reconstruct stories of the Fundamentalist church and its relationship to public speech and action, drawing links between the doctrinal and political commitments of Fundamentalist communities. The goal is to better understand the processes through which a set of private religious interests came to be invested with public significance and the demand for public speech over the course of the twentieth century. This will enhance our understanding not only of Fundamentalist communities and politics but also of the processes by which publics generally come to be constituted as such.

There has, of course, been excellent rhetorical work on sermons and other religious messages, and on the ways in which religious language influences political speech. Additionally, there have been a large number of studies, particularly in the social sciences, that analyze the structural and social elements of particular churches. Yet there has been too little work that explicitly considers the significant rhetorical role that churches play in historical and contemporary Fundamentalist rhetoric—both as symbolic elements within religious discourse and as the physical spaces within which such discourse often occurs. Given the increasingly public role that religious structures play in national and global political disputes—from a Catholic church in Qatar to a Muslim community center in Manhattan—it behooves us as students and scholars of communication to look seriously into their role not merely as scenes of religious speech, but as constitutive elements of religious and political identity. Toward this end, the following study traces different historical lines of Fundamentalist speech through their situated relationships to a particular "public symbol"—the Fundamentalist church.[3]

The church is both a physical manifestation of influence and a powerful symbolic frame for defining and securing Fundamentalist identity in and against the unbelieving world. Fundamentalist narratives often portray the world as a dangerous place where, at any moment, a believer might be lured away: Materialism calls out from every billboard and street corner; rock music and pornography function like drugs, dragging unsuspecting victims into a descending spiral of debauchery, fornication, and even rape and murder. The public schools and secular universities encourage children to abandon God and embrace paganism, socialism, and sexual perversion. Women have abandoned their proper, submissive roles, turned away from their families, and adopted dress and behaviors designed to challenge male authority and elicit male lust. Science teaches that human life has no purpose and value. Doctors murder babies. Homosexuals threaten the traditional family and express their sin with more and more impunity—seeking new victims to satisfy their perverted desires. In the midst of these storms, the believing community—the church—is a place of safety: a place that, though embattled, offers the only earthly hope for protection and rescue from a culture and a world that has abandoned God.

Fundamentalism is a manifestation of the belief that, in a context of many beliefs and many churches, there can be a "true church," defined not by organizational (i.e., denominational) distinctions, but by common commitment to a set of definable norms for belief, practice, and communication. Fundamentalism is in this sense unquestionably modern. It is a particular response within modernity to a problem of modernity—the need to maintain associational commitments in the context of pluralism—organized around an idealization of the local church as representative of an invisible but effective public association. In chapter 1, I focus on the irresolvable but constitutively productive tensions that mark the relationship between Fundamentalism and the state in secular modernity. I explore contemporary theories of publics and counterpublics, explaining how these can better inform work on Fundamentalism, and how an exploration of Fundamentalist politics can, in turn, enrich our understanding of public discourse and the constitution of public identities. I then examine the contested identity of "fundamentalism" as a descriptive category, offering an overview of contemporary scholarship and an analysis of the inability of this scholarship to adequately explain and situate Fundamentalist political engagement.

Idealizations of the church as a place of safety from and engagement with the world are as old as Christianity itself, manifested in repeated battles over heresy and apostasy, but its particular modern form—in which fundamental truth coexists with, and to some degree operates within, pluralism—developed among revivalist communities in the mid-1800s. In chapter 2, I consider the origins of this idea and its effects on the origin and development of Fundamentalist rhetoric and politics. I begin with the emergence of revivalist rhetoric in the eighteenth century and then turn to an analysis of the work of American revivalist Charles Grandison Finney in the mid-nineteenth century. I argue that by linking revivalist demands with "jeremiadic" conceptions of covenantal community, Finney redefined religious revival as a basis for public action, expanded the role of churches as both religious and political institutions, and laid a foundation for modern Fundamentalist conceptions of ecclesiastical and political life.

I focus my analysis on Finney's *Lectures on Revivals of Religion*, which he delivered between 1834 and 1835 at the Chatham Street Chapel in New York City. Chatham was a unique religious institution at that time in American history—arguably the first revival church. Where other churches at the time prioritized denominational affiliation and relied on annual pew rentals for their income, Chatham prioritized strangers over regular members—offering a permanent stage to promote revival speech. Led by Finney—then the most famous northern revivalist—Chatham became a prominent symbol of religious and political contestation, particularly as a center of abolitionist activism and controversy in New York. I argue that the chapel's political activities were intertwined with its revivalist rhetoric, which championed public persuasion as a divine demand and reimagined the revival church as a public actor within the emerging pluralism of American religious disestablishment. In this context, Finney's *Lectures* offered believers a new revivalist and Fundamentalist framework for evaluating speech and practice in modernity.

Revivalism at once translates the interpretive and rhetorical perspectives of the Fundamentalist and imparts a demand upon the private believer to adopt a public voice, speaking persuasively to the unconverted. Yet, if Fundamentalists had remained merely occasional proselytizers, it is doubtful that they would generate much interest today. The fearful fascination of Fundamentalism is not the small-town preacher with an altar call, or even the big-city revival in a sports arena. It is the specter of a system, the threat of a Fundamentalist institution that so haunts the modern imagination. And while its extent and unity are often exaggerated, it is true that systematization and institutional organization are the primary features distinguishing contemporary Fundamentalism from its revivalist roots.[4] By this I mean that the mark of contemporary Fundamentalists is an understanding that, as a community, they are not just addressing strangers, but addressing an organized confederacy of strangers—a world system whose norms of speech and evidence are very differently from, and often antithetical to their own. Although revival remains the organizing feature of Fundamentalism, the ideal of face-to-face persuasion—speaking to sinners—is no longer the norm. Individual speech is, increasingly, institutionally framed. The revivalist does not merely struggle to persuade but even to be heard. And yet that individual voice remains the idealized locus of credibility and authenticity—if I could only meet you face to face, many of these Fundamentalist narratives imply, I could, I would, persuade you. If, as Kenneth Burke argues, the essence of rhetoric is "identification," the perceived dilemma for modern Fundamentalists is that the means for attaining identification are continually delayed or elided by institutional norms of public address that restrict and threaten Fundamentalist speech.[5] At the same time, Fundamentalism articulates a refusal to submit to silence and a commitment to fight for the power to speak publicly. The church is the central figure in these narratives of struggle and resistance. Among contemporary Fundamentalists, stories of local churches speaking freely and transformatively to local communities are contrasted with warnings of public suppression and political takeover from national, elitist organizations. Collective resistance is thus presented as necessary in order to protect the freedom of local churches to speak and act publicly.

In chapter 3, I explore the emergence of this collective discourse within the World's Christian Fundamentals Association of the 1920s and its effects on revivalism and the imagination of the Fundamentalist church. I begin by providing a brief history of the events leading up to the establishment of the World's Christian Fundamentals Association at the end of the First World War. Following this, I explore the emergence of Fundamentalism through a set of what I am calling "oppositional condensation symbols" or "countersymbols." Using articles published between 1919 and 1922 in one of the most influential early Fundamentalist periodicals, I argue that narratives justifying Fundamentalist organization relied upon the symbolic condensation of diverse opponents into a "superchurch confederacy," in response to which, it was argued, local Fundamentalist communities needed to band together in order to preserve the idealized freedom of the local church. In the work of early Fundamentalist leaders like William Bell Riley, "modernists" and "liberals" were depicted as bureaucratic oppressors who threatened the speech and freedom of local churches through manipulations of national, denominational hierarchies. In contrast, Fundamentalists were depicted as defenders of local churches and their pastors. This dichotomy between superchurch confederacy and Fundamentalist fellowship left no neutral place for casual observers, and translated the private doctrinal and ecclesiastical commitments of Fundamentalist believers into a divinely authorized demand for counterpublic association.

In the early 1920s, this demand primarily manifested as a call to recapture and reform the denominations from which the Fundamentalist movement's leaders had emerged, primarily those of the Northern Baptist and Northern Presbyterian conventions. Yet it soon became obvious, as Fundamentalist historian David Beale argues, that the denominations were "beyond salvaging."[6] Having lost repeated battles to redeem their denominational conventions, Fundamentalism gradually changed from an activist to a separatist movement, and believers were called upon to abandon outside attachments and relationships and embrace, as far as possible, the exclusive company of the faithful. From the 1930s on, separation has become a dominant feature of Fundamentalist doctrine, and any attempt to speak or act publicly has to be negotiated within or against the separatist demand.

In this book, I identify separation as a framing ideal rather than a description of an actually existing community. This is not to deny that communities exist for which militant separation is a dominant doctrinal commitment, but to the degree that separatist commitments overwhelm revivalist demands, such communities necessarily abandon public speech for security, and in the process they abandon the revivalist orientation that is a defining hallmark of Fundamentalist identity. Thus, pure separation—if indeed such a thing were possible—is ultimately irreconcilable with the historical commitments of Protestant Fundamentalism. As Camille Lewis has demonstrated, even the most apparently separatist of Fundamentalist communities maintain some orientation to those outside in an effort to attract unbelievers into the believing community.[7] Separation is an ideal that orients, rather than eliminates, Fundamentalist publicity. It marks a tension through which and against which Fundamentalist rhetoric and politics are formed, justified, and reimagined. The final three chapters focus on different responses to, and negotiations of, this tension between separation and speech within Fundamentalist discourses—from apocalyptic narratives that dramatize total, visible separation while imagining new forms of publicity, to evangelical megachurches that work to accommodate themselves to the norms of outsiders while maintaining a definable language of separation and special purpose. These negotiations reimagine the purpose and content of the church in the world, and the relationship between private belief and public action in Fundamentalist speech.

In chapter 4, I examine how this tension is mediated through the idealization of the local church in apocalyptic narratives. Using a popular series of premillennial "Rapture" films from the 1970s and 1980s, I argue that apocalyptic narratives—particularly fictional narratives—translate political and social categories into Fundamentalist terminology and reimagine the local church and believing community as political actors. Rather than prioritizing national association or denomination, as early Fundamentalist rhetoric did, late-century apocalyptic fiction encourages local churches to network with one another, utilizing flexible methods and modern technologies to establish responsive and adaptable believing communities that can broadcast speech while maintaining tight doctrinal control. Rather than being—as many have argued—merely escapist fantasies that discourage believers from engaging in politics, these narratives encourage public action by articulating a critical role for the church in world events, reorienting Fundamentalism to a clearly defined Other, and helping to establish a discursive framework bringing together the spiritual work of the Fundamentalist church—the revivalist community—and the political redemption of a pluralistic and secular world.

In chapter 5, I explore how this apocalyptic framework operates within the rhetoric of "neo-Fundamentalist" activism, and consider how idealizations of Fundamentalist community as a flexible network began to flip the narrative of the "superchurch" on its head, transforming fears of anti-Fundamentalist confederacy into justifications for "church growth," superaggressive evangelism, and ultimately the establishment of national political organizations like the Moral Majority in the late 1970s. A great deal has been written on the Moral Majority over the years, but I explore how the discourse of the emerging Christian Right participated in, and was influenced by, ongoing concerns about the status and influence of the Fundamentalist church in the world. Using a sermon delivered by Jerry Falwell in 1971 and widely distributed through the 1973 book *Capturing a Town for Christ*, I consider how Fundamentalists reimagined the language of the superchurch as a means for negotiating the ideals of local-church freedom and interchurch cooperation in order to achieve a delicate, paradoxical balance between a desire for cultural legitimacy and concerns about the need to maintain separation and purity from the world. When combined with apocalyptic idealizations of flexible, technologically sophisticated networks, the rhetoric of superaggressive church growth offered a spiritual justification and organizational structure from which national political organizations like the Moral Majority would eventually emerge. Falwell became the first representative of political Fundamentalism to the non-Fundamentalist nation in the late 1970s, and his work combined with that of other national Fundamentalist leaders reoriented the Fundamentalist approach to political action. By combining global, apocalyptic pessimism with local triumphalism, neo-Fundamentalist leaders created affective space for new forms of spiritually and politically conservative ecumenicity.

Falwell's neo-Fundamentalism ultimately alienated him from both the more separatist Fundamentalists (who argued that he had gone too far in abandoning separation) and the more accommodative evangelicals (who came to argue that he was too inflexible and embarrassing for national politics).[8] In chapter 6, I explore how these inter-Fundamentalist tensions between resistance and accommodation have manifested in the rhetoric of evangelical megachurch leaders, who adopted methods of aggressive church growth while largely abandoning apocalyptic dichotomies and appropriating more public norms of speech. Using a 2009 sermon delivered at Willow Creek Community Church—arguably the best-known megachurch in the United States—I explore how the struggle to define and constrain accommodation has led to shifts within Fundamentalist communities and Fundamentalist politics. Willow Creek is explicitly accommodative in its approach to outsiders, yet at the same time its discourse points to boundaries—"fundamentals"—of belief and practice by which identity and action are defined. Thus, while explicitly opposed to the direct intolerance and anti-intellectualism of earlier Fundamentalist communities, megachurches like Willow Creek continue to operate within a Fundamentalist framework, and this understanding offers insights not only into the particular rhetoric of Christian evangelicals, but into the continuing influence of Fundamentalist narratives on other forms of public speech and association as well.

Chapter One

The Public and Its Fundamentalists

⌘

How and why are we, secular Americans, so deeply entwined with them, our dreaded fundamentalists?

—Susan F. Harding, "American Protestant Moralism and the Secular Imagination," 2009

In *The Public and Its Problems* (1927), John Dewey defended the ideal of strong publics. Challenging Walter Lippmann's pessimistic assessment that modern states were far too complex to be managed by their citizens, Dewey offered a fluid understanding of democracy and the state that highlighted the critical role of robust "public interests."[1] Yet, as his title suggests, Dewey's optimism was tempered by a sense that the modern public was in trouble. In the context of expanding technology, bureaucratization, and a dehumanizing standardization of action and association, the public, he argued, was fragmenting. The problem for Dewey, as Robert Asen argues, was not that there were multiple publics, but that this multiplicity was "uncoordinated."[2] The "art of communication" lagged well behind advances in transmission, and technological advancement produced mechanized mediocrity while reducing opportunities for public interaction.[3] As publics lost hold of the common ideals upon which their unity and consensus were once built, the balance between public and state was disrupted, and good states, Dewey warned, would be succeeded by uncoordinated expansions of government power and private interests that were no longer concerned with the public will or public good. Without effective means to "canalize" and "regulate" the "streams of social action," publics would become even more vague, fragmented, and ineffective at articulating demands and coordinating resistance. The result, Dewey argued, would be a troubling domination of "officials," who could no longer be held accountable to support and defend public interests, but would instead be left free to impose their own interests on an apathetic public no longer sufficiently organized to defend itself. In time, Dewey argued, people would come to perceive themselves as individuals only and lose the sense of being the individual-in-community that was for him the most basic unit of social and political life. Individuals outside public association would struggle to retain any sense of agency in a landscape of social issues that they would find increasingly difficult even "to find and locate in the vast complexities of current life."[4]

Dewey wrote *The Public and Its Problems* in the context of unprecedented technological innovation, economic expansion, and social conflict in the aftermath of the First World War. During the 1920s, radio was revolutionizing communication technology. The film industry had settled in California and gone mainstream. While the nations of Europe struggled to recover from the war, many in the United States were prospering. Yet it was also a decade that witnessed increasing inequity between rich and poor, rising tensions between rural and urban populations, and conflict between proponents of American expansion and the growing nativist and isolationist rhetoric of radical anti-Bolsheviks and groups like the Ku Klux Klan.

These broad social tensions were reflected in American Protestant communities as well. On the one hand, people were building churches and expanding ministries in ways unthinkable a few years earlier. Radio emerged as a powerful medium to transmit religious messages in the 1920s, and preachers like Aimee Semple McPherson, Paul Rader, and John Roach Straton began attracting thousands of new listeners through their broadcasts. Church buildings were growing at an astounding rate. It was the decade of the so-called "skyscraper church." In 1924, the twenty-three-story Chicago Temple Building was completed; housing a 1,200-seat sanctuary, it was then (at 568 feet) the tallest building in the city and remains the second-tallest church building in the world. That same year, the famous New York minister Harry Emerson Fosdick secured funding from John D. Rockefeller Jr. for what would become, in 1930, the Riverside Church—a gothic church exterior containing a functional twenty-four-story steel-frame bell tower. In 1925, John Roach Straton of Manhattan's Calvary Baptist Church began laying plans for a church-hotel skyscraper complex, which was completed in 1931 and remains arguably the most famous of New York's skyscraper churches.[5] Nor was all expansion upward. Massive "city temples"—some with seating for as many as 10,000 people—sprang up in major cities across the country, many of them having been originally constructed to house evangelistic revivals. In 1922, Paul Rader began preaching at, and broadcasting from, the Chicago Gospel Tabernacle (aka The Big Steel Tent), a temporary revival structure cheaply enclosed to create a permanent building. On January 1, 1923, Aimee Semple McPherson dedicated her 5,300-seat Angelus Temple in Los Angeles, the flagship of what would become the International Church of the Foursquare Gospel. In 1925, the 5,000-seat Moody Church was dedicated in Chicago.[6]

On the other hand, the postwar period was a time of unprecedented tension and disruption among American Protestants. In 1919, conservative Minnesota pastor William Bell Riley helped found the World's Christian Fundamentals Association, and the following year he led a conservative resistance movement within the Northern Baptist Convention to call for the convention's return to the "fundamentals of our New Testament faith."[7] In 1921, the Interchurch World Movement—a massively ambitious interdenominational project heavily financed and supported by John D. Rockefeller Jr.—collapsed less than two years after it was organized, leaving embittered church and business partners, and debts that would not be paid off for another three years. In 1925, the famous Scopes "Monkey" Trial in Tennessee pitted science and conservative, rural religion against one another in a battle for the future of public education. In 1926, the National Broadcasting Company (NBC), with strong input from an interdenominational Protestant organization called the Federal Council of Churches, agreed upon a set of policy standards for the distribution of free airtime to religious broadcasters, standards that largely excluded "nonrepresentative" religious groups—most prominently the loose, interdenominational association of conservatives who had come to be known as "fundamentalists."[8]

Such tensions between growth and fragmentation, visibility and invisibility were reflective of the problems of communication in modernity—problems that Dewey identified and that continue to weigh heavily on religious and secular thinkers alike. In modern democratic societies, associations must struggle for power and recognition in the absence of state-mandated authority. Thus, while they dominated urban landscapes for a time, the skyscraper churches and city tabernacles of the 1920s—like the so-called "megachurches" of today—operated in a radically different register than did the cathedrals of Europe, which stand now as silent witnesses to an established religion's social, political, and economic domination over a people. For much of Western history, the Christian church, like the feudal state, imposed such dominant, universal, and wholly communal values that, as Dewey argued elsewhere, "So far as life for the individual had a positive value, this lay not in living oneself out, but rather in the calm and the support afforded by the church."[9] Over time, however, the values of the church ceased to be the exclusive ideals of society—a process Charles Taylor describes as "disenchantment"—leading to "the underlying idea of society as existing for the (mutual) benefit of individuals and the defense of their rights."[10] In turn, the individual, rights-bearing subject provided a foundation for new kinds of political, moral, and religious associations, setting the stage for the modern state.

While premodern social cohesion was largely assured through collective conceptions of the self and the domination of feudal states and ecclesiastical institutions, modern publics must rely on other foundations for association and action. If individuals cannot create and maintain associations with one another, they cannot hope to defend their rights against political and business interests, or maintain justice and consensus in democracy. Indeed this was such a critical feature for Dewey that, as mentioned above, he began his study of the public with the individual-in-community, refusing to consider individuals outside of community as a unit of analysis. Such a perspective requires what Paul Ricoeur refers to as "imagination." Ricoeur says, "The truth of our condition is that the analogical tie that makes every man my brother is accessible to us only through a certain number of *imaginative practices*, among them, *ideology* and *Utopia*." By highlighting these two terms,

Ricoeur emphasizes that the analogy of association is always imperfect and incomplete. When an association becomes its own justification, it turns ideological and becomes a foundation for its own forms of domination against the unassociated. When this occurs, Ricoeur argues, our imagination must turn utopian in order to access possibilities for associations different from those we currently inhabit. Associations are necessary, but they are not natural and they need not be permanent.[11]

What Is a Public?

In his 1962 work *Strukturwandel der Öffentlichkeit*—which was translated into English in 1989 as *The Structural Transformation of the Public Sphere*—Jürgen Habermas develops a sociological and historical analysis of a particular epochal form of collective association in modernity—the eighteenth-century "bourgeois public sphere." What Habermas calls the public sphere involves "private persons" acting as critics of the state through the "public use" of "reason."[12] The distinction between a public and a private realm of human political existence is not recent, going back at least as far as the Greek distinction between *oikos* (the home) and *polis* (the city).[13] What Habermas describes in *The Structural Transformation*, however, is the emergence of a particular kind of middle space between the private realm and the political state. The bourgeois public sphere represented a space within which private citizens at the beginning of the eighteenth century—having no claim to nobility or official authority within the state—came to embody what Habermas regards as a critical check on state power through public reasoning and debate.[14] Through literary texts like newspapers and novels and meeting places like salons and coffeehouses, private people engaged in ongoing "organized discussion."[15] Departing from the feudal system, in which the engagement in public life was limited to the nobility and carried by inheritance, the public sphere acknowledged the political significance of the individual conscience, and it offered a realm within which the non-noble bourgeoisie could organize to make demands upon the state. Against both political and economic reification, the public sphere functioned as a "deliberative" public in which participation was determined by "rational-critical debate" and procedural rules, and through which a plurality of perspectives could be negotiated.[16]

The limitations of Habermas's rational-critical model have been discussed and debated at great length, and I will not replicate that work here. Crucially for this study, however, the Habermasian public sphere normatively excludes arguments grounded in nonuniversal religious or metaphysical assumptions. Following the Western tradition of political theory descending from Hobbes and Locke, Habermas interprets religion as an element of private human belief and practice—one that should be protected but that cannot be used as a basis for public argument and rational consensus. As a precondition to participating in the public sphere, Habermas argues, the religious believer must accept that "nothing in principle stands in the way of an autonomous foundation of morality and law—a foundation independent of the truths of revelation."[17] Since the publication of *The Structural Transformation* in the 1960s, Habermas has altered some of his arguments and increased the complexity of others. In his more recent work, for example, he has acknowledged the ongoing public significance of religious communities and suggested that "religious citizens" should "be allowed to express and justify their convictions in a religious language if they cannot find secular 'translations' for them."[18] Nevertheless, he has maintained the need for, and supremacy of, "rational-critical debate," and his suggestion that religious citizens be "allowed" to use religious language in particular instances retains an essential focus on secular institutions as the permission-granting loci of appeal. The ongoing importance of rationally circumscribed boundaries for Habermas points toward both the strengths and the weaknesses of his project. The rational foundation creates a strong basis for critique and resistance to political and economic domination, but it also institutes and maintains its own forms of domination. As Chantal Mouffe has argued, such a foundation is never neutral; rather "the expression of specific values," and the "antagonism" between these values and their opponents are not, ultimately, resolvable through appeal to reason or by any other method.[19]

These struggles for public legitimacy make clear that the boundaries between private rights and public concerns are not natural or fixed. For Dewey, the distinction between public and private activity was based on a recognition that the consequences of some human actions extend beyond the individual, and the status of practices and beliefs as public or private was based on an analysis of the extent to which these are publicly consequential.[20] For example, as Dewey argued, the exchange between doctor and patient has limited consequences beyond the individuals involved, but the general veracity and reliability of doctors have extensive public consequences—evidenced by the degrees, licenses, and regulations that surround the medical industry.[21] As this example illustrates, the privatization of activity has protective functions (e.g., shielding one's personal medical records from public view), but it also has the effect of excluding from public life actors or associations that are understood to be unreflective of, or dangerous to, the public interest. For Dewey, as for Habermas, religion was one such association in modern society. Dewey said, "As long as the prevailing mentality thought that the consequences of piety and irreligion affected the entire community, religion was of necessity a public affair." But he also argued that religion had become privatized in a modern context where the majority of people "no longer connected attitudes of reverence or disrespect to the gods with the weal and woe of the community."[22]

From the work of Dewey to the writings of John Rawls and Habermas, the notion that religious perspectives can be disconnected from modern politics continues to shape our academic and practical discussions about the public and political status of religious communities and arguments. As Cristina Lafont summarizes, "the liberal conception of democratic citizenship" is based on three assumptions: first, that "natural reason" is a sufficient foundation for moral judgment and political decision-making; second, that religious and secular citizens are capable of arriving at the same decisions by different paths; third, that secular reasons are universally available, while religious reasons are only available to members of religious communities.[23] The result of these assumptions has been a guiding principle that secular arguments can function as a neutral framework for public deliberation. Such a principle has, ideally, a protective function—shielding the rights of religious minorities and other marginal communities—but it also restricts or excludes those who cannot isolate out their rational-critical reasoning. Nicholas Wolterstorff, for example, argues, "It belongs to the *religious convictions* of a good many religious people in our society that *they ought to base* their decisions concerning fundamental issues of justice *on* their religious convictions. They do not view it as an option whether or not to do so."[24] Many Fundamentalist Christians are among those who find it impossible to isolate their "private" and public perspectives, and, as we will discuss in the chapters that follow, many of them have come to perceive secular institutions not as neutral frameworks for reasoned deliberation, but as representatives of a religio-political confederacy whose purpose is to marginalize or eliminate Fundamentalist communities. This perspective, in turn, has helped to spawn nodes of resistance to counter the perceived inequities of dominant or established publics and to enact alternative modes of publicity.

Like the relationship between the state and other forms of social interaction, the relationship between private and public is continually "wavering and shifting," and demands to privatize or publicize activities constantly circulate.[25] As Nancy Fraser argues, "What will count as a matter of common concern will be decided precisely through discursive contestation."[26] Yet these norms of contestation, at least as articulated by deliberative theorists of the public sphere, cannot incorporate many forms of speech and participation, and therefore, Fraser and others argue, they cannot effectively manage the struggle between what is private and what is public. This irresolvable tension within the public sphere, in turn, has led some undesired or marginalized social movements to enact alternative modes of publicity that Fraser calls "counterpublics." As Michael Warner describes them, counterpublics are defined "by their tension with a larger public."[27] To draw on Dewey, we might describe counterpublics as privatized associations that work within discourse to establish and create public consequentiality as a means of overcoming public exclusion and producing public legitimacy. Communication is directed both outward, toward dominant publics, and inward, toward the shifting imagination of the counterpublic community.

Counterpublic theory offers valuable tools to expand theorization beyond rational norms and acknowledge some of the challenges posed by a Habermasian conception of public sphere.[28] However, the scholarship on counterpublics retains an idealization of identity that threatens to reestablish Habermasian blindness to multiplicity and resistance in new forms. As Erik Doxtader argues, "The announced double *telos* of counterpublic theory, the desire to introduce oppositional argumentation into the public sphere but to do so in a manner that preserves the consensual nature of deliberative democracy, is underwritten by a 'weak idealism' that leads critique to assume precisely that which it sets out to explain."[29] This idealism is furthered by an object focus that often overwhelms critical theory and method. Studies of counterpublics remain dominated by work that is ideologically sympathetic to the movements being analyzed. While not individually problematic, the collective lack of critical distance leads to narratives that tend to instantiate counterpublics in undertheorized, binary opposition to the domination of state, economic, or social forces that further existing norms of public participation. The often conflated status of theorists as both observers and members of the communities they study tends to produce an untroubled analysis of counterpublic "counterdiscourses" and "oppositional interpretations" that inscribes a good/evil dichotomy and positions counterpublic communities as heroic challengers to oppressive state rule or public domination, with insufficient consideration given to these communities' historical, discursive, and often problematic relationships with their own "counter"-narratives.[30]

Following Doxtader, I suggest that many of these problems can be corrected by paying greater attention to the rhetorical practices and "counterpublicity" of social movements, an "inquiry into *how* particular situations lead groups to devise and employ forms of speech that turn between moments of opposition and moments of consensus in the name of remaking the collective good."[31] Counterpublic identity is constituted through discourse. Just as Robert Asen has argued that "citizenship" is a kind of engagement that individuals can take up or discard in various ways and based on various circumstances, I argue that counterpublics are intimately linked to the discursive action that organizes and sustains them.[32] Extending from Doxtader's definition and Asen's discourse theory of citizenship, I make three assumptions about counterpublic speech: First, rather uncontroversially, such speech does not preexist a discourse of exclusion from, or subordination within, the state or dominant public. Second, such speech always appeals to a discursively constituted universal that challenges exclusion. Third and most importantly, counterpublic speech is not stable, but must be continually reconstituted and redefined relative to the contingencies of exclusion and tension between alienation from and accommodation to what Doxtader calls "the dominant conventions of public deliberation."[33] To act as a member of a counterpublic is not equivalent to a priori marginalization. It is not, as Warner recognizes, merely to become aware of "subordinate status." Rather it is to *enact* subordination in speech.[34] Counterpublicity is a rhetorical process by which social movements continually rearticulate the boundaries of marginalization and resistance through discursive constructions of public exclusion and oppression. In part, this means that while counterpublic theory tends to focus on a priori relations of domination, often essentially conflating counterpublics with marginalized social identities, I will concentrate on the constructions of contestation and counter-contestation within and against which counterpublic associations continually redefine a "counter"-identity that is both institutionally regulated and discursively negotiated at the margins.

Who Is a Fundamentalist?

This study considers how American Christian Fundamentalists speak in public, negotiating tensions between public and counterpublic identity and action. However, the term "fundamentalist" requires some explanation. Broadly speaking, it has developed two distinct but interrelated meanings. On the one hand, Fundamentalism refers to a particular association or confluence of associations within American Protestantism, whose roots go back to the nineteenth century, but which came together as a coherent, national movement in the years immediately following the First World War.[35] This movement, which for the sake of clarity I have capitalized as "Fundamentalist" in this book, defined itself by a doctrine of biblical inerrancy—the belief that the Bible is authoritative and without error both in its accounts of God and in its accounts of historical or scientific fact—a "premillennial" and "dispensationalist" understanding of prophetic and eschatological narratives (see chapter 4), and a strong commitment to purity and separation from nonbelievers. It developed among frustrated churchgoers across denominational lines, built through networks of conferences, small groups, and schools called "Bible Institutes."[36] Its leaders wrote of Christian "fundamentals" that were being abandoned by "liberal" church leaders preaching a "modernist" doctrine and supporting a powerful "superchurch" confederacy. The initial movement has since fragmented into a number of broadly definable communities, some of which continue to self-identify as "Fundamentalists," while others, like the Christian "new evangelical" movements, began to abandon the term and some of Fundamentalism's more absolutist commitments around mid-century. For the purposes of this study, however, I identify these contemporary evangelicals as a subset of the category of "Fundamentalists."[37] In making this judgment, my purpose—as I hope will become clear—is not to conflate the contemporary communities or deny the diversity of spiritual and political perspectives among Fundamentalist and evangelical believers. Yet all of these groups are participants in a common discursive history, and the variations between and within these communities can be best understood as divergent responses to a set of common concerns, framed by a common hope for the eventual triumph of the "true" or Fundamentalist church over the unbelieving world.

Believers enter into Fundamentalist community through personal conversion—one's experience and testimony of individual transition from dark to light, damned to saved, slave to free. But conversion is not merely an affirmation of particular doctrinal beliefs. In claiming Jesus Christ as personal savior, the convert undergoes a change in belief but also a reimagining of identity, and a significant Fundamentalist distinction lies in the radical commitments implied by this new life.[38] Conversion involves the eradication of some old possibilities and the creation of new possibilities for constituting identity. It marks one's transition into a new narrative, a new story, a new community, in relation to which the conversion experience is interpreted and within which it is understood. This narrative includes not only a set of positively articulable beliefs, but a new tropology as well. The sixteenth-century Protestant reformer John Calvin famously described the new perspective and recognition of the convert by using the analogy of a person staring at the ground who turns to look up at the full, blinding light of the sun.[39] The sun reveals, but it also transforms perspective, orienting the human observer to a new world of light and shadow. This orienting perspective transforms the possibilities of metaphorization and, in turn, of narrative. The convert has access to a new set of metaphorical possibilities through which to describe and define the narrative of experience.[40] In turn, this reorientation of narrative opens up new possibilities for what we can call, in Kierkegaardian terms, a grounded or "mastered" irony;[41] the new convert becomes a new critic. Within the restraints of the converted perspective, the Fundamentalist critic challenges the unconverted perspective—solidifying the boundary between self and other.

Doctrines like biblical inerrancy are only comprehensible within this reorientation of tropology that enters the narrative at the critical moment of conversion. Fundamentalist salvation is marked as much by the recognition and assurance of the inviolable truth of Scripture as it is by recognition of one's need for redemption through Christ. On one level this inerrancy doctrine reimagines the Bible as a singular "Word of God." Thus, Bible teachers within the Fundamentalist tradition will sometimes engage in a unique oratorical style that combines teaching with a rapid-fire referencing of seemingly (to the outsider) disconnected Bible verses—a practice sometimes referred to as "proof-texting." These references are not explicated or explained; they serve only as evidence of the teacher's biblical authority. Fundamentalists often claim that these methods are purely inductive—proof of Scripture's inerrancy coming from an open analysis of the text itself. Yet only certain methods of reading are capable of yielding the inerrant truths that Fundamentalists ascribe to the text. Doctrines like dispensationalism, for example, require a particularly complex and rigid hermeneutical approach, since the dispensational framework has to be fully understood before the Bible student can read "rightly." As Timothy Weber argues, while Fundamentalists claimed to keep the Bible open for the people—in contrast to the elitism of "higher critics" outside the Fundamentalist community—they forced lay readers to remain dependent on Bible teachers and ministers for the frameworks that these "inductive" methods depended on in order to yield the proper results.[42]

Even where this referencing style is not employed, the continual presence of the Bible, whether physically or through reference, is essential to the authority of the Fundamentalist minister.[43] Once the Fundamentalist believer becomes saved into the recognition of the Bible as inerrant truth, this truth becomes the basis for all faith statements, and anything less than an inerrant text would admit the possibility of error into all dimensions of faith. As one author argues, "If any part of the Bible can be proved to be in error, then any other part of it—including the doctrinal, theological parts—may also be in error."[44] More importantly, to relinquish inerrancy would admit the possibility of error into the converted perspective. Therefore, true believers must, while diligently reading the Bible for themselves, also submit their individual rights of interpretation to the community. One author makes this explicit by contrasting the interpretive freedom of the "liberal" critic of Scripture with the commitment demanded of the "conservative," believing interpreter: "By claiming the right to sift [the text] . . . the critic cannot be true to the divinely inerrant nature of the biblical literature that is under scrutiny, and criticism is misapplied."[45]

Within these critical limitations, however, the Fundamentalist interpreter has access to vast resources for interpretive and intellectual development. Because the Bible reflects the singular mind and truth of God, it can be read back on itself as proof of its own truthfulness.[46] As one author says, "In seeking to understand the Bible, it is basic to listen to what the Bible says about itself."[47] And reading the Bible in this way will effectively demonstrate its inerrancy. As Jerry Falwell argued, "A thorough study of the Bible will show that it is indeed the inerrant Word of the living God."[48] Furthermore, because the living mind of God inhabits and translates the text for the believing reader, the Bible is a "living" word, whose narratives can be seamlessly conflated with contemporary time.[49] This inerrant, immediate text offers a limitless resource through which to directly access the mind and will of God. Fundamentalists are not, as many popular critics assume, uneducated or ignorant. Indeed many are, as Nancy Ammerman says, "voracious writers, publishers, and readers."[50] Many Fundamentalist communities also place an extraordinarily high value on reasoning and debate, calling on believers to "be ready always to give an answer" to those outside the believing community.[51] Despite frequent claims to reason inductively from evidence, however, the orienting perspective of conversion and the presupposition of biblical inerrancy and unity frame the Fundamentalist approach to argument.[52] The believer is called to read, study, and memorize the Bible on a daily basis. One Fundamentalist textbook says, "If the student has not read through the Bible twenty-five times, he should take steps to correct that. Of course, he certainly will not want to stop then."[53] In this intensive educational and critical training, the believing community—the church—is always part of the student's tropological and interpretive frame, guiding and managing the production of inerrant meaning.

In the American context, scholarly and popular narratives of Fundamentalism have been heavily influenced by public perception in the aftermath of the widely publicized Scopes "Monkey" Trial in 1925. This trial was, on its face, relatively benign—a biology teacher, John Scopes, had violated a Tennessee statute by teaching Darwinian evolution in his classroom. Scopes was guilty by his own admission, having been selected specifically to challenge the state law, and the verdict was a foregone conclusion. What sparked the national imagination, however, was the widely publicized ideological battle that pitted famous defense attorney Clarence Darrow against three-time Democratic presidential candidate, former secretary of state, and Fundamentalist hero William Jennings Bryan. And while the jury convicted Scopes, as expected, Darrow was widely regarded as the ideological victor of the trial in the national press—the voice of reason, speaking truth to "hillbillies."[54] Some Fundamentalist supporters declared Bryan victorious in the case he prosecuted, but for readers and radio listeners across the country, the "Monkey Trial" became an opportunity to make a mockery not merely of Bryan, but of Fundamentalism, rural ignorance, and the American South. As Robert Hariman says, "Despite its having no influence upon legal doctrine, the Scopes trial had a major impact upon American public discourse."[55] Undoubtedly the most vocal among the critics was the acerbic journalist H. L. Mencken, who famously said of the trial: "On one side was bigotry, ignorance, hatred, superstition, every sort of blackness that the human mind is capable of. On the other side was sense. And sense achieved a great victory."[56]

In the long term, Scopes helped to nationalize a narrative about Fundamentalist identity and to conflate that identity with rural and regional distinctions, which were, in turn, portrayed as out of touch with the modern, progressive, urban national consciousness and, thus, doomed to decline and die. Invoking evolutionary language, a *Christian Century* editorial in 1926 declared Fundamentalism to be a "vanishing" religion, saying:

> If we may use a biological term, fundamentalism has been a *sport*, an accidental phenomenon making its sudden appearance in our ecclesiastical order, but wholly lacking the qualities of constructive achievement or survival. Had there been no such person as William J. Bryan in American church life at that particular moment, fundamentalism as a threatening force of disruption would never have made its appearance.[57]

Bryan's death, shortly after his mixed and widely derided performance as prosecutor in the trial, helped to solidify the narrative that Fundamentalists were a species in retreat—an unfit and dying breed. In short, Scopes had the effect of simultaneously raising national awareness of Fundamentalism and condemning the imagined Fundamentalism of the press to an irreversible decline.

It was this narrative of marginalization and vanishing that was shattered in the late 1970s. Beginning in December 1978, a series of organizations emerged on the national landscape. Explicitly Fundamentalist and explicitly political, they were a devastating shock to many political secularists who were used to thinking of Fundamentalists (when they thought about them at all) as uneducated, rural isolationists, not as sophisticated political operators. The shock of political Fundamentalism derived less from the content of its message than from the fact of its existence. Its emergence challenged fifty years of secular theory. Susan Harding describes the rise of Fundamentalism as the nightmare of secularism, since the exclusion and erasure of the Fundamentalist was the basis for secular normativity: "If 'they' weren't dying out as a social category, 'we' no longer represented the natural, normal, secularizing outcome of modern history. 'We' no longer owned the future." This realization has transformed secular narratives of Fundamentalism. What had previously been invisible and ignorable became reinscribed as a malevolent cancer—not merely the Other, but the enemy of secular identity and modern progress: "our dreaded fundamentalists."[58]

Since the emergence of these conservative movements in the 1970s, "fundamentalism" has gradually acquired a second meaning. In addition to describing a particular Christian sect or interpretive tradition, (lowercase) fundamentalism has become popularly associated with a kind of universal, politically threatening religious or pseudo-religious militancy. This second meaning has traveled broadly across sectarian, social, economic, and political contexts—appropriated to describe that which is indefinable but fearful, radical, and repugnant in religious, economic, political, and ideological movements writ large.[59] In this sense, fundamentalism operates similarly to terms like "terrorism" and "demagoguery," naming an unnamable threat in a way that implies that we can know one when we see one.[60] Even to invoke the name is to invoke a term riddled with violence and contestation. In her book on liberal and fundamentalist communication, Sharon Crowley argues that "anyone who is not a fundamentalist is willing to entertain difference, to live with it, so to speak."[61] But, in naming "a fundamentalist"—establishing universal, impermeable, and conveniently vague boundaries between fundamentalism and the self—critics mark the limits of such self-assured perceptions. Fundamentalism thus described cannot be merely another difference in modernity, but is, rather, excluded in the act of naming. Fundamentalism is a difference that we cannot accept, for it threatens difference itself. It is, as another author has argued, "antimodern."[62] Divorced from any definable discourse or community, the fundamentalist name is retained as an ideographic marker of that which we consider malevolent and oppressive, a militant fringe, an intolerable cancer, and so forth. In this context, the street-corner evangelist, the neoliberal economist, the abortion-clinic blockader, the radical secularist, and the suicide bomber can collapse into one another—inhabiting marginally different places along an ill-defined "fundamentalist" continuum.

Modern liberalism is imagined as a tolerant frame within which, as Wendy Brown argues, individual subjects are free to draw personal comfort and conviction from their chosen religious and cultural paradigms, provided these remain isolated from political power and action. From this perspective, Crowley can say that the non-fundamentalist "is willing to entertain difference," but fundamentalism meanwhile represents the difference that can neither be entertained nor tolerated.[63]

When invoked to describe particular communities, this broad conception of fundamentalism carries the power to marginalize any undesirable speech as angry, militant, radical, or terroristic. The fundamentalist is marginalized and often infantilized—separated, as Crowley argues, from "good rhetoric" and reimagined as the ignorant, reactive, and dangerous fringe.[64] Reinscribed as what Brown calls "the barbarians," fundamentalists are associated with a priori intolerance and incivility and thus articulated as both normatively excluded from and fiercely antagonistic to public discourse and democratic norms. Such rhetoric has the unfortunate potential to impose injustice on those labeled fundamentalist, validating even extreme exclusions from public speech and political participation in the name of preserving order and civility.[65] Conversely, it may lead critics to ignore the relationship between fundamentalism and other forms of political and cultural resistance—implying that fundamentalist discourses are separated from and anomalous within normal democratic processes and thus need not be taken seriously.[66] Neither is a productive or sustainable response. The dream that fundamentalism would one day be swallowed by rationality or fade into civil platitudes has been irrevocably shattered. Fundamentalism, as Harding argues, has revealed itself to be "inside, not outside, our world, the polity, and 'us' as a social and political category."[67]

In encouraging a richer and more nuanced exploration of both meanings of "fundamentalism," I am not embracing fundamentalist ideals, and I do not wish to ignore or deny the very real violence and potential for violence that often underlies or accompanies fundamentalist speech. Instead, I hope to get behind the specter of the fundamentalist as pure Other, acknowledging that fundamentalist counterpublicity disrupts deliberative self-assurances and the ease with which democratic publics assert their tolerance, civility, and inclusivity. It is often at the point where definitional boundaries are most troubled that the most productive and imaginative work can begin. Fundamentalism troubles and will continue to trouble the boundaries of modernity and liberal subjectivity. My response is not to repudiate these boundaries or, necessarily, to redraw the lines of alienation and exclusion, but we must acknowledge, if only for the critical moment, the dreaded voice of the Other, which speaks back and challenges the assumptions that enable the act of naming.

Conclusion

Fundamentalism continues to play a critical and visible role in American politics. Its discourses are everywhere, and they compel us to consider seriously the ways in which Fundamentalists constitute identity, manage contingency, and justify public engagement in the modern world. Over the course of the past four decades, Christian Fundamentalism, in particular, has emerged as a dominant and maligned force in American public life and media, oriented around a complex of national and local networks, representing a variety of religious and political platforms and methods. There is no one Fundamentalism (and indeed there never was), but for all the variation, these movements and communities share a common hope and expectation that the true church will win in the end and save the public from itself. The world will be redeemed; the sinful and dangerous will be saved, cured, or eradicated; and the norms of public speech and participation will come to match those of the believing community.

Fundamentalism offers compelling narratives of conversion and reorientation, inerrancy and revival that enable believers to imagine a world where speech, community, and the norms of publicity are different than they are. By better understanding these narratives and the public symbols against which and through which the Fundamentalist community imagines itself, its enemies, and its future, we will gain insights that extend well beyond the consideration of a particular church or conservative organization. Fundamentalism is inseparably part of American political theater. As I write these words, the American political imagination is once again in flux. Economic and political insecurities have helped spawn new forms of political coalition. In the early months of 2009, for example, a "Tea Party" movement seemed to explode across the country, drawing together loose associations of economic libertarians, conspiracy theorists, nativists, and discontented conservatives. However we might define or describe it, there is no question that the

Tea Party's membership and its rhetoric were shaped and, at the time I am writing, continue to be shaped by many of the same communities and narratives that are the subject of this book. Tea Party coalitions define and justify activism through a kind of counterpublic speech that sets "We the People" against a confederation of political and intellectual elites whose ultimate intent is to suppress and eliminate conservative perspectives and establish a "socialist" state. A number of Tea Party participants, claiming little to no prior political experience, have described their entry into the movement as the fruit of intense research culminating in a kind of conversion experience—emerging, as one *New York Times* article described it, "as if reborn to a new reality."[68] Within this new reality, the convert has access to vast new resources for intellectual, critical, and even spiritual development, including books, classes, study groups, and rallies.[69] One author has described the Tea Party approach as "constitutional biblicalism"—treating the U.S. Constitution as a sacred text derived from Christian or biblical principles.[70] And certainly there is intense focus on discovering the original meaning of the text and the singular intent of its authors. Even the language of revival is present in Tea Party narratives. In a 2010 interview for the Christian Broadcasting Network, for example, U.S. Senator Jim DeMint described the Tea Party as "akin to the Great Awakening before the American Revolution."[71] The next year, DeMint wrote a book on the Tea Party titled *The Great American Awakening*.[72]

It is not my intention to overstate similarities between Fundamentalist discourses and those of the Tea Party or any other social or political movement. Rather, my point is to illustrate that, while this study is grounded in the history, language, and practices of a particular religious community, the critical frameworks I explore below are not limited to the rhetoric and politics of American Fundamentalism. As we consider themes of revival and apocalypse, conversion and countersymbol in the chapters that follow, I hope to encourage both a more nuanced understanding of Fundamentalist narratives and a richer discussion of the political complexities and consequences of both public and counterpublic speech.

Chapter Two

The Fundamentals of Revival

⌘

Success in saving souls is evidence that a man understands the gospel, and understands human nature, that he knows how to adapt means to his end, that he has common sense, and that he has that kind of tact, that practical discernment, to know how to get at people.

—Charles Finney, *Lectures on Revivals of Religion*, 1835

Revival speech is the foundation of Fundamentalist politics. At the heart of Fundamentalist efforts to remake the public—from abolition and temperance to contemporary struggles against abortion and environmentalism—is a desire to make a world in which the gospel message can be propagated and in which people will be more receptive to revivalist persuasion. For much of Christian history it was assumed that this transformation could only come "in the fullness of time," which had been preordained by God, but Fundamentalist counterpublicity derives from an emerging belief in the eighteenth and nineteenth centuries that human actions could affect God's plan and God's timing. It was a revolutionary idea that such a transformed world did not depend wholly on the mysterious intentions of divine will but could be brought into being through the persuasive speech of believers. It was this idea, more than any other, that transformed the landscape of religious politics in America.

Covenant Revival

The first Puritan settlers saw themselves as unique participants in God's design. As John Winthrop told Puritan colonists in 1630, God had called them to be "a city upon a hill" whose light would shine before all the peoples of the world. Quoting from the words of Jesus in the gospels, Winthrop invoked a metaphor that brought together the spiritual past and political present. The city he imagined was to be a place of light and unity, strength and security, ordered hierarchy under human rule, and equality before God. It was to be a fortress against sin and a light to pierce the darkness. It was to be a city of God—built by God and for God's glory.

It was also to be a city built on sermons. The Puritan saints were eager sermon consumers. Churchgoers typically heard two sermons each Sunday plus a midweek "lecture"—most lasting one to two hours—and many traveled to neighboring towns to hear more messages during the week. As an additional testament to their eager dedication to the spoken word, many of the Puritan sermons we have recorded today are based on the detailed notes of these listeners, who would carefully copy out the points of each message in order to reflect upon them further in the privacy of their own homes.[1]

These notes reveal a rigorously organized and systematic style that distinguished Puritan sermons from those of their predecessors.[2] The focus of these sermons was the careful articulation of biblical reason and truth. Although no distinctively American Puritan preaching manuals exist before Cotton Mather's *Manuductio ad Ministerium* in 1726, the Puritan ministers drew on a common set of organizing tools that were heavily influenced by the work of the sixteenth-century French logician Petrus Ramus and his followers.[3] Ramus located all disciplines within successive categorical pairings, which he laid out in complex charts. Having classified and arranged arguments through dichotomous pairs, the Ramist critic would bring two arguments together to form an axiom, and by setting multiple axioms "in their natural order," the critic could form the basis for Ramist discourses. The practice was intended to arrive at "objective truth" while encouraging plain justifications of common-sense claims.[4] In this process, Ramus elevated logic and grammar while reducing the status of rhetoric to a mere stylistic supplement.[5] For Ramist critics, rhetoric had no relation to the logical work of invention and organization. Rather, it was, as the Puritan-Ramist writer Alexander Richardson argued, a kind of ornament, which should only be used with caution and not in a way that distracted from the object or person being adorned. Rhetoric was viewed as a kind of seduction that, while useful to arouse a congregation's passions, was always in danger of turning those passions away from the plain rationality of biblical truth. While a measure of arousal was considered necessary in order to prepare the sinner's heart for conversion, such arousal was not be confused with conversion.[6] Rhetoric and emotion were to be employed by the ministers, but never to be emphasized.

This should not be taken to mean that the Puritans disliked emotion. They often used passionate—even florid—language in their writings and sermons, but they believed that emotions should only be invoked in the close, carefully organized interpretive framework of the believing community. Conversion, for the Puritans, was a deeply painful process, and some of their most lurid prose describes the agonizing struggle of dying to self and being reborn in Christ. It was also a process demarcated by a series of rigorous steps, which might take months or even years to work through. The emotions leading to true conversion, they believed, could only take place through careful, often excruciating confrontation with the sick depravity of one's soul. These emotions were not something that should be manipulated with words, for such manipulations might produce false hope and lead the sinner to shun the pain of the conversion process. Nor should these emotions be forced upon isolated individuals, who might fall into despair or even, as occasionally happened, take their own lives under the crushing burden of conscience. Rather, conversion was a process that was to take place within what Jerald Brauer calls the "nurturing community" of Puritanism.[7] When Puritan ministers displayed a Ramist sensibility and downplayed emotion and style in their sermons, it was not to avoid feeling, but to avoid the emotional manipulation they associated with rhetorical excess.

Critical to the functionality of the Puritan-Ramist sermon model was the presumption that saints—the already converted—were the primary audience, and all others were merely listening in, slowly absorbing the truth of God, which might, if God willed it, one day lead to their conversions. Although required by law to attend services, the non-converted were not members of the believing community, nor were they the primary audience of the community's sermons. They had no voice in either religion or politics, and they were expected to sit under the preaching of God's word in the hope that God's grace might reach them and allow them to understand and embrace God's rational and reasonable demands upon their lives and eternal souls.[8]

Yet this audience of the saints likely never constituted the majority of Puritan settlers. Perry Miller suggests that even in the 1630s, only a fifth of the people were church members, and those who were often did not reflect the unity of belief and purpose idealized in Winthrop's metaphor of the city upon a hill.[9] Early disruptions, like the heresy trial of Roger Williams in 1633 and that of Anne Hutchison in 1638, reflected how the efforts of Puritan leaders to create a pure, centralized, and authoritative theocratic community often conflicted with those who shared that community.[10] By the second generation, it was obvious that a church and state of saints alone would not survive. Many of the children of the Puritan founders remained only "outward" church members—meaning that they had been baptized into the church as children but had not shown signs of personal conversion as adults—and, because of this, their children were not eligible even for baptism. In 1662, in an obvious concession to the changing demographics of the churches and declines in church membership, the remaining first-generation leaders proposed a "halfway covenant," which would allow the children of these outward members to be baptized if their parents would assent to the teachings of the church and agree to outwardly follow the Bible and the church leadership. Neither these half-members nor their children would be eligible to participate in the sacrament of the Lord's Supper or vote in meetings, but they would be included in the church fellowship with the hope that they would eventually feel the Spirit's conviction and become converts. The goal of the halfway covenant was to make inclusion in the church as easy as possible, and this compromise altered the preaching situation for Puritan ministers. As ministers faced increasingly fragmented and vocally hostile congregations, the models of sermon making began to change.[11]

By the 1660s, the fragmenting effects of outsider resistance were obvious across Puritan communities, and Puritan ministers began turning more and more to "jeremiads" and revival sermons as they tried to restore community morals and reignite an ideal of common purpose among a disenchanted population. Jeremiads are what Sacvan Bercovitch calls "state-of-the-covenant" addresses, which condemn collective sin and pronounce judgment while reaffirming a people's unique calling and place in God's plan.[12] As in the writings of the Hebrew prophet Jeremiah, from which they draw their name, jeremiads balance harsh and violent denouncements of the community against the ultimate hope of redemption and restoration. Their form, as Bercovitch argues, was essentially and unshakably optimistic.[13] God's purpose, in the jeremiad, is not to destroy the covenant people, but to discipline them so that they will return to the path from which they strayed. Jeremiads imagine a community in process—looking to a future whose promised ideal remains unrealized but whose present conflict is always framed within the hope of eventual fulfillment.[14]

Intertwined with the jeremiad, which addressed the state of the community and the boundaries of belief and practice by which the community was to be defined, was the revival sermon, which expanded these boundaries by addressing those outside or at the margins and persuading them to become full participants in the community. These sermon styles have remained closely linked in American public discourse, and while more work has focused on the political effects of jeremiads in American life—effects that tend to be read as invoking "American myth" and sacred nationalism—the interrelated character of jeremiadic and revival rhetoric is critical for understanding how these discourses create meaningful and interdependent public communities.[15] Jeremiadic sermons begin with the failure of the community to meet the ideal upon which it was predicated and to which it is accountable, and they end with the hope of restoring that ideal. The ideal (whether envisioned as Winthrop's city upon a hill or what the English Puritan John Bunyan called the "Celestial City") is never reachable in the human realm but is always looked toward, and the community is warned not to fall back into apathy or stray again into sin as long as their journey toward that ideal continues. The ideal is framed as a journey into the future whose path is demarcated by the commonly held virtues and values of the past. It is this return to the past that leads critics like John Murphy to identify a troubling conservatism and insularity in jeremiadic rhetoric—an idealization of the past that "absolve[s] the system of blame" and institutes "a rhetoric of social control."[16] This insularity, however, is in part a function of the separation of contemporary jeremiads from the tradition of revival rhetoric. Revivals—which call upon the outsider to repent of personal sin and enter into the normative framework of the believing community—cannot rely on an idealization of the past (a past from which the outsider is excluded prior to conversion), but invoke instead a transcendent, ahistorical standard to which both believer and outsider are accountable. Revival speech at once clarifies the norms of the community—articulating a dichotomy between saint and sinner—and challenges those norms by introducing standards that exceed them. This challenge is not abstract. Sinners are called to join a covenantal relationship whose ultimate expression is only imperfectly reflected in the human community of believers, and this ongoing tension between the actual and the ideal has both spiritual and political significance. Saints are called to spiritual and political radicalism whose force derives from a transcendent ideal before which they are dependent, and through which they can challenge the practices and values of both the political age and the covenantal community.[17] The independence of the saint derives from the command of God, and this idea—one with roots in both Plato's *Apology* and the Christian New Testament—offers a basis for radical social thought. Yet, within this framework, the jeremiad continues to function as a communitarian force, which modifies radicalism somewhat by circumscribing the transcendent demands upon the individual within an idealization of the past and of covenantal norms. While the jeremiad separated from revival tends toward separatist insularity, the revival separated from jeremiad tends to abandon community norms for a fragmented individualism. To adequately constitute sustainable spiritual or political resistance, both are necessary, and the study of Fundamentalist rhetoric is, in large part, a study of the historical tensions between (and abandonments of) these two modes of address.

When fit together, neither revivalist nor jeremiadic rhetoric calls the saint to individual radicalism. Personal renewal presupposes a restoration and reformulation of community ideals. Although the individual sinner receiving the call to salvation is asked to abandon all earthly attachments for the sake of the truth, an essential feature of revival is a presumption of communal restoration. Revival sermons presuppose that the convert will not be an isolated pilgrim or a wandering radical; the new saint will join with a covenanted community who will invoke God's ideal to restore the spiritual and political life of the world around them.

These sermons are, by nature, addressed to an audience of the unconverted. While still professing the Puritan ideal of reasoned communication to the elect, pastors like Increase Mather and his son Cotton alternately railed against sin and pleaded with their congregations to return to the true path, preaching covenant renewal and revival in the second half of the seventeenth century. It was, however, a minister named Solomon Stoddard who created the first examples of what we might think of as religious "revivals" in a modern sense of the word. Between 1669 and 1729, Stoddard promoted a series of religious awakenings in his church and the town of Northampton, in the Connecticut River Valley. Preaching simple sermons without notes, Stoddard spoke to sinners, calling on the unconverted in his congregation to seek God's mercy, never knowing if God might hear them and save them from their sins. Abandoning the idealism of early Puritan rhetoric, Stoddard argued that it was impossible for ministers to distinguish saints and sinners. Thus all must be addressed as sinners, and this inability to know with assurance was what opened the way for the minister's call upon the people to actively seek the mercy of God.[18] In contrast to the Puritan model—which conceived of sermonic rhetoric as a frame within which divine truth could be made intelligible and allowed to take root in the hearts of those predisposed by God to accept it—Stoddard interpreted the sermon as a demand upon sinners requiring an immediate and active response.

Revivalism demanded that listeners accept the message without waiting for the growth of divine reason in their hearts. It demanded that listeners believe *now*—approaching the call of the gospel not as submission to divine authority, but as a foundational act of the will through which the believer could be assimilated into the covenantal community. Revival sermons prioritized rhetoric in that they demanded action in spite of the sinner's inability to know fully or obtain rational evidence of the truth on which he or she was called to act.[19] It was Stoddard, more than any other figure, who introduced this revival rhetoric into the New England colonies.

It was, however, Stoddard's grandson and successor Jonathan Edwards, along with the entrepreneurial Anglican itinerant George Whitefield, who invoked this rhetorical conception of revival as the foundation for covenantal restoration beyond local communities—restoration that involved strangers in a common ideal of spiritual and political renewal.[20] While Stoddard's revivals attracted converts, they never extended far beyond his own congregation. Edwards, Whitefield, and their contemporaries, in contrast, transformed revival from a localized to an "intercolonial cultural event."[21]

The first impetus for this change was the publication of Edwards's *A Faithful Narrative of the Surprising Works of God*, which described a series of revivals that took place at Northampton between 1734 and 1735. Although the Northampton Revival was a brief event and came to a sudden, tragic end in 1735—when Edwards's uncle slashed his own throat in a fit of despair over the state of his soul—it became an international symbol of God's work after *A Faithful Narrative* was published in 1737.[22] Filled with dramatic conversion stories, *A Faithful Narrative* depicted the revival as an unprecedented outpouring of God's Spirit, spreading well beyond Northampton as visitors to the town "had their consciences smitten and awakened" and carried revival to their own communities.[23] The text inspired readers throughout the American colonies and England. It promoted the idea that revivals could be regional and even national events, bringing communities together under the divine covenant and unifying churches around a common work. *A Faithful Narrative* prepared readers to pray for and expect revival, so that by the time the young George Whitefield appeared in New England in 1739, the people were ready to receive his jeremiadic and revivalist messages of judgment and restoration. And the revivals that followed in Whitefield's wake would permanently alter the landscape of American religious and political discourse.

Edwards's writings and Whitefield's oratory were the most public elements of a rhetorical revival that would fracture the American religious establishment over the last half of the eighteenth century. Revivals shifted the emphasis of preaching to the audience and prioritized individual interpretation over ministerial authority.[24] Community churches were fragmented by waves of revivalist fervor. After more than a century of essential unity, New England clerics split amongst themselves, separating into "Old Lights," who opposed the revivals as disruptive and questioned their value in promoting Christian virtues, and "New Lights," for whom the revivals were part of a great pouring out of God's Spirit.[25] Eventually, clergy on opposite sides of the debate began attacking each other so viciously that some lay members simply left their churches and formed their own sectarian communities.[26] Between 1742 and 1750, Massachusetts and Connecticut alone had seventy-seven "illegal separations" where sectarian groups abandoned their home churches to create new congregations. Often, the lay ministers who led these movements had no formal training or ecclesiastical authorization to preach.[27] In the period surrounding the American Revolution, itinerant preachers became symbolic of growing religious individualism.[28] Many of these itinerants, in turn, adopted the writings of Jonathan Edwards for their own purposes, establishing his posthumous reputation as one of the great theologians of American evangelicalism while simultaneously reducing his status among the "Old Light" congregations.[29]

Oratory and Architecture

Revivalism continued to change the face of American Protestantism in the nineteenth century. As Nathan Hatch relates, between 1775 and 1845 the number of ministers increased from 1,800 to almost 40,000, and the number of denominations doubled, most of them led by revivalists and other lay ministers.[30] While older, established churches struggled to remain viable, populist sects like the Baptists and Methodists rapidly expanded their influence.[31] While congregations in the east continued to rely on educated ministers and local government support, itinerants often wore their lack of formal education as a badge of honor—preaching a plain gospel to "ordinary" people. With educations comparable to the rural populations they served, these ministers were both more willing to preach on the frontier and more capable of communicating to frontier audiences.[32]

Camp meetings flourished along the southern and western borders. Originally held in churches or on church property, these meetings soon spilled out into the fields, often drawing such large crowds that several preachers were employed at the same time, addressing different groups around the camp.[33] During the first decades of the nineteenth century, hundreds of these meetings drew thousands of people each year across Ohio, Indiana, Illinois, Kentucky, and Tennessee. Often lasting for weeks during the summer, camp meetings combined regular doses of singing and fiery preaching with carnival accoutrements that included vendors, sideshows, and, undoubtedly, plenty of romantic and sexual dalliances in the tents and wagons around the camp perimeter. Yet the distractions and temptations of the camps only lent greater urgency to the revivalists who plied their audiences' emotions with the immediate demands of Christ and dangers of damnation. Camp meetings and revivals popularized and institutionalized a new standard of preaching as a persuasive art for the common sinner.

The effects of revivalism transformed established churches as well. From a relatively cohesive and coherent set of denominations at the turn of the century, American Protestants fragmented into hundreds of churches, revivals, societies, and sectarian communities in the first few decades of the nineteenth century. As churches competed for members among themselves and with itinerant revivalists, elocution became an increasingly valuable commodity, and powerful preachers drew larger and larger crowds. To fill their churches, older ministers learned to follow the revivalists' lead in abandoning complex arguments for audience-focused oratory, and younger ministers were trained in the art of simple and adaptive preaching. Nineteenth-century rhetorical training manuals synthesized the work of theorists like George Campbell, Hugh Blair, and Richard Whately into a system that championed rhetoric's power to adapt messages to all manner of purposes, audiences, and occasions, and sought to apply rhetorical insights to all forms of communication.[34] Where Puritan ministers spoke with divinely ordained authority, nineteenth-century preachers needed to grab and hold their audience's interest through speech and performance alone. Where Puritan ministers could focus on the slow and steady growth of grace in the human heart, confident in a captive audience, nineteenth-century preachers needed to engage the emotions of an increasingly mobile and transient population, not abandoning logic or reason altogether, but subordinating reason to clarity in order to provoke passion and action among the common listeners.[35] On the one hand, such oratorical preaching could and often did become a means unto itself. As Richard Whately remarked in his *Elements of Rhetoric*, preachers could be admired for their preaching without their congregations gaining any understanding of the subjects upon which they preached.[36] On the other hand, simple eloquence and adaptive oratory offered increased opportunities for understanding in the audience, and thus, it is unsurprising that by century's end the "great revival preachers" had become the standard against which preaching effectiveness was measured.[37] By teaching speakers to adapt basic rules to a wide variety of audiences and contexts, rhetoric offered a path to upward mobility, and revival preachers were determined to offer their upward path from sin to salvation to the widest possible congregation.[38]

The effects of revivalism also began to be reflected in church architecture. Particularly in and around urban areas, popular churches were expanded and new churches built to accommodate the growing crowds who pressed to hear from the most famous and eloquent preachers. The architecture of these late-eighteenth- and early-nineteenth-century churches reveals remarkable adaptations to meet the changing demands of an audience-focused revival culture. In the United States, the famous American architect Robert Mills introduced the round or "auditorium" church with his design for the Circular Congregational Church in Charleston, South Carolina, which featured an eighty-three-foot diameter rotunda covered by a copper-plated wooden dome. The auditorium design maximized acoustics—using the domed roof to project a speaker's voice across the large room—and extended the seating capacity for the congregation.[39] The design was most clearly realized in Mills's second auditorium church, the Sansom Street Baptist Church in Philadelphia, which was completed in 1812 for Pastor William Staughton and featured a ninety-foot rotunda with seating for 2,500 people. As one attendee said of the Sansom Street Church: "The largest church gatherings I have ever seen under one roof were there, and regularly, too, for many years."[40] Though churches like these remained a distinct minority in the first few decades of the nineteenth century—as, indeed, they are today—they point to the growing influence of revivalism, and to changing views of the public role of a church, from the undisputed center of a community to one institution among many competitors. New designs extended revival churches' external presence and internal capacity in order to draw greater crowds, and in succeeding over competing institutions, they simultaneously elevated themselves above the competition and lowered themselves to the level of camp meetings, lyceums, and other speaking and entertainment venues.

It was in this context of competition and transition that a young revivalist named Charles Finney began his preaching career.

The Revivalist

In his *Memoirs*, Charles Finney recalled sitting in a church balcony as a young man and looking down on the minister in his high pulpit fumbling awkwardly with his Bible and notes:

> As he proceeded he would read the passages of Scripture where his fingers were inserted, and thus liberate one finger after another until the fingers of both hands were read out of their places. I observed that when his fingers were all read out, he was near the close of his sermon. His reading was altogether unimpassioned and monotonous. And although the people attended very closely and reverentially to his reading, yet to me, I must confess, it was not much like preaching, or to say the least not much like that which I thought preaching ought to be.[41]

The bad preacher story contrasted older assumptions of church authority against emerging ideals of revivalist populism. Traditional Protestant churches elevated the pulpit above a congregation seated in boxes or in flat, parallel rows. Ministers were chosen by God to speak for God, and thus they were positioned above their congregations, occupying a space between the divine and human realms. The congregation looked up at the preacher as at one who mediated between themselves and God—standing apart and impermeable in his pulpit fortress.[42] Yet in his anecdote, the young Finney, sitting in the balcony and thus looking down from an even higher vantage, recounted seeing not a divinely appointed authority, but a bumbling and inept orator "reading" not the Bible but "his fingers." Scripture was trapped in Finney's description, unable to capture the audience and demand their allegiance or their action. The minister, bound inside an enclosed pulpit, had likewise trapped God's truth between his fingers, unable or unwilling to set it loose upon the bored, if reverent, congregation.

In contrast to the bad preacher, Finney understood revivalism as demanding ministers to become effective orators, moving the emotions of their audience in order to provoke the inner workings of God's Spirit. As a revivalist, Charles Finney mastered the art of adapting messages to audiences. Although trained as a lawyer, he refused to adopt the style of the bench or of the pulpits of his childhood, but instead used that same "crude and vernacular speech" that had become a hallmark of itinerant and camp-meeting preachers.[43] Finney gained a reputation for clarity. Once, having heard him speak, someone supposedly remarked, "He doesn't preach; he only explains what other people preach."[44] His messages were direct, unadorned, and unrefined—Finney saying that he "studiously sought to avoid the use of any word that would not be understood by the common people without reference to their dictionaries."[45] In his revival meetings, he concentrated on music, prayer, strong emotions, and simple sermons. He preached practical messages and adapted his style—variously described as "flamboyant" and "severe"—to his audience and situation. Although he never carried a revival further south than Delaware, Finney brought the southern oratorical style of the previous generation's camp meetings to the northern states.[46]

As a theologian, Finney was an amalgamation of perspectives, availing himself, as one of his critics said, "of Calvinism on the one hand, and of the flexible passions of men on the other."[47] He consistently privileged audience response over doctrinal and denominational loyalty. Although originally ordained a Presbyterian minister, he later claimed not to have read the Presbyterian Confession before his ordination examinations, and said that after reading the Confession's doctrine of election, he was "absolutely ashamed of it."[48] Doctrine was only useful for Finney insofar as it produced the "fruits" of conversion, and apart from those fruits, it was useless.[49] Although Finney would remain nominally Presbyterian until 1836, his revivals were always deliberately interdenominational.[50]

Finney had been converted in October 1821, and from the mid-1820s through the early 1830s he traveled primarily around Massachusetts, Pennsylvania, and New York, concentrating his work on the rapidly growing towns up and down the newly completed Erie Canal, which had opened in the fall of 1825. Between 1825 and 1826, he led a famous series of revivals in Oneida County, New York, and in 1830–31 he led another major revival in the city of Rochester. His efforts brought "multitudes . . . into the churches" wherever he went, but his "new revival methods" also provoked harsh criticism from other ministers, who accused Finney of promoting fanaticism, allowing women to pray publicly, and reflecting poorly on the authority of established churches and ministers.[51]

After Rochester, Finney had offers to come and preach from all across New England, but the constant traveling had strained his health, and he was searching for a more permanent place to settle down with his wife and children.[52] So in 1832, he accepted an offer from brothers Lewis and Arthur Tappan—a pair of wealthy silk merchants, revivalists, and abolitionist leaders—to become permanent pastor of their latest financial and spiritual endeavor: a "free church" to be built in a rented theater with a tawdry reputation in one of the worst neighborhoods in New York City.

The Tappans were part of a group of wealthy bankers and merchants who called themselves "An Association of Gentlemen," and who for a number of years had been working to promote revivals in New York. In March 1830, the association launched a four-page weekly paper they called the *New York Evangelist*, which they intended to be "the advocate of Revivals . . . Temperance and Anti-slavery."[53] Later that same year, in an effort to open churches up to revival, the Tappan brothers and other association members financed the first of what would become a series of "free churches" in New York City.[54] Reflecting their revivalist populism, the free-church advocates argued that churches should not rent out their pews, which was the normal practice, but should instead remain "free to all" and welcoming to all social classes. Such churches, they argued, should be established in the poorer areas of the city where "the population is densest."[55] As Lewis Tappan described it, the free churches were intended to be "the means, under God, of drawing in large numbers of persons who are too often excluded from houses of worship, in consequence of the pews being owned or occupied by those who make no direct efforts to accommodate persons of humble life, or those who need to be urged to attend public worship."[56] People of different social classes mingled together in the free-church pews, and church ministers agreed not to take a regular salary, but to be supported by congregational gifts.[57] The First Free Church was organized on September 22, 1830, with sixteen members, but by October 1831 the congregation had expanded so rapidly that they had outgrown two locations and settled into a new building that could seat 800 to 1,000 worshippers.[58]

Given the remarkable success of this first experiment, the free-church advocates quickly moved to establish a second congregation, and on February 14, 1832, thirty-nine members organized the Second Free Presbyterian Church of New York. Initially the church met in Broadway Hall, but later that same year the Tappan brothers leased a nearly bankrupt theater on Chatham Street in lower Manhattan, "in the heart of the most irreligious population of New York."[59] Thus the church would come to be more commonly known as the Chatham Street Chapel. Substantial renovations—which included raising the pit area and creating a sloping floor on the ground level—increased seating from 1,300 to approximately 2,500.[60] It was an ambitious and expensive undertaking, and the association members needed a preacher whose reputation could fill all those seats. It is hardly surprising, therefore, that they approached the most popular itinerant revivalist in New York and offered him their new church.

Although skeptical of the project and concerned that Chatham's location was "too filthy . . . for decent people to go there,"[61] Finney eventually accepted the offer and was installed at Chatham on September 28, 1832—his first permanent pastorate. It was not, however, an auspicious beginning. A cholera epidemic had broken out in New York City during the previous summer, and Finney, already in poor health, was "taken ill" during his installation service and could not preach again until the spring of 1833.[62] Yet, although he remained weak, within a few weeks of returning to Chatham he had started a new series of revival meetings and was preaching every night to large audiences. Finney treated Chatham as he would any other revival stage and sent volunteers door to door to advertise services.[63] After a little less than three weeks, the chapel had received five hundred new converts, and the congregation had grown so large that it sent out a "colony" church, which was organized as the Fourth Free Church on January 5, 1834.[64]

Chatham was a unique space combining auditorium design with free-church social ideals—conflating revivalist and ecclesiastical sensibilities. For a number of reasons, the chapel's lessees refused to remodel it to look more like a typical Protestant church, choosing instead to maintain the former theater's three gallery levels and full stage. Rather than elevating the pulpit above a congregation sitting in parallel rows, Chatham consisted of raked amphitheater seating, rising up from a large stage without a permanent pulpit. The stage allowed the preacher to remain mobile and active throughout the sermon—a design that privileged the dramatic performance style typical of revivalist preaching. The body and not merely the word of the preacher mattered. As Jeanne Kilde says,

> This decision resulted in a significant alteration of relationships between minister and congregation within this building. For services, a portable lectern most likely was placed in the middle of the stage for preaching purposes, and Finney's trademark anxious bench was set below the stage. The result, of course, was that perhaps for the first time in U.S. religious

> architecture, the preacher was fully released from the cage of the elevated pulpit and given the physical performance space that a secular orator commanded. Although the visual link to a higher authority was severed, the preacher now had access to the performative authority of the actor.[65]

The chapel, in other words, physically reflected the social emphases of the free-church movement and the performance focus of revivalist preaching. Prior to Chatham, elevated pulpits gave the minister a privileged position between the congregation and God. In contrast, by lowering the minister *below* the congregation, Chatham's design prioritized the congregation as audience and accommodated the minister to their needs, embodying a new, democratic ideal of religious practice.[66] By refusing to rent pews—opening their services to a socially and even ethnically varied congregation—the revivalists transferred camp-meeting ethics into a church. The camp meeting, as Ellen Eslinger argues, "formed a world unto itself as rich and poor, man and woman, black and white, joined to worship together."[67] Within the camp's "society in microcosm," people were forced into close proximity with those outside their normal social circles.[68] In similar ways, Chatham's design encouraged social mingling and made members of all classes visible to the gaze of all others. As in illustrations of camp revivals—which often depict men and women mingling with, talking to, and observing one another while a revivalist preaches in the background—Chatham's half-moon amphitheater uniquely exposed the congregation to itself, allowing audience members to observe one another, even as it permitted the minister to see every member of the congregation.

The raked amphitheater seating introduced at Chatham would become a common feature during the late nineteenth century. Coinciding with the suburbanization of a growing American middle class, these churches became gradually more ornate, integrating lavish comforts of upper- and upper-middle-class homes into their designs.[69] In reimagining church as both stage and home, these churches modeled a new kind of religious public. Rather than emphasizing separation—between minister and congregation, human and divine—the amphitheater church modeled an integration and continuation between sacred and secular life. The theater-church offered a model of idealized civic community that persisted throughout the century—democratic but well-ordered and hierarchically organized based on aptitude and ability rather than predetermined class. What M. Christine Boyer says of theatrical representation applies to revival churches like Chatham as well: "[It] carried a sense of moral order within its aesthetic forms, bringing a memory of a harmonious society to public review."[70]

As a more practical matter, the amphitheater design made Chatham's sanctuary an invaluable multipurpose space, further redefining the relationship between sanctuary and society. To make up for the loss of pew rentals, Chatham's lessees rented out the building for both social and sacred activities throughout the week.[71] Outside the work of revival, therefore, the chapel quickly became a central meeting space and an important public symbol for a number of religious and political groups. Over the next few years, Chatham's guests included the American Bible Society, the American Tract Society, the American Education Society, the American Seaman's Friend Society, the National Convention of Sabbath School Teachers, and the American Board of Missions, as well as Sunday school unions, concerts, exhibitions, and public meetings on topics including labor, temperance, abolition, and philanthropy.[72]

The boundaries between Chatham's religious and social roles had been a major source of contention since its founding—particularly in relation to its abolitionist activities—and these boundaries were most severely tested in the summer of 1834. Attendance at the chapel's services had declined in late 1833, when Finney again left Chatham for health reasons—this time setting off on a six-month voyage to the Mediterranean—and left his uninspiring co-pastor, John Ingersoll, in charge.[73] During the summer, while Finney was still abroad, Chatham became a focus of anti-abolitionist mob violence. Finney, like the chapel's founders, supported abolition and refused to offer the sacrament of communion to slaveholders, saying, as one visitor recalled, "he could not recognize as christians [*sic*] those who held men in slavery."[74] The Tappan brothers were far more active in the abolitionist cause than Finney, however, and they had, from the beginning, invited abolitionist groups and activists into the chapel. Indeed, such was the chapel's reputation that in April 1834, the first women's anti-slavery society in New York City named themselves "The Female Anti-Slavery Society of Chatham Street Chapel."[75] A month later, in May 1834, the American Anti-Slavery Society celebrated their first anniversary at the chapel. Two newspapers in New York, the *Courier* and the *Enquirer*, began dismissively referring to the city's anti-slavery "fanatics" as the "Saints at Chatham Street Chapel,"[76] and the *New-York Spectator* called Chatham a "desecrated edifice" after reports of racial intermingling in its services.[77]

In Finney's absence, Chatham's founders, particularly Lewis Tappan and *New York Evangelist* editor Joshua Leavitt, grew more aggressive in using the chapel to promote abolitionist causes. For the Fourth of July celebration at the chapel in 1834, the *Spectator* reported that "the rows of seats back of the orchestra were filled *alternately* with blacks and whites," a display that was "clearly intended to outrage public taste and feeling." Whatever the intentions, some members of the public were outraged, and a small riot broke out at the chapel on that occasion.[78] Three days later, a much more serious riot erupted when members of the biweekly meeting of the Sacred Music Society, who had earlier agreed to move to a smaller room in the chapel that night so that the auditorium could be used for a church function, found that "instead of being occupied *for church purposes* . . . it was thronged by a congregation of blacks assembled to hear a black preacher." The Music Society members angrily demanded their room back, and when the black congregation refused to move, a fight broke out. In the escalating dispute, furniture and lamps were broken, and six men were arrested after the police arrived.[79] Part of the mob, after being thrown out of the chapel, vandalized the home of Lewis Tappan.[80] The mob riots continued, off and on, for several days, and the damage to the building was considerable.[81]

By the time Finney returned to New York City in late July 1834,[82] he found Chatham overrun with "mob excitement," and in frustration and continuing poor health, he left again after only a few days, traveling to his family's vacation spot in northwest New York for the rest of the summer.[83] When he returned to Chatham in November 1834, Finney faced more bad news. Joshua Leavitt told him that the *Evangelist*, which had grown increasingly abolitionist in tone, was now on the brink of financial collapse. Although still weak from his long illness, Finney agreed to deliver a series of weekly lectures at Chatham and allow Leavitt to record and publish them in an effort to increase subscriptions.[84] In the twenty "Lectures on Revivals of Religion" that he gave between December 5, 1834, and May 2, 1835, Finney combined jeremiadic and revival rhetoric in order to promote revivalism as a new foundation for healthy religious and political community. He condemned the apathy and inaction of the past, while pointing to a transcendent standard of renewal for the future. He argued that revivals were not miracles beyond human agency, nor were they the exclusive purview of camp meetings and itinerants. Rather, he described them as human inventions, promoted and maintained through artful persuasion. Finney called the Chatham community to repentance while arguing that a restored and reinvigorated free-church model of revival ought to be the defining and unifying feature of all Protestant churches. The revival church was, in turn, reimagined as the center of covenantal and political life.

The Revival Church

Finney opened his *Lectures* as a jeremiad. In the Puritan tradition, as Kurt Ritter argues, jeremiads utilized a basic four-part structure, which involved the preacher naming and describing the sin of the community, linking scriptural prophecies of divine judgment with present events, urging repentance and renewal of the covenant in order to avert further punishment, and offering hope of God's restorative blessing.[85] Finney began his first lecture by quoting a passage from the Hebrew prophet Habakkuk: "O Lord, revive thy work in the midst of the years, in the midst of the years make known; in wrath remember mercy."[86] In response to this verse, Finney said:

> It is supposed that the prophet Habakkuk was contemporary with Jeremiah, and that this prophecy was uttered in anticipation of the Babylonish captivity. Looking at the judgments which were speedily to come upon his nation, the soul of the prophet was wrought up to an agony, and he cries out in his distress, "O Lord, revive thy work." As if he had said, "O Lord, grant that thy judgments may not make Israel desolate. In the midst of these awful years, let the judgments of God be made the means of reviving religion among us."[87]

Speaking at Chatham—to a congregation recently embroiled in the social upheaval and violence of New York's summer of 1834—and to the reading audience of the floundering *Evangelist*, Finney linked the prophetic passage to his own day. He offered up the prophet's prayer that God would not allow these events to destroy the free-church movement or the work of the *Evangelist*, but would, instead, make these judgments the motivators of revival. Everything that followed in these *Lectures* was an extension of this prayer, a sustained call and plan for the community to repent of their sins and return to their covenantal relationship with

God by embracing "the means" of revival that God, even in his wrath, had so mercifully offered.

Finney argued that in order to be restored, the community needed to obey God and use the means he had provided to promote revivals, persuade sinners to come to Christ, and expand the kingdom of God throughout the earth. Only through active promotion and expansion could the covenant be restored and the community redeemed. Such a demand would have been unthinkable for the Puritans or even for those revivalists of the previous generation. Oriented by a Calvinist orthodoxy that subordinated human action to divine will, earlier revivalists were given to describing revivals as miracles, outpourings, awakenings, or, as Jonathan Edwards called them, "*Surprising Works of God*"—special and unpredictable manifestations of the divine Spirit. Finney, in contrast, defined them as "a purely philosophical result of the right use of the constituted means."[88] For Finney, revivals were not surprises or miracles, but natural excitations of religious emotion based on the work of human agents. By linking revival and agency, he opened the possibility of revivalism as a site for collective action, and he categorized the promotion of revivals within those demands that God could legitimately make on the believing community. So long as revivals were "surprising," they remained private events that were fundamentally rooted in the spiritual relationship between individual believers and God. While a minister might call upon his congregation to pray for revival, such prayers would be contemplative rather than active. Believers could hope for an outpouring of God's Spirit, but they could not act to make that hope a reality, encourage others to act, or expect that any actions they might take individually or communally would have any predictable results. In contrast, Finney not only encouraged, but demanded human action to promote and sustain revivals, and, in so doing, he made these actions an element of obedience to God through which the community could be restored. While earlier descriptions of revivals had presented them as means for temporarily elevating community feeling, Finney presented them as means for the restoration, redefinition, and expansion of the covenantal community itself.

In these lectures, Finney compressed his community's mission to a single standard—their ability to convert sinners and bring them to a decision for Christ—and he linked this revival focus with the hope for both spiritual and political transformation, arguing that revivals were the only means to "restore religion to the place it ought to have in the estimation of the public."[89] Reimagined as a jeremiadic demand upon the community, revival was associated with new forms of ecclesial association and political engagement. Inspired to action by the judgment of God, a revivalist church could counter existing political and religious institutions while advocating a new kind of covenantal community whose goals included the kind of economic, social, electoral, and international reform that would, ultimately, usher in a radically different form of government under the kingship of Jesus Christ.

Countering Secular Emotion

Revivals provoke strong emotions. From the eighteenth century to the present day, revivals have brought to mind images of men and women falling to their knees or flat on their faces—weeping and pleading with God and a preacher to save their souls. When delivering his infamous "Sinners in the Hands of an Angry God" at Enfield, Jonathan Edwards reportedly had to stop preaching and ask his wailing audience to quiet down so that he could continue.[90] Such displays have led critics to accuse revivalists of fanaticism, manipulation, impropriety, and dangerous emotional excess. Finney acknowledged these critiques and condemned "thoughtless levity," but he argued that revivals must stir the emotions if they were to be effective. Perhaps someday, he mused, the Christian community would become so "enlightened" that the "torrents of worldliness" would no longer threaten spiritual growth, and the emotional drama of religious revivals would no longer be necessary.[91] However, until that future time, the spread of the Christian message depended on the "excitements" of revivalism. Chiding his audience, Finney said, "Instead of priding yourself in being free from such [emotional] extravagances, you ought to hide your heads." Lack of emotion, for Finney, indicated a lack of commitment to Christ or a lack of belief in the realities of eternal damnation for those who have not accepted Christ. To save sinners, the risk of excessive emotion was far more desirable than the risk of emotionless rationality that failed to adequately experience God. To be pious without emotion was "superficial." Feeling was an essential sign of true faith—proving that one was a follower and not merely a "professor of religion." Finney equated loss of feeling with spiritual backsliding. If a convert did not feel saved or have a continuous desire to save others, it indicated that her conversion might not have been genuine. "We do wrong," Finney said, "if we let the fear of impulses lead us to resist the *good* impulses of the Holy Ghost."[92]

Such concern about emotions is not new. On the one hand, emotions are disruptive and excessive; they seem to distort reason and promote thoughtlessness and gullibility. They transform crowds into mobs and threaten social fragmentation. On the other hand, emotions call upon our capacity to pay attention to the world around us. Aristotle described the emotions as things "accompanied by pain and pleasure,"[93] which disrupt our placidity. In an emotional moment, our immediate experience is not proceeding as usual, and the disruption of normalcy produces a mental and physical response. When we are emotional, we react. We take action, and this action provides a basis for public engagement. For Finney, emotions were to be judged on their efficacy in leading sinners to act on the gospel message. Good emotions brought salvation, while bad emotions deluded sinners, distracting their attention or lulling them into a false sense of security. Emotions were fickle, and the devil would try anything to keep the sinner out of heaven. Thus, "We must have exciting, powerful preaching," Finney said, "or the devil will have the people."[94] Even a crying infant or an uncomfortable pew might be enough to distract the sinner and keep her from submitting her soul to Christ.

Among all these distractions, Finney identified the emotions attached to business and politics as particularly damaging. The complexity of politics, for Finney, was yet one more way for the devil to distract sinners and keep the hell-bound on the path to destruction, while keeping churchgoers focused on bad emotions that were at odds with the gospel. He said:

> The great political, and other worldly excitements that agitate Christendom, are all unfriendly to religion, and divert the mind from the interests of the soul. Now these excitements can only be counteracted by *religious* excitements. And until there is religious principle in the world to put down irreligious excitements, it is in vain to try to promote religion, except by counteracting excitements. This is true in philosophy, and it is historical fact.[95]

In this passage, Finney summarized his theory of emotions and the role revivals could play in countering political distractions and refocusing attention on those good emotions that would lead to Christ and conversion. He argued that God calls ministers to create emotional experiences, breathing feelings into their congregations. The minister must not be a logician—a "professor of religion" who seeks abstract wisdom or deeper doctrine at the expense of souls—but rather a consummate rhetorician. And it was the Spirit of God that functioned as a kind of rhetorical teacher, guiding the revivalist to "use means wisely, in a way adapted to the end, and to avoid doing hurt." Like politicians, revivalists were to be masters of persuasion who could "drive [sinners] away from every refuge" until their words and "manner of speaking" had so compelled the unconverted souls that they were eager to join the cause. Revival religion propelled the individual convert into a new kind of church community, which appropriated and redefined emotion and persuasion to further the cause of Christ and "build up the kingdom of God." Emotions compel action, and the skillful revivalist was to use all the emotional tools at his disposal to compel the sinner to accept Christ and join the battle against the devil's politics.[96]

Countering Religious Establishment

Just as there were good and bad emotions for Finney, there were true and false churches. The true church was a revival church. Throughout the lectures, Finney described churches and denominations that had been "cursed" by God for failing to promote revivals. These churches focused on ornament and education. They sent their young ministers to seminaries where all enthusiasm for revivals was taken out of them. Finney, who had neglected his own theological training, was dismissive of theology schools throughout the lectures. The dangers of religious education were similar to the dangers of politics. In both cases, a potentially good thing had been captured by the devil and used as a tool to distract Christian workers from the task of saving souls. Indeed, he warned that some education, at least that coming from "professors of religion," might eternally damage the souls of students, driving them away from God and straight to hell. In the seminaries, Finney said, "blind and stupid" experts dismissed emotion and the saving power of God. They interpreted faith but failed to experience it. In contrast, he argued, the true church and true followers of Christ were to learn from practical experience. Formal education was unnecessary for revivalists. To start a revival, believers did not need to understand theories or abstractions; they needed a practical understanding of persuasion and emotion, together with a "plain common sense" understanding of the Bible. Formal education was what turned actors into passive thinkers, and Finney repeatedly warned his listeners to think of the thousands or millions of souls that had gone to hell in the past because evangelists were not equipped to act and to persuade them, while living, to come to Christ.[97]

In their obsession with ornament and tradition, meanwhile, Finney compared these false churches and seminaries to the Roman Catholics and their "strange and ridiculous" practices. Protestants condemning Catholics was, of course, nothing new, but by conflating Catholic and Protestant identities, Finney adopted an approach that became a commonplace and critical tactic of twentieth-century Fundamentalists. By invoking this distinction—setting revivalist churches on one side, and Catholic and non-revivalist Protestant churches on the other—Finney indicated the critical role he understood revivalism to play as a counter religious discourse. Revivalism was a fundamental principle of Finney's religion, which marked not merely the difference between obedient and disobedient churches, but the difference between true churches and those false Protestant institutions that could be dismissively equated with the unquestionably apostate Catholics. Revivalism offered a fundamental foundation for a unified, interdenominational Protestant, counter-religious community, which represented an idealization of already existing practices embodied in the free-church movement and Chatham Street Chapel. Although he maintained that denominations "should labor by themselves" if they could not reach productive agreements with each other, Finney idealized a unified, revivalist Christianity beyond denominational "prejudice." He described true Christians coming together to construct new churches, like Chatham, that were built with revival as their goal. The true church, he argued, must be a revival church, and revival was the fundamental element around which true churches could unite together in common community.[98]

Finney's search for fundamentals by which true churches could be united and false churches excluded was an inevitable consequence of the fragmentation produced by denominational disestablishment and political controversy, and by revivalism itself. It is hardly surprising therefore that, although the term "fundamentalism" did not become common until the 1920s, references to "fundamentalists" date back at least to the period when Finney was delivering these lectures. In

1842, the Cincinnati-based *Catholic Telegraph* described a "Class of the Fundamentalists" who believed that "those who hold the fundamental points of religion continue in the doctrine of Christ, though they differ, toto cœlo, in every thing [*sic*] else."[99] The author described these Fundamentalists as trying "to reconcile the unity and oneness so strongly inculcated in the New Testament, with the protestant principle of private interpretation and its consequences [*sic*] variety of opinion."[100] In other words, lacking the strong hierarchical unity of Catholicism, American Protestants in the nineteenth century struggled to locate common norms upon which to construct ideals of community and practice. By using the call to revival persuasion as a jeremiadic standard against which beliefs and practices could be measured, Finney translated revivalism into a "fundamental," which transcended denominational and ecclesiastical boundaries while splitting Protestant believers and churches into two camps. Across denomination, doctrine, and region, Finney implied, true believers could unite as members of the true church—the revival church—and stand against the evils of the false church and its professors of religion.

In order to counter these false churches, Finney again invoked the revivalist as rhetorician. False ministers promoted their education, but they had lost their ability to communicate practical truths. When it came to revivals, they were likely to either ignore them or to treat them as miraculous and surprising events that were outside human control. Finney attacked this ideal and argued at great length that a revival was "not a miracle." Throughout these lectures, he rejected as "absurd" the idea that religion was exempt from the natural laws that govern every other human activity. Religion did not exceed "the ordinary powers of nature," but instead "consists entirely in the right *exercise*" of these powers. Churches were not merely called to pray and trust God for revivalist fervor; they were called to bring about revivals in their communities. Explicitly opposing earlier revivalists, like Edwards, who emphasized the inability of human beings to respond to Christ without God's grace, Finney defined conversion as a matter of human will, saying, "When God commands us to do a thing, it is the highest possible evidence that we can do it." Sinners could not blame God for their sin, and revivalists could not blame God for the lack of emotion and conversions in their churches. Finney said that church people used to think revival was "an interposition of Divine power which they had nothing to do with," but he urged his listeners to accept revivals as natural human events "to be *promoted*." He did not wholly discount the role of God, for "without the blessing of God," revival was impossible. However, he reimagined God as an audience approachable through human persuasion. In order to generate revival, he argued, churches needed to direct their persuasion both outward, stirring the emotions of sinners—and upward, persuading God to bless the work with his convicting Spirit. Persuasive, or "effectual," prayer adopted the same methods as persuasive speech. Finney said, "The spirit of prayer is a state of continual desire and anxiety of mind for the salvation of sinners. . . . It is the same, so far as the philosophy of the mind is concerned, as when a man is anxious for some worldly interest." Believers were to come to prayer as interlocutors before God, and thus Finney imagined God offering a rhetorical model for revival persuasion through the act of prayer. The revivalist was not controlled by God, but was to follow God's model in order to achieve predictable and effectual results. Rather than suspending "the laws of matter and mind," revival was to follow naturally from the established means of persuasion. Therefore, since revival was rhetorical and accessible to human agency, Finney deemed it appropriate to regard regular revivals as a fundamental practice for all true churches and to make a jeremiadic demand that churches adapt these means, create revivals, convict sinners of their sin, and bring believers into the revival church. Salvation of the covenant community required that community to save souls, and the political and spiritual dimensions of church life were inseparably linked to the revival of religion.[101]

Redefining Political Community

Just as there was, for Finney, a true and false church, there was right and wrong in politics. Speaking to an audience that had so recently been involved in political conflict, he stressed that revivals were more important to true churches and true religion than any social or political efforts. He argued, for example, that while churches must oppose and speak out against the sin of slavery, they must also avoid "angry controversy" on the subject. The church's fundamental focus was not to be abolition but revival, and the church had sinned by reversing this focus. This did not mean that a return to revival meant abandoning politics, but for Finney, revival was the comprehensive category, involving personal repentance of sin (including slavery), a religious commitment to save souls and break the devil's power over them, and a political commitment to further "the reformation and salvation of sinners." Just as education without revival made actors into passive "professors," social change without revival would "only make it worse" for sinners who had not been converted. By making sinners more comfortable in their unrepentant sin, Finney warned, well-meaning Christians might be unintentionally condemning them to an eternity of suffering. Politics without revival was dangerous.[102]

Nevertheless, Finney argued that revival churches needed to adopt a correct and consistent stand on political issues, saying, "God cannot sustain this free and blessed country, which we love and pray for, unless the church will take right ground. Politics are a part of religion in such a country as this, and Christians must do their duty to the country as part of their duty to God."[103] Having once defined revival as a fundamental demand upon the true church, Finney could speak to that church as both a religious and a political association. Outside of the true church and its revival-centered perspective, politics was a devilish distraction that would keep churches from winning converts and keep sinners out of heaven. However, once churches were united around the common call to revive religion, they would be free to determine a common politics through which revival might be most easily propagated. Indeed, Finney recognized that a united Protestant church could have profound social, economic, and political consequences. Such a community could "regulate the commerce of the world" and "sway the destinies of nations, without involving themselves at all in the base and corrupting strife of parties." All the church had to do was "let it be known that Christians are united" around a common cause, and the political world would soon match their ideals.[104] By offering revival as a fundamental standard for religious unity, Finney also articulated a space for a united, revivalist politics.

For Finney, right religion and right politics were ultimately intertwined so that the true church's political activities would have profound spiritual implications for society. Specifically, Finney argued that political regulation on behalf of religious revival would hasten the salvation of the world's people and the millennial return of Christ to reign on earth. This is a doctrine known as "postmillennialism." During the nineteenth century, postmillennialists championed a belief in the steady improvement of the human condition through reason, and the "dominion" of nature through religious and technological advancement. Beginning with the work of Edwards and continuing throughout the nineteenth century, revivalist narratives were heavily inflected with postmillennial fervor, and revivals were understood as proof that God's Spirit was advancing his work in America. For Finney and other postmillennial revivalists, revival growth was an indication of God's advancing kingdom—a metaphor that effectively conflated religious and political manifestations. The postmillennial believer knew that the nation and the world would belong to the true church in the future, and this knowledge authorized collective political action in the present in order to secure that future.[105]

Conclusion

Finney's lectures saved the *New York Evangelist* as 2,500 new readers subscribed to the paper between December 1834 and May 1835 to get reprints.[106] In book form, the lectures became a bestseller in both the United States and in England. Finney's narrative of a unified revival church struck a powerful chord with the popular imagination, and his arguments spoke to a troubled Anglo-Protestant culture struggling to rectify the ecclesiastically atomizing effects of sectarianism, itinerancy, disestablishment, immigration, and slavery. After Finney, revival came to be widely seen as a way of repairing denominational and, later on, political divisions.[107] As one example, seeking to rebut European claims about American denominational disunity, Robert Baird argued in 1844 that "the main branches of the evangelical Protestant Church . . . ought to be viewed as branches of one great body, even the entire visible Church of Christ in this land."[108] In this context, Baird argued, like Finney a decade earlier, that belief in revivals constituted a mark of true faith so that anyone who would oppose revivals was to be regarded as an infidel, a heretic, or a backslider—in short, "an enemy to spiritual religion itself."[109]

Finney's lectures became the standard text of a new preaching culture. His vision of a common church united around the principles and politics of revival powerfully influenced the next generation of ministers who combined the oratorical skills of the previous generation's camp-meeting preachers and circuit riders with the social savvy and urban flair of a rapidly expanding middle class. The methods of these "princes of the pulpit"—men like Phillips Brooks and the famous Henry Ward Beecher—carried, in turn, into the media-saturated ministries of late-nineteenth- and early-twentieth-century figures like D. L. Moody, Billy Sunday, and Aimee Semple McPherson, and ultimately, these performer-revivalist ministers and their large churches laid a foundation for contemporary Fundamentalist megachurch culture in the United States.

In his *Lectures*, Finney envisioned a new kind of religious public. Called to common repentance for their sinful neglect of revival, the imagined covenantal community of the revival church stretched across denominations, drawing together a diverse body of believers around a common commitment to pursue the available means of persuasion for the salvation of souls and the transformation of society. These, in turn, gave meaning to a fragmented social landscape, providing a set of communally defined tools with which to critique and act upon the world. Finney's proto-"fundamentalism" responded to rapid changes taking place in Anglo-Protestant hegemony and American society as a whole in the first few decades of the nineteenth century. His revival-church vision offered a sphere within which change could be interpreted, values discussed, and action enabled. This sphere operated in public, reaching new converts and working through personal, social, and political means to transform all of society into an unreachable but always hoped-for ideal—the kingdom of God on earth.

Chapter Three

Countersymbols and Confederacy

⌘

> Those who make the plain teaching of the Bible the rule of all faith and practice look upon this age as the "Church period," a period in which the Holy Spirit is the Administrator of God's earth plans; and they recognize in a true church a "called out" company, who have found in Christ . . . the only place of safety from judgment.
>
> —William Bell Riley, "The Great Divide or Christ and the Present Crisis," 1919

Fundamentalism has its roots in revivalism, but the Fundamentalist movement of the twentieth century has emerged as a radical reformulation of revivalist idealism. When Charles Finney addressed listeners and readers in his 1835 *Lectures on Revivals of Religion*, he warned of individual enemies that the revival church would have to confront and overcome in order to establish Christ's kingdom on earth. He warned of "professors of religion" who would dismiss and speak against the work of revival. He warned often of a personal devil who conspired to keep sinners out of heaven. When he spoke against institutions and systems, however, it was more as distractions than as deliberate threats to revivalism. Seminaries could distract would-be revivalists and turn young "doers" of God's will and God's word into mere professors. Business and political interests—even good interests—could lead believers to seek after the things of this world and neglect the things of God. Churches with uncomfortable pews or badly run prayer meetings could drive sinners away and keep them out of heaven. For revivalists like Finney, however, these things did not constitute evidence of an organized threat. There was not a coordinated effort to destroy revival; it was merely the loss of personal faith and disciplines that led believers astray. True, Finney mentioned institutional opponents like Catholics and Unitarians in his *Lectures*, but these were clearly positioned as foils to the work of individual revivalists. They offered a needed contrast to the true church and true believers, but they did not represent a systemic or organized threat. They were, Finney argued, "ignorant" and "ridiculous," but while their teachings threatened the souls of potential converts, they did not threaten the stability or security of the revival church as a whole. Throughout Finney's lectures it was individuals, not institutions, that posed imminent risk to the church.

By the 1920s, however, the discourse of revivalism had changed. It was now institutions and systems that were the threats, and individuals were largely defined through their relationship to organized associations of belief and practice whose goals were not merely to distract true believers, but to destroy true belief and the systems supporting it. While continuing to idealize revivalist speech that was directed at the individual, resistance groups within some of the major Protestant denominations were constructing narratives of an emerging conflict between "a confederacy" of religious and political elites and a new "counter movement" of plain-spoken believers who were organizing to fight for the "fundamentals" of their faith.[1] The essentially public speech of revivalism—which presupposed the freedom of speakers to reach and persuade audiences—was gradually being replaced with resistant counterpublic speech that both idealized this freedom and declared it under siege.

On May 27, 1919, a loose association of Protestant ministers, evangelists, and church leaders convened the first World Conference on the Fundamentals of the Faith. In front of a purported gathering of more than seven thousand attendees, they announced the formation of a national body, the World's Christian Fundamentals Association. Less formally, the association was called the Fundamentalist Fellowship, or the Christian Fundamentals Movement,[2] and by the early 1920s, members were referring to themselves simply as "Fundamentalists." The effective life of the World's Christian Fundamentals Association was short-lived, but the name and the identity survived. By the mid-1920s, Fundamentalism had become a commonplace name for a definable, interdenominational movement whose members advocated cooperative resistance as a means of countering perceived threats from religious and political "modernists" or "liberals."[3]

Expansion and Ecumenicism

The kingdom of God was a central metaphor in revivalist rhetoric. It represented both a continuation and a perfection of the existing revival church community. It described the ideal political state that was to be the culmination of revivalist speech. Revivalists like Finney portrayed the kingdom as an earthly reality, intertwined with the revival community and advancing through the divinely appointed means of persuasion. Revivals were only a temporary calling for the church. Like scaffolding, they surrounded the growing edifice from which Christ would eventually reign on earth. The role of the revivalist, in the meantime, was to remain flexible, adapting the means of persuasion to the particular needs and cases they encountered. Revivalists, above all, presupposed that their audience was composed of individual sinners who needed to be brought into the community of faith and added to the edifice of God's kingdom.

In the latter decades of the nineteenth century, however, such a positive vision of the kingdom became harder to justify. The decades of disputes that culminated in the Civil War left denominations split along regional and abolitionist lines.[4] In the military camps, denominational identities did not disappear, but sectarian loyalties seemed far less significant, and many of the army chaplains tried to incorporate the rhetorical styles of revivalist and camp-meeting preachers in an effort to appeal to the denominationally diverse and easily distracted soldiers under their care.[5] Membership declines and leadership vacancies, particularly in the South, left many churches financially destitute and their church buildings abandoned.[6]

In the decades leading up to the war, changing perspectives on the slavery issue forced an increasing number of church members and church leaders to reexamine their understanding of the Bible's explicit and tacit endorsement of slavery in various forms. In particular, many moderate abolitionists—who believed that slavery was wrong but did not want to abandon their reliance on Scripture—began adopting new strategies of reading and interpretation. As Molly Oshatz argues, "The slavery debates gave rise to ideas that would become the hallmarks of liberal Protestant theology: God's revelation unfolded progressively through human history, moral action had to be considered in its historical and social context, and the ultimate source of Protestant truth was the shared experience of believers rather than the letter of the biblical text."[7] New divinity schools challenged long-held assumptions about the accuracy and authority of the Bible, and the growing diversity of the U.S. population challenged the exceptional status of Anglo-Protestant churches in social and political life. In May 1881, the Revised Version of the New Testament was released to huge public demand. This represented the first significant challenge to the Authorized (or King James) Version in America, and, more significantly, it opened up for the first time the process of Bible translation to the general public—revealing the fragmented nature of the documents, lack of true originals, etc. The result was that, after the Revised Version, public knowledge of modern Bible criticism began to increase, and the obvious trustworthiness of the biblical text came under broader scrutiny.[8] Even as the scope of the revivalist kingdom grew larger, the dream that Finney had expressed of a unified revivalist-Protestant voice in politics seemed more and more remote.

Postwar industrialization led to a surplus of American products, which in turn led industrialists to seek new, international markets for American goods. Revivalists also developed an international vision, and foreign-missions efforts were expanded, with a growing number of Protestant missionary associations organized to carry the Christian gospel around the world. In 1867—after a twenty-year delay caused by slavery controversies between Northern and Southern churches—the United States joined the Evangelical Alliance, an international association of Protestant leaders that had been first established in London in 1846. In 1875, American revivalist D. L. Moody began what would become a twenty-five-year ministry in the United States, having achieved breakout success in Britain. In September 1893, a World's Parliament of Religions was held in connection with the World's Columbian Exposition (aka Chicago World's Fair) and gave masses of Americans their first exposure to representatives and teachers from many non-Western religious traditions. The World's Parliament did not produce the "universal fraternity of virtue and morality" that its leaders had hoped for, but it did, instead, provoke a large number of American Protestants to search for new ways to extol their relative superiority among the world's religions. A month after the parliament, the Evangelical Alliance sponsored the International Christian Conference in Chicago to discuss the status of American Protestantism, and the future of its evangelistic and social efforts to effect the "salvation of the world."[9]

Narratives of evangelism, consumerism, and political conquest often overlapped, as in Josiah Strong's best-selling *Our Country* (1885/1891), Albert J. Beveridge's famous "March of the Flag" speech (1898), and John R. Mott's *The Evangelization of the World in This Generation* (1900). Military and industrial language combined with revivalism to justify American international expansionism. Josiah Strong, for example, declared that "The Christian religion, by rendering men temperate, industrious, and moral, makes them prosperous." And George Northrup, president of the American Baptist Missionary Union, called on believers to "conquer for [Christ] all the kingdoms of the globe."[10]

Meanwhile, American industrial demands for cheap labor fueled rapid immigration growth across the second half of the nineteenth century. As Strong told his readers: "During the last ten years we have suffered a peaceful invasion by an army more than four times as vast as the estimated number of Goths and Vandals that swept over Southern Europe and overwhelmed Rome."[11] For many political, industrial, and religious leaders, immigrants were a necessary but insidious force whose presence challenged American exceptionalist and expansionist narratives. Industry leaders followed the dictates of an emerging social-evolutionary science—which defined workers' abilities through racial categories—in an effort to minimize worker rebellion and maximize output. Workers from the same country were often separated from each other, so as to minimize collective associations.[12] The immigrant population, Strong and others argued, was predominantly ignorant, narrow-minded, and often criminal.[13] For the safety of the nation and the advancement of civilization, immigrants needed to be contained within (and, when possible, converted into) the existing order.

In this context, conversion took on new meanings. Among the Puritans, narratives of spiritual conversion were used as tests of membership—a testimony to God's convicting work in the souls of the saints, which brought them into the religio-political community. Among revivalists, as we have seen, this convicting work was redefined to include the rhetorical relationship between the sinner and the revivalist, and conversion was reimagined as what Finney called "the right employment of the sinner's own agency."[14] As with revival, what once was a wholly mystical connection between God and the human soul was reimagined as a natural and expected outcome of well-constructed rhetoric. The actual moment of conversion still required some level of divine intervention, but human agents were now primarily responsible for persuading sinners to come to Christ. By taking conversion out of the divine realm and locating it in human persuasion, revivalists opened the door for the secularization of conversion narratives, and late-nineteenth-century authors like Strong and Mott both preached and embodied the conflation of spiritual and social conversion. Strong, for example, wrote *Our Country* to promote the cause of home missions, and published the book through the American Home Missionary Society. As Congregationalist minister Austin Phelps said in his introduction to the 1891 edition of *Our Country*:

> By natural sequence, the *localities* where those elements of powerful manhood are, or are to be, in most vigorous development, have been the strategic points of which our religion has taken possession as by a masterly military genius.
>
> The principles of such a strategic wisdom should lead us to look on these United States as first and foremost the chosen seat of enterprise for the world's conversion. Forecasting the future of Christianity, as statesmen forecast the destiny of nations, we must believe that it will be what the future of this country is to be. As goes America, so goes the world, in all that is vital to its moral welfare.[15]

Linked to agency and persuasion, revivalist conversion narratives created the possibility of conversion as a tool for political interpellation. Political conversion narratives emphasized holistic redemption—the spiritual, social, and political person could be redeemed. As spiritual narratives had come to demarcate the boundaries of church membership, political narratives became required markers of American identity. Participation in the "American dream" involved conversion to the established American ideals of religion and commerce, and the dream's purveyors were religio-political revivalists, drawing foreigners and immigrants into the national fold.[16]

Beginning in the late nineteenth century, proponents of the "social gospel" movement preached revival and conversion as means for moral, social, and economic improvement. The social gospel leaders helped to establish large "institutional churches" in major cities across the United States that tried to extend the kingdom-building work of the church across the whole week and offer social alternatives for the urban poor.[17] Housed in free-church modeled, multifunction buildings, these institutional churches were designed to restore the church to the center of community life in the rapidly expanding urban context. Combining sanctuaries and Sunday school classrooms with gymnasiums, swimming pools, and, later on, space to view the hundreds of early films that were produced explicitly for church audiences, these churches, which typically included office or hotel space that they rented out for extra income, created programs throughout the week that were intended to redeem the social, moral, spiritual, and political values of the working-class and immigrant populations surrounding them—creating, as one institutional church pastor said, "a material environment wherein the spiritual Christ can express Himself . . . by planting itself just where Christ stood and worked when He was on earth—in the midst of publicans and sinners."[18]

In many ways, institutional churches functioned as prototypes for the contemporary megachurch. They were products of large cities. They were adaptive and audience-focused. And they created an early version of what one megachurch scholar and promoter has called the "seven-day-a-week church."[19] As a whole, then, the social gospel and institutional church leaders were united by a common and expansive continuation of Finney's vision of the revival church at the center of the modern world, guiding the nation to become God's kingdom on earth. As social-gospel leader Walter Rauschenbusch said,

> Where a really Christian type of religious life is created, the intellect and its education are set free, and this in turn aids religion to emancipate itself from superstition and dogmatism. Where religion and intellect combine, the foundation is laid for political democracy. Where the people have the

> outfit and the spirit of democracy, they can curb economic exploitation. Where predatory gain and the resultant inequality are lessened, fraternal feeling and understanding become easier and the sense of solidarity grows. Where men live in consciousness of solidarity and in the actual practice of love with their fellow-men, they are not far from the Kingdom of God.[20]

Such expansive ambitions, however, were stymied by the fragmented reality of Protestant denominations at the turn of the century. Strong, for example, morosely contrasted the strength of the "Roman Catholic hierarchy" with the American Protestants who remained mired in denominational and regional disputes.[21] Promoting expansion abroad and cooperation at home, prominent Protestant ministers and periodicals began systematically promoting interdenominational unity as the necessary path to continued Protestant relevance.[22] Without cooperation, it was argued, there could be no kingdom.

Mere revivalism seemed an inadequate foundation upon which to construct a united Protestantism capable of extending the kingdom of God around the world. While revivalists like Finney had promoted revivals as a way to unify local denominations around common evangelistic efforts, these events were neither systemic nor sustainable. Denominations that cooperated for a momentary revival would then return to their separate identities, and there was nothing to encourage cooperation beyond the revival event. Therefore, in the latter decades of the nineteenth century, along with the social-gospel and institutional-church movements, there emerged a series of cooperative efforts among the largest Protestant denominations, which were intended to permanently instantiate an interdenominational Protestant identity that could stand up to global challenges and counter-religious competition. In the absence of an established American denomination, Robert Schneider argues, "the ecumenical organizations claimed for themselves the role of an informal national establishment."[23] The leaders of these movements reimagined revival unity in the form of a more permanent institution that could maintain Protestant credibility and influence in an increasingly pluralistic environment, and they called for "federation" and "unity" among the churches.

By 1919, as the nations of Europe absorbed the realities of the Armistice and the end of the First World War, two American ecumenical organizations were vying for supremacy. One was the Federal Council of the Churches of Christ in America, which had been established in 1908 with approximately four hundred members representing thirty denominations. Although similar in some ways to previous associations, such as the Evangelical Alliance, the council was much more explicit in linking religious and political activism, adopting the language and critiques of the social-gospel movement.[24] While the council's first decade was, as William Hutchison argues, only a "mixed success," by 1919, revitalized by the critical role its General War-Time Commission of the Churches had played in recruiting military chaplains and organizing interdenominational support for the war effort, it had gained dramatic international visibility.[25]

Competing with the Federal Council was the newly minted Interchurch World Movement, established immediately after the Armistice, chaired by John Mott, and financially supported by John D. Rockefeller Jr.[26] After witnessing unprecedented displays of interdenominational unity during the war, the movement's leadership became convinced that the time was ripe for an international ecumenical organization—rooted in the United States—that could restore Christian dominance on the global landscape and serve as a mechanism for worldwide missionary and social work. The Interchurch World Movement was in some ways more ambitious and certainly more aggressive than the Federal Council, advocating a complete centralization of Protestant leadership and resources, reflected first of all in its unprecedented drive for denominational money. Ultimately, the movement's leaders misread the postwar religious landscape, and their ambition would be their downfall. The movement proved to be a financial disaster, which raised only a tiny fraction of its projected funding, incurred massive debts, offended powerful business interests, and completely collapsed by 1921.[27] During its year and a half in existence, however, the Interchurch World Movement seemed likely to dominate the ecumenical landscape and replace the Federal Council as the premier voice of the American Protestant church. The speed and aggressiveness with which the movement organized led some critics to label it a "superchurch" or a "Protestant Papacy."[28]

Ecumenicism, and in particular the Interchurch World Movement, became dominant sources of what I am calling "oppositional condensation symbols" or "countersymbols" among members of an emerging resistance movement within the established denominations. In speeches and writings, leaders of the World's Christian Fundamentals Association warned of a growing "confederacy" effort to compel interchurch cooperation; manipulate government leaders; collaborate with Germans, Catholics, Jews, and Bolsheviks; and in various other ways dismantle local churches and replace them with a repressive, anti-American, religio-political regime.[29] In response to this confederacy, they argued, Fundamentalist believers needed to form a "new fellowship" in order to preserve the freedoms and secure the interests of local churches and church members against what early Fundamentalist sympathizer J. Gresham Machen would describe as "the centralization of power which is going on in the modern Church."[30] One significant result of these arguments was that doctrinal, sectarian claims took on increasingly public and political significance in the rhetoric of the emerging Fundamentalist community.

Countersymbols

In her book *Verbal Behavior and Politics*, Doris Graber says: "A verbal condensation symbol is a name, word, phrase, or maxim which stirs vivid impressions involving the listener's most basic values. The symbol arouses and readies him for mental or physical action."[31] Condensation symbols do not operate at the level of the sentence or proposition but of words. They cannot make or support claims. They have no rational or critical dimension, and as such, they are difficult to critique in and of themselves. To argue against the meaning of a condensation symbol is to miss the point. These symbols are, instead, closely related to what J. G. A. Pocock calls a "happening" in language, which does not attempt to persuade propositionally but to establish "patterns of choric incantation shared by the speaker and his responding audience."[32] The power of condensation symbols rests in their being continually recognized and identified as constitutive calls that frame response and provoke action. The common stirring of a crowd in response to these symbols establishes an emotional foundation for collective association, which, because it is not grounded in propositions, is not subject to counter-propositional argument.

The precise referent of a condensation symbol is, as Graber says, in part dependent on the interpretation of the responding listener, and this ambiguity allows the symbol to perform its condensing function, bringing together often-heteronomous ideas and ideals, which, as

David Zarefsky argues, "might diverge if more specific referents were attempted."[33] Condensation symbols create unity out of "political differences"; however, such unity is often achieved only through untenable abstraction at the level of the symbol. When people use the same term to describe different beliefs, perspectives, or experiences, such condensation does not make the differences go away.[34]

Condensation symbols rely on tropes of contiguity to simplify concepts and increase audience investment. As Paul Achter says, "The concept of a 'condensation symbol' subsumes a variety of rhetorical concepts from metaphor to synecdoche, that is, a variety of rhetorical figures that shrink and reduce complicated concepts into simple, manageable, or memorable forms."[35] An opening call out to "my fellow Americans" in a speech asks those called to recognize themselves as participants in a common bond, belief, or destiny and so establishes a manageable foundation of identity for the propositions to come.

However, as Achter acknowledges, the condensation symbol is not merely metonymic or synecdochic, and it does more than reduce and manage complexity. It also, in Graber's terms, "arouses" investment and action at a particular point along a chain of contiguous relationships. Such points of investment involve a turning to metaphor, a claim emphasized by recent studies in rhetoric and psychoanalysis. Drawing on Jacques Lacan's theory of tropes, for example, Christian Lundberg defines metaphor as "a function whereby certain metonymic connections become particularly significant points of investment, exerting a regulatory role on a chain of signifiers by retroactively organizing the series of metonymic connections in which the metaphor is nested."[36] In this sense, condensation symbols do not merely "subsume" a variety of rhetorical concepts; they function as particular moments of tension between metonymy and metaphor—specifically as moments of metaphoric symbolization along a chain of metonymic condensations. Furthermore, as Joshua Gunn argues, condensation symbols do not merely simplify existing relationships; they often create relationships by standing in for impossible, and ultimately unsymbolizable, desires for unity.[37] Condensation symbols create the language with which to describe and imagine a unity that is at once necessary and unrealizable.

Such imagined unity has political effects. In a seminal 1980 article, Michael Calvin McGee theorizes a particular kind of condensation symbol, which he calls an "ideograph."[38] Essentially, an ideograph is a condensation symbol linked to an ideological commitment. More specifically, it refers to words—or, as has been more recently considered, images—that non-propositionally invoke the ideology of a particular dominant group or culture. McGee uses as examples words like "freedom," "religion," and "the rule of law," which might on the surface seem ordinary or natural, but which carry strong affective power in their correlation with ideological communities or commitments, beyond whatever part they might play in propositional statements. Because they are invoked to further the agenda of a particular ideological interpretation at the expense of alternate interpretive communities, ideographs are inherently divisive, while appearing to invoke natural and uncontestable ideals within the normative framework from which they emerge. As McGee says, "such 'talk' *separates* us from other human beings who do not accept our meanings, our intentions."[39]

Although he focuses on positive terms in his analysis, McGee acknowledges that ideographs "may guide behavior and belief negatively by branding unacceptable behavior."[40] Drawing on McGee, a number of authors, particularly in the past decade, have appropriated the term "negative ideographs" to describe words like "terrorism" that are invoked to further the ideological commitments of the public or the nation against its enemies.[41] Like its positive counterpart, a negative ideograph refers to "an ordinary-language term found in political discourse," which is linked to specific but poorly defined normative goals, and which "warrants the use of power" against behaviors branded as unacceptable.[42] In both positive and negative forms, the ideograph invokes the norms of a dominant public against particular deviance from those norms, but this is different from what I am calling a countersymbol.

I am resistant to invoking ideographs when considering resistance movements and counterpublic speech. While such movements also define normative values and authorize the use of power to resist those who oppose these values, they do this, as we considered in chapter 1, from a perspective of perceived marginalization from, and contestation with, what Michael Warner calls "a larger public."[43] Counterpublic speech denaturalizes and disrupts dominant discourses in order to create a space for resistance, and in this sense their use of oppositional condensation symbols is deliberately non-ideographic.[44] In contrast to ideographs, countersymbols are words that mark their strangeness—provoking collective resistance through a discursive explication and framing of an unjust and unbalanced public landscape—a world in which the right or capacity of a community to speak is being suppressed or denied.

Countersymbols differ from negative ideographs in at least three respects: First, they invoke prior intimacy—pointing toward a previous (if unsymbolizable) unity between normative and resistant communities. Second, they negate this intimacy while retaining the ghost of the prior intimacy beneath the negation, embodying a split that constitutes a new difference. This difference is a betrayal of the initial imagined unity, and it is identified as such because it retains within itself elements of that unity. Morphologically, countersymbols implicate and negate the resistant discourse that forms around the constitutive call of their appropriation, embodying the contestation they name. A politician, for example, might call on supporters to combat the manipulations of a "radical Right." The "Right" in this case implies a Left and points toward an imagined, unsymbolizable unity, while "radical" indicates a zero-sum struggle in which the identity of the naming community is defined through its symbolizable but ultimately unrealizable separation from its Other. Third, countersymbols establish, in Pocock's words, "patterns of choric incantation" that invoke and call for a new unity against the difference, constructing a new communal identity rooted in resistance to, and difference from, that which has been negated. To put it another way, while negative ideographs identify certain behavior as "unacceptable" to the public, countersymbols identify certain behavior as betrayal of a common, prior unity between public and counterpublic, against which counterpublic speech is directed. While ideographs mask their ideological commitments, countersymbols make their commitments visible in order to constitute, within the landscape of the public sphere, a space for effective resistance.[45]

Theorists of social movements and protest movements have long recognized that resistance requires the articulation and definition of a crisis against which, and through which, the resistant community is formed. Leland Griffin, for example, argues that all rhetorical movements will undergo "*a period of rhetorical crisis*" in which the balance between groups is disrupted and group members are forced to pick sides.[46] Griffin—drawing in part on Kenneth Burke's description of humans as "inventor[s] of" (or invented by) "the negative"—describes this watershed moment as culminating in an act of saying "no," which he defines as a prophetic move by a "Saving Remnant" who identify what is wrong with the old order and "foretell the coming of the new."[47] What I have been describing is an extension of these earlier arguments. Countersymbols act to justify an act of negation and division by defining the new as a recovery of original principles—or fundamentals—corrupted by the old order. Thus the "new" is not new, and resistance becomes reimagined as an act of restoration and return.

The emergence of American Fundamentalism in the years immediately following the First World War offers a good case study for us to consider the role that countersymbols play in the formation of resistance communities and counterpublic speech. Dating the emergence of a social movement is in most cases an impossible and unnecessary task. Movements do not spring forth ex nihilo, and the symbols and discourses they appropriate to describe their origins only further blur their histories and render more opaque their moment(s) of creation. I am thus not interested in dating the emergence of Fundamentalism as an object of inquiry, but rather in considering the particular discursive framework within which Fundamentalist rhetoric came to supersede other rhetorical forms for a particular subset of American Protestants. This framework can be productively explored through an examination of two dominant countersymbols: apostasy and confederacy.

Apostasy

Although it had long been a negative ideograph justifying the use of church power against religious deviants, apostasy came to function as a countersymbol within the emerging Fundamentalist movement. As countersymbol, Fundamentalists directed the charge of apostasy against church and denominational leaders—accusing those in power of betraying the values upon which that power was based. Apostasy gestured to unity as a spiritual ideal while negating the possibility of its political instantiation. As early as the 1870s, Bible and prophecy conferences, which would eventually serve as models for the World's Christian Fundamentals Association, were warning of apostasy in the American churches. The 1878 creed of the Niagara Bible Conference, for example—a document that influenced the doctrinal statements of a number of subsequent Fundamentalist organizations—predicted "a fearful apostasy in the professing Christian body."[48]

Apostasy was originally an act of naming that defined individual behaviors as seditious—as deviance against the community, requiring community response. In Greek, the word *apostasis* connotes both abandonment of one's obligations and rebellion against established authority. According to Henry Liddell and Robert Scott, the Greek root was commonly applied to those who instigated political revolt or to those with "power to dissolve an assembly."[49] Apostasy is related to defection and desertion,[50] but it is also, as John M. G. Barclay argues, a nonobjective measure of deviance and "*a blatantly judgmental term employed by 'insiders' in excluding others*." One cannot be apostate "in essence," but only "in relation to others," and specifically in relation to the standpoint of those naming the apostate as such.[51] Similarly, Stephen Wilson describes apostasy and heresy as "social labels applied by others (usually, but not always, those in authority) to those with whom they disagreed."[52] Among Christians, apostates came to be identified with "teachers of a false doctrine" who had the power to challenge and corrupt the language and practices of orthodoxy from within.[53] For example, writing in the second century, Irenaeus, the bishop of Lyons, says of such teachers: "Setting up the name of Christ Jesus as a kind of decoy . . . they bring many to destruction, spreading their evil teachings under a good name, and by the sweetness and beauty of the name [of Christ] offering them the bitter and evil poison of the serpent [Satan], the prince of the apostasy."[54]

Apostasy exists at the intersection of religious and political identities. The apostate is one who inhabits and distorts orthodox language and thus destabilizes the boundaries of orthodox belief and community. While such orthodoxies are most commonly identified with religious doctrine, apostatizing rhetoric is not limited to religious communities. Any orthodoxy can spawn apostates. In his well-known work on civil religion, for example, Robert Bellah uses apostatizing rhetoric when describing struggles between American political orthodoxy and resistant movements. He says, "For all the overt religiosity of the radical right today, their relation to the civil religious consensus is tenuous, as when the John Birch Society attacks the central American symbol of Democracy itself."[55] Although he never uses the word apostasy, Bellah presents "Democracy" as an article of faith, and members of "the radical right" as seditious opponents, emerging from that faith, who ought to be resisted. In a similar vein, Michael Lee argues that conservative politicians, pundits, and commentators draw on a "canon" of texts that provide common ground for collective action while offering different conservative "sects" the resources for identifying "imposters and apostates" among their ranks.[56]

Ambiguity and secrecy are central to the apostate threat, whether this threat is conceived in religious or secular terms. Apostasy threatens community from within, and in the name of opposing apostasy, communities sacrifice their own members, symbolically and, in some cases, physically exorcising and purifying the body and redefining the boundaries of fidelity. Such language, used in the past to exclude individuals or small groups of undesirables from the halls of ecclesiastical power, was, among the emerging Fundamentalists, turned against those who held that power. In the notes of his 1909 Reference Bible, early Fundamentalist leader C. I. Scofield describes the threat of apostasy in terms similar to Irenaeus: "Apostates depart from the faith, but not from the outward profession of Christianity."[57] Yet, while Irenaeus focuses on individual acts of rebellion against church authority, Scofield, throughout the notes of his Bible, links apostasy to church leaders who have become participants in "modern pseudo-Christianity" and "the greed and luxury of commercialism."[58] By naming leadership and institutions as apostate, emerging Fundamentalist authors were beginning to define a separate, resistant identity that was mediated through the articulation of an imagined Other.

In addition to Scofield and the creed of the Niagara Bible Conference, other early texts invoked the systemic spiritual and political threat of apostate leaders. Most famously, between 1910 and 1915, a twelve-volume series called *The Fundamentals* was published, and approximately three million copies were distributed to pastors and church leaders across the country. The series was funded by California oil millionaires Lyman and Milton Stewart and featured articles by prominent conservative Christian scholars and evangelists.[59] These authors were broadly united in their support of the doctrine of biblical inerrancy and their opposition to the "higher criticism" of the Bible being advocated by many of the denominational seminaries and schools. Such criticism, they argued, reduced or eliminated credence for the supernatural, offering naturalistic or mythic explanations for the various miracles described in the Bible. It also minimized doctrinal commitments to Jesus Christ as the divine Son of God and redeemer of human sin while focusing its attention on the moral, cultural, and economic issues favored by proponents of the social-gospel movement. Many of the authors in *The Fundamentals* argued that the prominence and popularity of higher criticism had the effect of delegitimizing "biblical" arguments, so that, as one author argued, a God-defying human philosophy had been embraced by "the theological machinery of our ecclesiastical systems"—ultimately leading to *"the greatest national apostasy that has ever taken place."*[60] Here, as with Scofield, apostasy served as a powerful countersymbol within the not-yet-fully constituted Fundamentalist movement, and it drew together religious and political categories of betrayal in defense of an emerging resistant identity. Apostasy was presented as a "national" and not merely spiritual problem, and this offers an early indication of the anti-federalist conservatism that would later become a dominant feature of Fundamentalist political discourse.

The lion's share of *The Fundamentals* was devoted to protesting the marginalization of conservative scholarship and assuring readers that the claims of conservative scholars were reliable—providing evidence from archeological or historical research that affirmed biblical claims for the divinity of Christ or the historicity of supernatural events. The audience constituted by these articles was assured, on the one hand, that their speech and their desire to speak were reasonable, and, on the other hand, that their ability to speak was being systematically marginalized by political and spiritual elites. The continual references to "higher critics" and higher criticism served as evidence of a systemic, hierarchically driven suppression of the ordinary, respectable, and reasonable speech of conservative believers. Thus these articles invoked the need for resistance—articulating equivalences of belief and practice whose continued existence was threatened by the apostate—but they did not make the additional step of adopting a collective "Fundamentalist" identity among the various conservative churches. While broadly united in opposing higher criticism, the authors of the series agreed consistently on little else. Some opposed Darwinian evolution, for example; others suggested that it might be an acceptable theory within limits. Some warned about the dangers of modern science; others argued that it should be applied to evangelism. In one notable essay, the author suggested that it was possible to be a Christian and a socialist—a notion that would become inconceivable in later Fundamentalism. The overall effect of *The Fundamentals* was not to constitute a Fundamentalist identity, but to address a diverse community of conservative pastors, Bible school administrators, and denominational leaders. Indeed, *The Fundamentals* had only a modest effect on conservative coalitions at the time and only became significant later as a sign, for Fundamentalists of the 1920s, of early conservative cooperation.[61]

Confederacy

If apostasy focused attention on the intersections between doctrinal and political division and indicated betrayal of fundamental values by spiritual leaders, "confederacy" pointed to the institutional structure of that betrayal, and paved the way for arguments in favor of a national, organized countermovement. Apostasy was an ancient, arcane charge, steeped in a long and complex history of ecclesiastical power and doctrinal language. Confederacy, on the other hand, was a modern charge, linked to concerns over local values and community associations in the context of an increasingly urbanized, technological, and interconnected national and international landscape. Also, while individuals could be apostates, confederacy could only exist collectively. As Fundamentalist countersymbol, confederacy was linked to an increasing focus on centralization among the largest and most powerful American Protestant denominations.[62]

In the aftermath of the First World War, it was a Minnesota revivalist named William Bell Riley who led the charge to resist interchurch and ecumenical efforts and forge a countermovement among conservative believers, writing in a 1919 article: "The Confederacy movement of this moment is a challenge, and those men and women who are loyal alike to the Lord and to His Word, can neither ignore nor neglect it."[63] In this passage, "Confederacy" performs the countersymbolic work of invoking and negating the resistant community. Among conservatives, "confederacy" was originally appropriated as a positive call for unity. In 1915, Herbert Booth—the son of Salvation Army founder William Booth—published *The Christian Confederacy*, in which he called for "a more perfectly organized attack upon the powers of evil." In 1917, Riley published *The Menace of Modernism*, in which, like Booth, he called for a "Christian confederacy . . . a close fellowship, yea, even an organization, of true and evangelical conservatives" that could stand up to the united threat of ecumenical federation.[64] Yet Riley colorfully denounced confederacy in the 1919 article, calling it an aid to "that infidelity which is forcing its way beyond the very altars of our churches, and which has already slimed our schools with its deadly saliva." Interchurch confederacy, as Riley was invoking the term in 1919, represented a distortion and betrayal of cooperative community, and an apostate institution that was bent upon the "obliteration of denominational barriers."[65] In Riley's rhetoric, the word had come to represent a corrupted, polluted version of itself. Such confederacy both embodied and distorted the ideal of Christian unity. The image of infidelity getting behind the altars and dripping saliva inside the schools pointed to the grotesque intimacy that was being forced upon Fundamentalist believers. Just as the danger of apostasy derived from its close association with orthodoxy, the confederacy movement was dangerous, Riley argued, because of its close associations with the institutional structures of local churches and public institutions. He said, "We are ready to protest against the destruction of honorable denominational titles by a coalition that renders them meaningless."[66]

Prior to the First World War, there seemed to have been a general attitude among conservative believers and revivalists that they still had a voice within their particular denominations and a platform from which to address their grievances. Works like *The Fundamentals* were primarily designed to be tools for pastors and church leaders to better defend against doctrinal or organizational changes at the local level. The diversity of perspectives between the various articles reflected variation among localized conservative movements and a general acceptance of that variation within a common, loosely defined framework of fundamental principles and demands. As long as local movements could voice their resistance and articulate a hope of gaining headway with denominational leaders, there was little need or motivation for any stronger association. In describing the unignorable challenge of "the Confederacy movement," however, Riley indicated to his audience that that voice and platform were disappearing—confederated infidelity was taking over the churches and the schools—transforming the discursive opportunities for Fundamentalist believers. The denominational and doctrinal risks of apostasy were invested, through the threat of confederacy, with public urgency. As countersymbol, the precise referent of confederacy was less important than the demand for action that it placed upon its audience.

What action was possible? Riley had already said that confederacy excluded the speech of Fundamentalist believers. If they were faithful to conservative doctrine, they would not be heard. Therefore, the only option was to bring believers together in a kind of resistant community or, as Riley said, a "NEW FELLOWSHIP [that] will necessarily run counter to that confederacy which will unite an apostate Church and world-improvers."[67] Riley introduced confederacy as the countersymbolic betrayal against which his proposed countermovement would stand. He assured them that, while the conservative association seemed small, there were great, untapped forces that would rally to the cause if properly motivated. "Hundreds of the most eminent preachers of the world" were already part of the countermovement; Bible schools and colleges had emerged across the country as bases for training and motivating action. Indeed, Riley claimed that the movement had already forced the confederacy to take notice. He said, "A veritable flood of evangelical and premillennial literature is pouring from the present-day press; and the magnitude of it is giving much annoyance to the Confederacy company; and the popularity of it, with the true people of God, is proving at once its spiritual power and the promise of victory for the cause of our Christ."[68]

As a further demonstration of believers' strength, Riley and other conservative leaders convened the first World Conference on the Fundamentals of the Faith in 1919, and he declared that the size of the event was proof of a great, though previously silent, community of the faithful who had not succumbed to the interchurch "tapeworm" that was infecting churches and denominations around the country. Reports of the conference described the event and the new World's Christian Fundamentals Association as a response to confederacy as represented by the Interchurch World Movement. The conference report from the Committee on Resolutions said, for example:

> We note with interest the determined endeavor to force the various and evangelical denominations into a federation in which the "fundamentals of the faith" will play little or no conspicuous part. We believe that the accomplishment of such a religious corporation at the cost of truth would provide a flashing spectacle of apparent church success to be speedily succeeded by the most colossal failure that has characterized Christianity since the dark days when an ecclesiastical corporation (the Roman Catholic Church) controlled the religious thinking of the world, and we voice our determined protest, and as members of the various evangelical denominations hereby declare our utter unwillingness to enter into any such federation movement, and in the instance of its formal adoption by our respective denominations, our fixed determination to find for ourselves *a new fellowship* in which the

> Bible will be authoritative, the deity of Christ undisputed and the faith once for all delivered the basis of our confession and of our conduct.[69]

If, as I have been arguing, "confederacy" functions as the dominant countersymbol in these texts, the words "corporation" and "federation," above, are linked to that dominant countersymbol through the rhetorical figure of *polyptoton*, functioning as extending countersymbols and highlighting the bureaucratic, impersonal structure of the interchurch threat, which contrasted with the populist, cooperative "fellowship" of Fundamentalist believers.[70] Even while they met in a national conference, to propose a national association, the discourse of the emerging Fundamentalist movement set local communities against national federation and global corporatization. Such language conflated spiritual and political categories—reflected most clearly in the comparison of the interchurch movement to the Roman Catholic Church of premodernity. The comparison implied that truth and freedom were with the new fellowship of believers. Confederacy, not Fundamentalist believers, would turn back the clock on human progress, returning civilization to ignorance and ecclesiastical oppression, and ultimately, Riley argued, it would destroy the (always-already existing) Fundamentalist community.[71]

This argument has had profound consequences for Fundamentalist publicity and politics. Over the early decades of the twentieth century, the populism of Fundamentalist believers shifted from one that saw national government as a means for social and economic liberation—typified in the work of William Jennings Bryan—to a localized populism marked by anti-government conservative and even isolationist attitudes. There are, of course, many factors that account for this change. Global war, immigration, racial tensions, and the Red Scares must all be considered, but the role played by counter-ecumenical rhetoric, and its accompanying countersymbols, must be taken into account as well. Early Fundamentalist speeches and writings effectively positioned "the people" as counter to federation—setting the rural and the local against an imagined religio-political bureaucracy. Interchurch movements were defined as apostate institutions, while the conservative countermovement idealized local communities and rural, traditional identity. Even while building a counter-ecumenical and counter-political community, Fundamentalists did not adopt the language of a national counter-council. Riley and other leaders emphasized that the new fellowship was merely a response to the confederacy threat and an extension of local cooperative efforts that already existed among regional Bible conferences and conservative churches. But, for the first time, national resistance and public argument were the organizing principles.

The Activating Call

At the 1919 World Conference, William Bell Riley was elected the first president of the World's Christian Fundamentals Association. In his presidential address, Riley called for Fundamentalist churches to separate from confederating denominations. He declared that the "hour has struck for the rise of a new Protestantism." By seeking "Confederacy," the established denominations had issued a direct challenge to the integrity of the church, but this threat also represented an opportunity for the believers to unite with one another against the systemic opposition of the enemy. "Let them form it!" Riley declared. "That will leave the men who believe in 'the faith once for all delivered' in a new fellowship as delightful as desirable." Through countersymbols of confederacy and federation, Riley's audience was offered both a justification for separation from the established denominations and an absolution of the responsibility to define the separation. Riley validated the proposed fellowship through its mere-ness. It was not, he argued, an aggressive, power-seeking organization, but only that which was left when apostate churches had confederated together against what Riley described as the "fundamental" question: "Is Christ the Son of God or no?" Critical to emerging Fundamentalist resistance was the claim that they were only responding to outside forces. The "Great Divide" between bureaucratic, institutional "Federation" and mere "fellowship" framed Riley's speech.[72]

Within this frame, Riley set out the interchurch threat in terms that conflated spiritual and political identity. He equated confederated speech with concealment and deception, saying, "One Modern theologian so defines sin as to give . . . special point to Talleyrand's remark, 'Speech was given to man to disguise his thoughts.'"[73] Riley compared complex and wordy modern definitions with simple "biblical" declarations, adopting the position that modern speech implied trickery and sought victory over the plain truth. He used the words "silly" and "foolish" to describe denominational opinions of Fundamentalist believers, language that both implied an anti-populist authoritarianism among the confederated denominational leaders and affirmed the rightness of the believers' position, since it would recall for his listeners the declaration of the Apostle Paul that God chose "the foolish things of the world to confound the wise."[74] Riley thus assured his listeners that Fundamentalist beliefs and believers would win in the end.

In the short term, however, confederacy not only threatened churches; it threatened the nation as well. Riley defined it as anti-American—a political threat linked to both German militarism and Bolshevik revolution. On the one hand, Riley compared modern theologians to German thinkers, implying that the former supported and enabled the kind of military aggression that Riley's audience would associate with the latter. This was certainly not a new comparison. A year earlier, during a speech delivered at the 1918 prophecy conference where the initial plans for the World's Christian Fundamentals Association had been drawn up, Riley had argued that Germany, with its emphases on higher education and efficiency, had been so overrun by "Darwinism," "Modernism," and "Militarism" that the country had risen up to strike a "deadly blow" against Christianity. He argued that Germany illustrated the dangers of collectivism and confederacy since the prosperous and well-educated German people had been no match for "the evil caldron of the universe" unleashed by her leaders, who denied the divinity of Christ and the authority of the Bible.[75] Similarly, in his presidential address, Riley implied that the teachings of the confederacy movement would have been "a delight" to those German thinkers who supported their nation's war against the world.[76] On the other hand, Riley described the confederacy movement as "theological Bolshevism" that sought to expand power by abolishing truth and freedom.[77] As countersymbol, confederacy incorporated both the violence of the recently ended war and the imagined perils of the emerging Red Scare. The fate of Christianity and the nation were intertwined, Riley implied, and by joining together in solidarity, Fundamentalist believers were performing both a spiritual and a patriotic duty.

Linking comparisons to the Germans and the Bolsheviks was Riley's argument that interchurch confederacy was totalitarian. He argued that "the Federation movement . . . is seeking to capture denominational conventions" and that it would manipulate or force church leaders into joining its organization. If not opposed, he argued, confederation would lead to "the practical abolition of all 'fundamentals of the faith.'"

Cooperative separation was, therefore, a necessary response. Such a conception of Fundamentalism positioned it as a negative association, born of a recognized marginalization and the threat of further suppression.[78]

The Fundamentalist Fellowship

As early as 1920, conservative pastors and church leaders began following the call of separation that Riley had laid out—abandoning their denominations to form independent congregations. For these, in particular, the Christian Fundamentals Movement offered a "counterpublic" in Phaedra Pezzullo's sense of an arena for organizing resistant speech and imagining resistant identity.[79] In the context of the movement's anti-ecumenical rhetoric, local associations, and particularly local churches, became the dominant public symbols of both the risks of interchurch confederation and the advantages of Fundamentalist fellowship. And as it became increasingly clear that Fundamentalists were losing power in their denominations, the discursive emphasis on local strength, cooperation, and organization became even more significant, and ultimately it helped to ensure the survival of Fundamentalist language and identity beyond the 1920s.

Stories of struggling local churches and interchurch abuses further cemented the idea that the confederacy movement was everywhere, infecting every level of society and extending an anti-conservative and anti-American regime that would soon endanger every local church and every Fundamentalist believer. In a March 1920 article for Riley's *School and Church*, for example, West Virginia pastor W. S. Bradshaw argued that the leaders of the Interchurch World Movement were using church consolidation to create "a steam roller . . . before which no man, even the fanatic, would dare attempt to stand." The steamroller metaphor combined fears of mechanization, urbanization, bureaucratization, and violence—reimagining the Interchurch Movement as a crushing, urbanizing force that would suppress freedom and difference in its quest for "world reason" over local beliefs and community practices. Bradshaw emphasized this by quoting an unnamed church leader who described a county-level interchurch organization that was trying to pressure all the local churches into joining them. "God helping me," this church leader said, "I would rather part with my right arm than to comply with these [interchurch] requests! But the [*sic*] most of the ministers of the county have fallen into line, so far as I know."[80]

Small rural congregations had been from the beginning of the ecumenical movement a major source of contention between interchurch leaders and the emerging Fundamentalists. Confronted with a large number of closed or leaderless rural congregations surrounding his Minneapolis-based headquarters, Riley's response was to mobilize his forces, exciting his students about the mission field of the rural church. Upon graduation, many of these students went on to reopen formerly closed rural churches, a trend that put Riley in direct conflict with the policy of the interchurch movements and major denominations that wanted to consolidate these churches in order to handle their resources more efficiently. Ecumenical leaders argued that local denominational prejudice could be overcome by focusing attention on social service and de-emphasizing points of doctrinal dispute. Instead of many weak churches, a few strong, centrally located congregations could be organized to serve the physical and spiritual needs of their communities. From a bureaucratic perspective, such policies made sense perhaps, but they paid little heed to the will of rural populations.[81] Although most of the rural church reformers had come from farms and small towns originally, few showed any interest in returning there—seeking instead to improve rural church conditions from the outside. Thus, James Madison argues, they "tended to instruct rather than listen to the people they so wanted to help." Consolidation threatened to strip small towns of important religious and civic institutions and force townspeople to travel greater distances for church services. In addition, these populations were resistant to social-gospel collectivism and denominational efforts to achieve consensus by eliminating doctrinal differences. Consolidation decisions, as it turned out, could not be effectively enacted from above.[82] The genuine bureaucratic risks of the consolidation efforts, combined with the aggressiveness of ministers like Riley and their closer connection to the rural populations, began to transform a number of previously quiet country churches into aggressively Fundamentalist "gospel tabernacles" that would, over the course of the twentieth century, form the most stable foundation for the sustained growth of institutional Fundamentalism.

As an ecclesial and political movement, Fundamentalism set local freedoms against demands for greater centralization and invested local communities with the power and responsibility to sustain the

Fundamentalist fellowship against liberal confederacy. As Bradshaw argued—invoking the military language of the recent war—"While Moderns are constructing their Big Berthas, let Conservatives get busy with their Mausers." Unlike the steamroller, this metaphor enacted marginalization while offering assurances that marginal speech could triumph—though perhaps only violently—over a bloated and oppressive public that was unprepared for resistance. Key to this triumph, however, was a restoration of revivalism and persuasive revivalist preaching, and thus Bradshaw argued, "The great outstanding preachers of America are orthodox. Their great congregations are with them to a man."[83] Just as Riley had implied that cooperation could provide safety and security for the marginal Fundamentalist communities, Bradshaw implied that there could be safety in a strong, independent local church—framed within the context of a Fundamentalist community—and the larger the church, the greater the safety. In the context of expanding ecumenical control, these large churches—often referred to as "temple" or "tabernacle" churches—seemed to offer hope for the survival of Fundamentalist speech and effective fortresses against spiritual and political assault.

Undoubtedly, the city temple and tabernacle movements were at least partially influenced by the institutional church congregations described above, but Fundamentalist advocates resisted the comparison. For example, a 1921 issue of *School and Church* showed an illustration of "The Institutional Church," which featured a cutaway of a church building, showing a gymnasium, bowling alley, swimming pool, dance hall, pool hall, boxing ring, and movie theater. High in the steeple, physically separated from the fun, a pastor and three women were assembled in the "Religious Dept." The caption underneath included a quote from a former institutional church pastor, bemoaning the money that had been wasted on the "machinery" of social activities and arguing for a return to simple faith and evangelism. The condemnation of machinery resonated with Fundamentalist critiques of the confederacy movement as impersonal, irreligious, and mechanistic in contrast to their own local, personal, and populist approach. Where modern churches and confederacies were, as Bradshaw argued, committed to "passing shows" and "moving pictures," Fundamentalist churches were presented as rooted in the plain and unalterable truth of the Bible.[84] The temple and tabernacle churches would become, over the course of the twentieth century, prominent symbols of ongoing Fundamentalist resistance and centers of Fundamentalist speech.

Bradshaw and his church embodied this resistance when they issued a "declaration of independence" and officially separated from their Baptist denomination, becoming an independent Baptist church within a larger Fundamentalist movement. In the declaration, which was reprinted in the April-June edition of *School and Church*, Bradshaw's church condemned the Interchurch World Movement, calling it "a menace to pure Christianity and the liberties of Christians in coming days." They argued that the Northern Baptist Convention's "New World Movement" campaign—a campaign begun in 1919 to raise $100 million over five years for the educational and missionary work of the denomination—had become the denominational arm of the Interchurch World Movement, the two organizations becoming "so interwoven that it is not possible to co-operate with one and not with the other." Therefore, Bradshaw's church declared that they were separating from the denomination, so that no further money would go from them to fund either the New World Movement or the Interchurch World Movement. This declaration, and the fact that it was reprinted in *School and Church*—one of the dominant forums for the Christian Fundamentals Movement—point to an emerging collective identity among Fundamentalist believers. Bradshaw's church did not simply abandon its denominational identity for isolated independence; it entered into a new form of identity and a new space for social and spiritual community.[85]

Twenty years later, in a 1940 dedication message for the Fort Wayne Gospel Temple in Indiana, Riley praised the tabernacle churches for being nondenominational, saying "Denominationalism, as born itself in a come-out movement, has now grown big and correspondingly bigoted." He denounced denominations as "ecclesiastical bosses," and he argued that tabernacle churches were returning to the simplicity of New Testament worship and Gospel truth. He praised their commitment to tradition and orthodoxy, which derived, he argued, from their willingness to build "plain buildings"—sacrificing ornament for capacity—and preach to "plain people." In other words, independent churches represented the strength of the people pulling away from the demands of interchurch confederacy and the denominations it represented and returning to the fundamentals of the Bible. Fundamentalism became a kind of cooperative community within which these independent churches could create meaning and constitute a public, post-denominational identity. Though often institutionally independent, the Fundamentalist church became symbolic of the larger Fundamentalist fellowship, which challenged the power of bureaucracy and confederacy in the church and the nation—idealizing the local, the plain, and the fundamental in the context of a mechanized and impersonal confederacy.[86]

Conclusion

By mid-1921, the Interchurch World Movement had collapsed, and Riley trumpeted its death in his address at the third national conference of the World's Christian Fundamentals Association, saying, "And let not the Liberals forget that the greatest single endeavor ever attempted by them went down to signal if not disgraceful defeat, when the 'Interchurch' came to signal, if not disgraceful disintegration."[87] Yet the countermovement that had acquired its national form through its symbolic battles with interchurch confederacy survived. Although the Fundamentalist movements of the early 1920s remained tied up in interdenominational disputes and struggles for regional control, the countersymbols of these early movements became a foundation for national Fundamentalist identity and discourse throughout the twentieth century. Countersymbols of "apostasy" and "confederacy" continued to set plain, local people against national federation, and they challenged interchurch bureaucracy while inspiring and legitimizing their own bureaucratic institutions. The emergence of Fundamentalism marked a split that continues to define American Protestantism. Since 1919, as Kristy Maddux says, "the two parties—private and public, soul-winners and social gospelers, moral reform and social justice—have defined American Christianity."[88] In the space of a few years, a diverse collection of schools, denominations, institutes, and conferences was transformed into an identifiable social movement, and while its associations (and fortunes) rose and fell over the years, a Fundamentalist identity remained, invoked as a common forum for speech within a common narrative of marginalization and suppression.

The Fundamentalist movement that emerged at the end of the 1920s was qualitatively different from the Christian movements that had fought for suffrage and temperance around the turn of the century. There was an increased pessimism about public speech, an increased suspicion of both church and state federation, an increased focus on apocalyptic narratives of rescue, and an increased call for separation.

Fundamentalism emerged from struggles with the Interchurch World Movement profoundly distrusting of both national and international cooperation and, particularly, of any efforts to achieve cooperation through secular means.[89] As Markku Ruotsila has demonstrated, Fundamentalist arguments opposing the Interchurch blended frequently with their opposition to the League of Nations—an organization also established in 1919. Both Interchurch advocates and their Fundamentalist opponents described the Interchurch World Movement and the League in similar and cooperative terms, and, as we will touch on in the next chapter, this religio-political perspective continues to influence the Fundamentalist community's distrust of the League's successor, the United Nations, to the present day.[90]

There was also, significantly, a displacement of denominations as the primary mediating frame for Fundamentalist disputes. Prior to the First World War, "Fundamentalism"—to whatever degree it can be said to have existed—functioned as a mode of internal dispute within a handful of denominations. From the 1920s on, however, Fundamentalists increasingly broke away from the denominational establishments—either creating new denominational associations or following the gospel-tabernacle pattern of large, self-sustaining congregations. In the absence of denominational identities, Fundamentalism remained as a coherent social movement, enabling communication across regional and ecclesiastical divisions that had not previously existed, even as the Fundamentalist concept of "the church" expanded in the subsequent decades from denominationally authorized institutions to the independent superchurches and megachurches, "house churches," and online communities that we will consider in the coming chapters. At the same time—isolated from the established denominations, and, until the mid-1970s at least, all but invisible to outsiders—Fundamentalists continued to craft political arguments, stage "public" debates (often with imagined opponents), and articulate a vision of social, spiritual, and political revival that they claimed would restore the fundamentals to the center of American life and upend "the Apostate Christendom" for the good of the local church and the revival of an unbelieving nation.[91]

Chapter Four

The Superchurch Revealed

⌘

> The days in which we live are seeing many prophecies being fulfilled that we have never seen fulfilled before, and surely this serves to remind all of us that the time is short at best, and if we would be followers of Jesus Christ, we must join his band now.
>
> —*A Thief in the Night*, 1972

Fundamentalism is largely defined by narratives of confrontation with and marginalization within the larger social landscape. To be at rest or at peace is incompatible with Fundamentalist identity because the Fundamentalist church must have enemies. It should come as no surprise, therefore, that Fundamentalist narratives frequently highlight the alienation of believers from the world they inhabit and the enemies the church must overcome. Arguably most prominent among these narratives are those connected to the apocalypse—the imagined final conflict between Fundamentalist believers and their enemies culminating in the triumphant return of Christ to ensure believers' victory. From the various editions of the *Scofield Reference Bible* in 1909, 1917, and 1967 to Hal Lindsey's *The Late Great Planet Earth*—the best-selling nonfiction book of the 1970s—to the runaway success of Tim LaHaye's and Jerry B. Jenkins's *Left Behind* novels at the turn of the millennium, apocalyptic narratives have dominated and continue to dominate the Fundamentalist market. And while we should not conflate Fundamentalism and apocalypticism—for the two are not synonymous—we must account for the influence of these narratives on speech about the Fundamentalist church and its perceived role in spiritual and political contestation.[1]

The relationship between apocalyptic and political narratives remains a source of considerable discussion and debate. For example, in his book *The Prophetic Tradition and Radical Rhetoric in America*, James Darsey argues that American reform rhetoric has substantial roots in the prophetic works of the Hebrew Bible, but he differentiates the activating prophetic from what he sees as a pacifying apocalyptic voice. Prophecy, he says, presents specific threats of divine judgment within a framework that is ultimately optimistic. It does not offer a stable escape from history, but a more "strenuous" call to repentance and action.[2] Darsey argues that apocalyptic narratives, in contrast, present evil as a powerful but external force in the world—a conception that transfers the burden of moral responsibility from human beings to God, whose task it becomes to intervene in history, rescue believers, and destroy evil forever. Darsey defines apocalypticism as a retreat from public action that "does not seek to make the current world morally legible" but to escape from the world by means of divine intervention and the eradication of evil.[3] Thus described, apocalyptic narratives resist both prophetic critique and political action, responding to oppression and fear with an indeterminacy that conflicts with judgment and engagement in the public realm.

Darsey's argument is somewhat similar to the critique offered by the Jewish philosopher Martin Buber, who argues that while the prophet urges us to change this world, the apocalyptist urges us to look for change in the next world.[4] If applied to Fundamentalist movements, at least part of this argument makes sense. By separating from the major denominations and retreating into counter-ecumenical and counter-political communities by the mid-1920s, Fundamentalists abandoned many options for direct engagement with the world. Fundamentalist speech also became far less likely than revivalist speech to demand collective repentance on the part of its audience, being more likely to define the Fundamentalist community as the righteous defenders of the faith against a religio-political confederacy. This fits an argument that divides prophetic critique from apocalyptic passivity. Buber also argues that the apocalyptic leaves no room for the notion of community repentance or "turning." For the apocalyptic writer, he argues, "the prophetic principle of the turning is not simply denied in its individual form, but a turning on the part of the community is no longer even thought of. The turning is nowhere acknowledged to have a power that alters history or even one that manifests itself eschatologically."[5] Within the apocalyptic frame, the believing community is relieved of many of the burdens of jeremiadic and revivalist rhetoric with its calls for self-critique and self-reform. Instead, pronouncements against the false church, the totalitarian state, and the unbelieving world come from a place of spiritual and ideological security. We are in the right, the apocalyptic community is assured, and God's fiery judgment will confirm our rightness in the end.

This lack of community introspection is certainly significant, and it is a topic we will return to in considering both Fundamentalist evangelistic methods and the temptation to violence within Fundamentalist communities. However, this distinction between the prophetic and the apocalyptic does not mean that apocalyptic communities are politically passive, or that apocalyptic rhetoric is antithetical to public speech and involvement. In order to identify apocalyptic rhetoric with political passivity, Darsey seems to assume that evil is faceless or, at best, vague in apocalyptic narratives—a productively abstract malevolent force before which believers simply wait for divine intervention. Stephen O'Leary offers a similarly broad perspective on evil in his book *Arguing the Apocalypse*, where he contends that "apocalyptic functions as a symbolic theodicy." O'Leary's work provides an important critique of Barry Brummett's argument that apocalyptic narratives are irrational and reactionary; however, O'Leary's perspective remains too broad to give a sufficient account of the connection between apocalyptic narratives and specific calls to political action.[6] O'Leary focuses on apocalyptic narratives as philosophical efforts to resolve and explain the problem of evil in the world, whereas I argue that apocalyptic narratives, and particularly fictional narratives, provide not only a philosophical rationale for engaging evil, but a plan or map for practical politics. By recreating doctrine and politics in a structured form, apocalyptic fiction allows pessimistic

Fundamentalists to tell optimistic stories of Fundamentalist takeover and to imagine what the church's triumph in and over the world can and should look like.[7] It is not enough for evil or malevolent forces to exist in the world; they must directly affect the rhetorical situation. They must, as we discussed in the previous chapter, both invoke and negate the community being addressed.[8] Thus, the evil in apocalyptic narratives is often very specific—an extension of ideologies and institutions that figure heavily in Fundamentalist political discourses and are rooted in particular moments in time. Despite, as Buber and Darsey indicate, promoting a kind of self-directed passivity, apocalyptic rhetoric both supports and encourages forms of political action by framing that action as collective resistance to specific manifestations of evil in the world.

In contrast to those who argue that apocalyptic rhetoric promotes passivity, Sharon Crowley is perfectly willing to accept that apocalypticism motivates political action; however, her argument moves toward the opposite extreme, leading her to all but collapse Fundamentalism and apocalypticism into one another. In supporting her claim that apocalypticism is a dominant feature of Fundamentalism's ruthless efforts to seize political hegemony and dominate the public sphere,[9] Crowley relies heavily on a supposed conflation of "premillennial" and "postmillennial" doctrines in contemporary Fundamentalism. This argument is by no means unique to Crowley. Indeed it has been repeated so often in recent scholarship that it has virtually acquired the status of "truism."[10] Yet it is a simplistic, unnecessary, and ultimately inaccurate claim that only contributes to the confusion surrounding the relationship between Fundamentalist politics and apocalyptic narratives. The root of the claim is that "premillennial" apocalypticism—which teaches that Christ will return to destroy the evil in the world and establish a thousand-year (millennial) kingdom on earth—is, as Darsey argues, suppressive of political action. Therefore, the argument goes, Fundamentalist politics can only be justified if premillennialism is blended with "postmillennialism," which is normally rather loosely defined in this scholarship as a positive doctrine of Fundamentalist advancement in the world.

The essential problem with this argument is that it misunderstands Fundamentalist reading practices and presumes a tremendous lack of sophistication and capacity for invention among Fundamentalist readers. To argue that premillennialists cannot appropriate these narratives to motivate political action is to assume that readers approach these texts only in a strictly "literal" sense—as preordained, doctrinally defined events before which believers need only wait passively. Yet these narratives have never been merely literal doctrines among Fundamentalist believers. Crawford Gribben has recently demonstrated that apocalyptic fiction and apocalyptic doctrine have intermingled throughout the twentieth century.[11] And the fictional accounts have functioned as both literal—if inventive—articulations of doctrine and allegorical adaptations of apocalyptic prophecy to contemporary events. This often paradoxical intermingling of the literal and the allegorical is perfectly consonant with normal Fundamentalist approaches to reading and interpretation. When appropriating stories and characters from the Hebrew Bible, for example, Fundamentalists demand that these events be interpreted as literal, historical truth—insisting, for example, that the historical Moses did in fact walk his people through the middle of the Red Sea after God parted the waters. Yet they also read these events as Christian allegories, illustrating deeper truth—in this case, the truth of Christ leading believers from spiritual bondage to spiritual freedom through baptism. In other words, the Fundamentalist doctrine of biblical inerrancy should not be mistaken for a simplistic historicization of all biblical events or doctrinal elements. It is, instead, a complex, multifaceted reading strategy that continually invokes the stability of biblical truth and yet continually allegorizes, adapts, and rearticulates that truth in the context of changing spiritual, social, and political demands and conditions.

If we understand that apocalyptic narratives function both literally and allegorically for Fundamentalist audiences, we can begin to clear up a great deal of confusion about the public and political functions these narratives perform. We can begin, in particular, to identify in the apparently escapist fantasies of premillennialism valuable tools for articulating and motivating narratives of cultural and political resistance to a perceived religio-political confederacy. And the dominant frame within which this ideological and motivational work is performed is, as we saw in the previous chapter, the local church.

Both Darsey and Crowley offer problematic conceptions of the role and function of the church in apocalyptic narratives. Crowley seems to overdetermine the church as a physical institution and undervalues its constitutive role in the articulation of Fundamentalist publicity—a role she primarily assigns to various prominent leaders who are, she argues, essentially manipulating apocalyptic narratives in order to dupe their followers.[12] The church, for Crowley, serves two main functions. It is, first, her counter to the "state," which reinforces the hegemonic dichotomy between "liberalism" and "fundamentalism" that runs throughout her book. Second, it offers evidence of Fundamentalists' physical (and thus ideological) dominance—manifested, for example, in the rather outdated argument that "church bells ring in nearly every American neighborhood on Sunday mornings."[13] In contrast, I argue that apocalyptic narratives tend to denigrate the dominance of the church as a physical institution. Where the rhetoric of city temples and tabernacles that we considered in the previous chapter tended to elevate the physical structure as a practical tool for revivalism and a symbolic representation of Fundamentalist resistance, apocalyptic narratives tend to eradicate the physical and institutional elements of the church while idealizing a pure community of true believers. This reflects a critical tension within Fundamentalism. By understanding this tension between the idealization and denigration of the physical/institutional church, we can better interpret the rhetoric surrounding the emergence of Fundamentalist superchurch and megachurch congregations, as well as the recent emergence of church narratives in network and online forms.[14]

In contrast to Crowley's overemphasis on the physical church, Darsey sets apocalypticism outside the community of believers, rendering it as an individualizing discourse that fragments the possibilities of productive, active publicity. This is particularly reflected in his claim that apocalypticism "shatters the identity of its author,"[15] creating narratives that seem to emanate directly from God and thus restrain human authority and agency at the moment of articulation. In considering the limitations of this claim, it is helpful to turn to Paul Ricoeur's discussion of "threefold mimesis" in the construction of narratives. In *Time and Narrative*, Ricoeur distinguishes between three different kinds of mimetic activity. Mimesis$_1$ refers to that which precedes the creative act of composition. Mimesis$_2$ is "the mimesis of creation," which mediates between Mimesis$_1$ and what Ricoeur calls Mimesis$_3$—the engagement of the reader or spectator with the narrative. Darsey's analysis examines apocalyptic narratives in the movement between Mimesis$_1$ and Mimesis$_2$, concluding that the lack of a definable, human creator hampers the abilities of these narratives to speak constitutively and persuasively in human social and political contexts. However, I argue that these narratives are never understood to be complete in their composition. Even the structure of apocalyptic writings demands that we conceive of the reader or listener not as a passive recipient of information, but as an active participant in the construction of meaning and action in the narrative. In the New Testament book of Revelation, for example, the Spirit of God speaks to the prophet, who inscribes the divine words with the caveat "He that hath an ear, let him hear what the Spirit saith unto the churches." This phrase, repeated seven times in the book, establishes a critical foundation for apocalyptic narration as oral performance—a perspective on the text advocated by scholars like David Barr.[16] However, beyond its role as oral drama, the phrase points to the role of "the churches" as recreators of meaning within the text. Apocalyptic narratives, like the book of Revelation, do not "shatter" the author's identity; they reinscribe that identity in the figure of the preacher/prophet addressing a particular instantiation of the church community. This is not to deny that Bible prophecy teachers and pastors obscure their interpretive role behind an inerrant reading of these texts.[17] Nevertheless, apocalyptic narratives are only complete as they are prophetically invoked—calling out to the community of believers for response and action and thus remaking the "hearer" as author—at the level Ricoeur calls Mimesis$_3$.[18] These narratives do not simply snatch the church out of an unsalvageable world, nor do they simply expand the church in the world. They do both. In premillennial apocalyptic narratives, the last vestiges of an institutional Fundamentalism are stripped away as true believers are taken up to heaven and the false church joins with the state to create the ultimate, confederated superchurch. However, in these narratives the focus is on new believers—post-Rapture converts who recreate the Fundamentalist community as an adaptive network, independent of both institutional church and bureaucratic state. It is this "re-creative" demand that is most obvious in those most "recreative" forms of apocalyptic narrative—the popular novels, dramas, and films that translate divine doctrine into human stories.

A key framework for these fictional narratives is the loss of one kind of community *in order to enable* the imagination of new social and political possibilities. They depict not the end of the world, but the dramatic passage of a community beyond the limits of the end, into a new social landscape that fully incorporates the interpretive standards of the community into the structure of the world itself. They function, therefore, as a form of persuasive and public communication, which restructures the narrative world in order to create new grounds for spiritual and political organization. They extend counter-ecumenical and counter-political contestation into a future social landscape, which allegorically clarifies existing boundaries and defines the political stakes of the public in ways that often idealize counterpublicity in the present.

In this chapter, I use a popular series of apocalyptic films as a case study to demonstrate how apocalyptic narratives negotiate a space between separation and speech for Fundamentalist believers by reimagining spiritual and political contestation as a dichotomy between two kinds of church—the deinstitutionalized, Fundamentalist church and the institutional, federated church of the "Antichrist." In these narratives, the need for separation is clarified through threats of violence and eternal damnation, yet at the same time, Fundamentalist believers are portrayed as the primary public actors in a global struggle for survival—raising the stakes of public engagement and making political as well as spiritual demands upon Fundamentalist audiences. Ultimately, these narratives idealize Fundamentalist cooperation through flexible and responsive networks of believing communities, which use modern technologies to unify Fundamentalists and bring about spiritual and political revolution.

Dispensational Politics

Critical to Fundamentalist separatism in the middle decades of the twentieth century was the belief that Fundamentalists would not long have to struggle to defend their identity in the world. Separation is a siege mentality and is thus only reasonable as a short-term position. The idea that churches would function as fortresses against the onslaughts of the outside world was only sustainable if that function was temporary. Separation depended on the expectation of rescue from the situation in which believers found themselves. Thus, for a majority of Fundamentalists, separation went hand in hand with the doctrine of an imminent "Rapture" of believers. The Rapture has been a central tenet of most forms of separatist Fundamentalism in the twentieth century. In essence, the doctrine predicts that all true believers will be rescued from this present world and its struggles by a sudden and miraculous "snatching-up" of the true church to be with Christ. The Rapture, as Nancy Ammerman says, "lends both urgency to the evangelistic task and comfort to persecuted believers."[19]

The Rapture is a central feature of the most dominant modern variant of Fundamentalist premillennialism, called "dispensationalism." The origins of dispensationalism go back to Ireland in the 1820s and 1830s, when a former Church of Ireland priest named John Nelson Darby—a member of a schismatic group called the Brethren and later a leader in an inter-Brethren schism called the Plymouth Brethren—adopted premillennial views and also took the additional step of dividing the Bible into seven historical periods or "dispensations," arguing that God revealed himself differently and established different rules for social and religious organization in each of these dispensations. Like other premillennialists, Darby believed that the end of the world would culminate in a seven-year period of global tribulation, during which time all the nations would be governed by a single, evil world leader known as the Antichrist or "the beast."[20] However, using 1 Thessalonians 4:17 as his "proof text," Darby argued that Christ would rescue or rapture the true church before the tribulation events could take place.[21]

Darby's ideas circulated among premillennialist communities in Britain and America throughout the latter half of the nineteenth century. However, in the United States, dispensationalism acquired its greatest mass appeal following the 1909 publication of the *Scofield Reference Bible*, which popularized and lent authority to the doctrine by describing it in notes uniquely integrated into the text of the Bible. As Randall Balmer argues, "For generations of fundamentalists ever since [its publication], the Scofield Bible has served as a kind of template through which they read the Scriptures."[22]

Among the complex doctrines of dispensationalism, one idea is critical to understand. For dispensationalists, the present dispensation—commonly called the "Church Age"—is interpreted as a kind of "pause" in biblical chronology whose existence was not revealed to the Hebrew prophets. They believe that this pause will end when Christ raptures the church into heaven and restarts the biblical clock, bringing to pass the prophetic events recorded in the books of Daniel and Revelation.[23] The church is thus separate from Bible prophecy in dispensational theology, called only to gather as many converts as possible while holding fast to the true faith in expectation of a sudden rescue from the world. The apparent rise of apostasy and ecumenical confederacy, which we discussed in the previous chapter, fit perfectly with this narrative. Dispensationalists believe that apostasy in the church is a significant sign of the coming tribulation—an indication that the Church Age is coming to an end and the Rapture will soon take place.[24] And after believers failed to redeem the denominations from interchurch confederacy in the early 1920s, separation seemed to make perfect prophetic sense.

Dispensational narratives appeared to clearly support the separation of Fundamentalists from public life; however, these narratives were not as straightforwardly separatist as they might at first appear. And this is particularly evident in dispensational texts produced in the second half of the twentieth century. Around mid-century, three changes took place in the religious and political landscape that challenged and reshaped the doctrinal and narrative direction of dispensationalism. The first was the official establishment of the state of Israel in 1948. As Gribben says, "Until 1948, leading dispensationalists had uniformly insisted that the rapture would be the next event on the prophetic calendar. But for many of these writers, the establishment of the state of Israel offered a 'proof of prophecy' that would be of foundational importance in their attempt to prove the reliability of their interpretive system."[25] Gradually Fundamentalist theologians and authors began to revise the dispensational system to integrate certain prophecies into the narrative of the pre-Rapture church. These new interpretations were given a certain amount of doctrinal credibility through the revised *New Scofield Bible* in 1967 and were popularized by Hal Lindsey's bestseller *The Late Great Planet Earth* in 1970. These doctrines, Gribben argues, "undermined the coherence of dispensational ideas."[26] In particular, as Lindsey's book demonstrated, they opened a path to increasing sensationalism in prophetic narratives on the one hand, and justified a new dispensational investment in the political world on the other. By investing prophetic meaning in pre-Rapture events, Lindsey's work made particular political demands upon the reader. For example, he argued that the establishment of the Jewish state in 1948 was one of three events that set the stage for the coming seven-year tribulation period. The second event was the Jewish repossession of Jerusalem in 1967. The third event, Lindsey argued, would be the rebuilding of the Jewish temple on the site where it once stood. Acknowledging that such a temple cannot be built while the Dome of the Rock shrine still stands, Lindsey nevertheless declared, "Obstacle or no obstacle, it is certain that the Temple will be rebuilt. Prophecy demands it."[27] If the Rapture was, in fact, not the next event on the prophetic calendar, Fundamentalists were given leave to uncover all kinds of new links between prophetic narratives and current world events. Far beyond issues specifically related to Israel, this shift gave dispensational believers a new investment in current events and a new role as interpreters of the political and social landscape.

The second change was the reemergence and reinvigoration of Protestant ecumenicism in the aftermath of the Second World War. As we discussed in the previous chapter, ecumenical movements served a critical constitutive function for early Fundamentalism, invoked as a direct assault on the freedom of Fundamentalist believers and the values of the Fundamentalist church. In the 1920s, the Federal Council of Churches and the Interchurch World Movement were the chief representations of this threat. By 1950, however, these had been replaced by two new organizations: the World Council of Churches, conceived in the 1930s but officially established in 1948, and the National Council of the Churches of Christ in the U.S.A., which was established in 1950 and absorbed the struggling Federal Council of Churches as well as a number of other ecumenical organizations.[28]

Condemnation of these new organizations was immediate. Even before they were officially established, Fundamentalist authors were already describing the World Council as the "church of the Antichrist,"[29] and referring to the National Council as a "dangerous monopolist move" and "a huge superchurch."[30] In 1948, Fundamentalist provocateur Carl McIntire created an organization called the International Council of Christian Churches specifically to combat the World Council, and every year he scheduled the date and location of his annual meeting to coincide with that of the World Council's, forcing the latter to do extra advertising in order to prevent local press from confusing the two organizations. Seven years before, in 1941, a group of Fundamentalists, under the leadership of McIntire, had officially organized the American Council of Christian Churches (ACCC). The ACCC directed its energies toward exposing the threat that ecumenical movements posed to Fundamentalist freedom and values, warning that a coming worldwide superchurch would replace sound Bible doctrine with hierarchically mandated church "unity."[31]

Like William Bell Riley, a generation earlier, McIntire compared his efforts to the Protestant Reformation, calling it the "Twentieth Century Reformation Movement." By abandoning the fundamentals of the faith and working for common communion with Catholic and Orthodox churches, McIntire argued, the World Council had committed apostasy and was actively working to annihilate the true Protestant faith from the inside: "We are witnessing a sustained attack by Protestants on their own houses."[32] James DeForest Murch, a leader within the National Association of Evangelicals—a group that, for the most part, rejected the name "Fundamentalist" and sought to separate themselves from what they saw as McIntire's extremism—nonetheless made similar charges against the ecumenical movement, arguing that the National Council was part of a "sinister plan" that was working against evangelical interests, eliminating revivalist and evangelistic preaching, and establishing "an unholy alliance between super church and state."[33] Other authors accused the World and National Councils of "carrying on a subtle, insidious Satanic brainwashing" to persuade Americans to deny the true faith and embrace a Catholic and Communist superchurch,[34] a "One-world government,"[35] and the "blind acceptance of a Communist directive entirely outside the church."[36]

Anti-Communist and anti-ecumenical narratives intertwined within the emerging Cold War rhetoric in the United States. For Fundamentalists and other conservatives, the formation of the World Council of Churches was final proof of the ecumenical movement's long-suspected "Red" leanings.[37] ACCC president W. O. H. Garman warned that the "first intent" of the World Council was to establish a "super church organization which will dominate world politics."[38] McIntire claimed that the council stood with the Communist governments of "the East," against the political and religious freedom of "the West."[39] Furthermore, in this battle between East and West, he argued, the ecumenical movement was more dangerous than other political threats because ecumenicists had access to the churches and their members and thus unprecedented power to sway the American public away from capitalism and Christianity and toward the false faith of the Communist order. He said, "The World Council has entrance to the minds of people in the West whom Stalin could never reach."[40] Billy James Hargis, friend of McIntire and leader of a prominent anti-Communist movement called the Christian Crusade, charged that "Millions of honest Christians in National Council denominations think their money is being used for God's work and are unaware that much of it is being used for leftwing political purposes."[41] The ACCC similarly argued that the ecumenical councils were disguising their true motives, saying:

> Many Christian Americans do not realize that the National Council of Churches claims their support and uses it in their various un-Christian and un-American policies and activities. A great deal of money given by

> well meaning Christians to their local churches for use in God's work, ends up with the National Council for their use in their un-Christian and un-American policies and activities.[42]

Ecumenical support for state engagement on issues like labor reform and civil rights were denounced by Fundamentalist leaders and radical conservative groups, such as the John Birch Society and the Circuit Riders, as representative of a "superchurch run by a clerical coterie of fuzzy-minded pinkos and Red infiltrators."[43] Chief among these critics was Hargis, who produced a number of books and pamphlets charging the National Council with promoting Communist ideology, encouraging open borders, and discouraging military preparedness in a way that made them "responsible" for the Pearl Harbor attack in 1941.[44] He said, "A superchurch serving as the arm and herald of a one-world supergovernment is at work in the form of the World-National Councils of Churches."[45] Such narratives inevitably presented the National and World Councils as agents of religious and political suppression that would eventually lead to persecution and annihilation of religious believers—first locally and then globally. Counter-ecumenical rhetoric brought together religious and political interests around a common perceived threat to Fundamentalist, conservative, and national identity, so that, as McIntire argued, Fundamentalists needed to become politically involved in order to rescue both church and state in the West.[46]

These political narratives were inevitably linked to apocalyptic narratives that predicted a coming Antichrist, superchurch confederacy, and one-world government. National Association of Evangelicals' leader James DeForest Murch explicitly linked the ecumenical movement with apocalyptic prophecies of the Antichrist: "Outwardly their ideology appears to be Christianity of the highest order. Since, however, they would impose it by political force upon an unregenerate world they are but laying the groundwork for the cataclysmic events prophesied by the apostle John."[47] Similarly, in *The Late Great Planet Earth*, Hal Lindsey argued that the National and World Councils had abandoned good doctrine for Communism and political violence, predicting that after the Rapture these organizations would unite all religious systems into a single, apostate world religious organization.[48] It is in the context of these changing narratives of political engagement, ecumenical confederacy, and Communist threat that we can best understand the role of apocalyptic narratives generally and of fictional narratives in particular.

More than revivalist scare tactics or escapist fantasies, these stories are intertwined with disputes about the status and role of the true church in the world and changes in the political culture of dispensational Fundamentalism.

A Thief in the Night

Directed by Donald W. Thompson, *A Thief in the Night* (1972) was one of the first films to take on Fundamentalist apocalyptic narratives within a fictional motif. Produced for $68,000, the film brought in approximately $4.2 million in its first decade on the market—a blockbuster by Fundamentalist standards at a time when such films were funded almost exclusively by voluntary audience donations and were not expected to turn a profit.[49] The film tells the story of Patty, a young woman who dreams that she has been left behind in the Rapture—only to discover in the end that it was not a dream. With a nonlinear script that effectively built tension, and utilizing lightweight Panaflex cameras that created an intimate realism, it is not hard to understand why the film became such a hit with Fundamentalist audiences.[50] Featuring an opening song by Larry Norman—the most popular Christian rock artist at the time—and marketed as an evangelistic tool for younger audiences, *A Thief in the Night* was seen by millions of people in churches, camps, and youth groups across the country.[51] The film's success led Thompson and producer Russell S. Doughten to make three sequels: *A Distant Thunder* (1977), *Image of the Beast* (1981), and *The Prodigal Planet* (1983), each of which continues the story of those left behind to endure the tribulation period after the Fundamentalist believers have been raptured.

Unlike the *Left Behind* novels, *A Thief in the Night* remains virtually unknown outside Fundamentalist circles, but Thompson's and Doughten's films created the media and publishing standard for all the apocalyptic fiction that followed them. More than any other apocalyptic text of that period (with the possible exception of Lindsey's *The Late Great Planet Earth*), *A Thief in the Night* and its sequels profoundly influenced the discursive makeup of contemporary Fundamentalist rhetoric, media, criticism, and politics. As Randall Balmer argues, "It is only a slight exaggeration to say that *A Thief in the Night* affected the evangelical film industry the way that sound or color affected Hollywood."[52] And Heather Hendershot says,

> It would be hard to overstate the influence of Thompson's films on evangelical culture. Today many teen evangelicals have not seen *A Thief in the Night*, but virtually every evangelical over thirty I've talked to is familiar with it, and most have seen it. . . . [E]vangelicals who grew up in the 1970s and early 1980s often cite *Thief* as a source of childhood terror, in part because the film shows people who *think* they are saved but are not and therefore are not raptured with their families.[53]

This childhood fear has led to a good deal of anger among former Fundamentalists who remember the film as a traumatic experience. Because it was an evangelistic film, screenings of *A Thief in the Night* were often accompanied by a message from a pastor or youth-group leader assuring teenage viewers that the events depicted in the film would really happen, and urging them to repent and accept Jesus before it was too late, and this context only heightened the trauma. Rocker Marilyn Manson lists the film's novel among the apocalyptic obsessions of his Fundamentalist childhood.[54] Amy Johnson Frykholm describes watching *A Thief in the Night* as an evangelical high school student—her first exposure to apocalyptic popular culture—and being angered by "the thought that fear might be used to motivate belief."[55] Yet, as Hendershot says, "Interestingly, for every person who says this film drove them away from the church for good, there is another who says he or she was saved immediately upon seeing the film. I have found that *A Thief in the Night* is the only evangelical film the viewers cite directly and repeatedly as provoking a conversion experience."[56]

The action of *A Thief in the Night* is framed visually by a ticking yellow clock that slowly fades into focus at the beginning of the film and fades out at the end, a visual cue whose meaning is reinforced by the Bible verses that accompany the clock and remind the audience that Christ could return at any moment. "Don't let me find you sleeping!" the words of Jesus warn as the camera focuses on the clock.[57] That Patty is, literally, asleep throughout most of the film reinforces the audience's understanding that she is spiritually asleep as well. In her dream, the true believers are raptured up to heaven, and Patty discovers what has happened when she finds her husband's electric razor buzzing in the sink where it fell when he vanished. In the chaos following the mass disappearances, a global military government takes over. Called UNITE (the United Nation's Imperium of Total Emergency), the new government requires all citizens to put a "mark" on their right hand or forehead to demonstrate their loyalty to the new world order. This is, as Fundamentalist viewers would immediately recognize, the "mark of the beast"—a symbol of loyalty to the Antichrist, which offers temporary salvation from the trials of the tribulation while damning those who take it to eternal hell.[58] Patty, though not a true believer, is afraid to take the mark, and the forces of the new world government chase after her. At the very end of the film, running from one of her old friends, Jerry, who is now a government agent, Patty slips off a bridge and falls toward certain death, at which point she wakes up—only to stumble out of bed and discover her husband's electric razor buzzing away in the sink. As Patty starts screaming—realizing that her nightmare has come true—the camera again finds the yellow clock, and the viewer is reminded that "The End . . . Is Near!"[59]

As is often the case in fictional series, the first film was designed to stand on its own, while the other films in the series adopted that original story to a larger narrative. In this case, the narrative of the series moves from the Rapture event to the constitution of a post-Rapture community of believers. Bridging the critical years between 1977 and 1983—a period when the so-called "New Christian Right" was emerging on the national stage—these films reflected changing attitudes and interpretations about the status of the Fundamentalist church in society and the role of Fundamentalist believers in the world. The second film in the series, *A Distant Thunder*, picks up where *A Thief in the Night* left off. Patty has been left to struggle through the tribulation; angry with God but afraid to take the mark of the beast, she has almost decided to accept Jesus as her savior. But the film ends when she is betrayed by one of her best friends and is forced to watch as another friend is beheaded on a guillotine for refusing to take the mark. As the camera focuses on Patty's screaming face, the screen fades to black and the words of John 3:16 appear: "For God so loved the world that He gave His only begotten son, that whosoever believeth in Him should NOT PERISH but have EVERLASTING LIFE."[60] Traumatized by the experience of watching her friend die, Patty is strapped to the guillotine at the beginning of the next film, *Image of the Beast*. Given one last chance to take the mark or accept Jesus, Patty screams out that she wants the mark, but a sudden earthquake scares the soldiers away, and she is left helpless as the earthquake shakes the guillotine blade loose. Having turned away from Jesus, the audience is meant to understand that Patty has been sent to hell.

Patty's story arc is designed to traumatize viewers. Unlike many of the villains in apocalyptic stories like *Left Behind*—who are portrayed as purely evil and deserving of their fate—Patty is a sympathetic character, a good person, who is sent to hell for being too scared to be martyred for the sake of her soul. The audience who has followed her over two films is meant to sympathize with her and feel agonized at her loss. It is one of the oldest and most controversial tactics available to the revivalist. Like Jonathan Edwards adopting the position of a malicious child dangling his metaphorical spider over the flames, Thompson uses sadism to save. In his analysis of the *Left Behind* series, Christian Lundberg suggests that there is sadistic enjoyment linked to the pleasure readers derive from these novels—the pleasure of "assuming the position of the victim and of working this position through by assuming the position of the tormentor."[61] But we never take the position of tormentor in relation to Patty. This is not a horror film where the knife is placed, perspectivally, in the audience's hands. We are, instead, victimized by her victimization—forced to watch helplessly behind the unyielding screen that separates us. Just as the blade falls, we are shown the guillotine from Patty's perspective, and as it ends her life we take her place. It is an effective, upsetting, and infuriating moment. It is also a critical transition in the narrative arc of the series. Just as revivalist preachers would call would-be converts to abandon their old life of sin and embrace new life through Christ, this scene calls upon its audience to abandon Patty. Only by accepting the narrative and refusing to become lost in Patty's confusion and indecision can the audience break free from sin and enter into the believing community. Only by sacrificing human sympathy on the altar of divine judgment can we be saved. It is a moment equivalent to the scene at the cross in John Bunyan's famous Christian allegory, *The Pilgrim's Progress*, where the focus of the narrative shifts from the agony of a burdened sinner to the trials of a believer—trials that, for all the suffering they cause, are only minor delays on the Christian's inevitable path to God's kingdom. In the same way, with Patty's death, the allegorized focus of the series shifts from the suffering of those left behind to the progressive organization of a post-Rapture church. There is still suffering, but it is no longer meaningless, being now part of the Fundamentalist church's inevitable progress to victory.

Following Patty's death, in *Image of the Beast*, the focus of the narrative shifts to a man named David Ryan, who, together with a woman named Kathy, her three-year-old son Billy, and another woman, escapes from prison after the earthquake that killed Patty also opens the prison doors. A computer expert, David designs a counterfeit mark that will fool the authorities, but his plan backfires when he and Kathy try to buy food, and he is captured. At the end of the film, Kathy's son is converted to Jesus and then killed by the authorities, and David is shown calmly walking toward the guillotine, apparently facing execution.[62]

The final film, *The Prodigal Planet*, opens by saying that it is a story of a few people in the wilderness. Over a shot of earth from space, a voice intones, "The planet earth is dying. The disease is sin." Then Russian-accented voices accompany shots of missiles launching and nuclear bomb blasts. As the explosions fade, we return to the action of the previous film. David is rescued at the last moment by Connie, a member of the "Believers' Underground." As they drive through the charred, post-nuclear landscape, Connie tells David that the underground was impressed by his ability to make a counterfeit mark, and they rescued him because they needed someone with his technological ability. She says, "We need you to construct a special computerized transmitter. This will create an instantaneous, worldwide communications linkage to underground believers." She also gives him a coded message that will supposedly lead them to the believers' secret hideout. Armed with this code, they set off across country, picking up others along the way and trying to evade the government agents pursuing them—a group led by Patty's former friend Jerry. Except for the regular breaks in the narrative for characters to witness to one another, this last installment of the series is a fairly typical post-apocalyptic road-trip movie, complete with an abandoned city, car chases, and roving bands of "mutants." After Connie—who turns out to have been a double agent—is killed, the group arrives at the believers' hideout, where David installs the transmitter and plays some notes from a Christian hymn, which overload the UNITE computers. Then, as one of the characters prays to accept Jesus, an earthquake and hailstorm destroy the government's headquarters. In the final scenes, a hymn is sung in the background as Jerry crawls out from under the wreckage, sobbing. He tears off his government armband and throws it down, crying louder as he looks around—terrified. Then explosions destroy the buildings, and the fire fades to a shot of outer space, with stars moving past the camera. The words of Jesus appear over the stars: "The rain came down, the streams rose, and the winds blew and beat against the house; yet it did not fall, because it had its foundation on the rock."[63]

These are films about religious and political community. Despite the obligatory asides—particularly prominent in the middle two films—where pastors and teachers use a complex series of maps and charts to explain the sequence of events that God has predetermined for the last days, the focus of these films is not God's control over human events or even the end of the world. Instead, this is, paradoxically, a "literal" account of Fundamentalist escape to the next world and an allegorical account of Fundamentalist resistance in this world, one in which the true church grows from dispersed individuals in *A Thief in the Night* to an international resistance network at the end of *The Prodigal Planet*. While divinely appointed events play out in the background, human choices drive the narrative. As people choose to either accept the mark or accept Christ, they take their places as members of warring communities, and they become part of a political struggle with eternal consequences.

The narratives of these films conflate spiritual and political identity. The UNITE government combines Fundamentalist fears of confederacy with an allegorical illustration of anti-Communist sentiment. Originating from the United Nations, which Fundamentalists had long condemned for enabling Communist ideology and Communist governments,[64] UNITE is a military government, and in the first film, its soldiers wear drab green uniforms, or white shirts with black ties, and red armbands, which evoke images of both Nazi and Communist paraphernalia. In the subsequent films, the soldiers all wear drab green with yellow armbands, which are particularly reminiscent of Cuban military uniforms. Like Riley's sermon that we considered in the previous chapter, the UNITE government combines anti-fascist and anti-Communist sentiments under a unifying fear of a totalitarian state. To join with this world government is to deny Christ and damn one's soul. To remain outside the Fundamentalist community, as Patty does, is to ensure both persecution and damnation. Passivity is not an option; choice and action are demanded of every believer. Furthermore, this struggle does not simply involve government institutions. The true church and the false church are portrayed as central to political events. As allegory, the series highlights the dangers of the ecumenical movement. Over the course of the films, ecumenicists move to the center of the totalitarian government, linking church and state in the violent suppression of Fundamentalist freedom. In the first film, there is mention of a "church confederation" whose chairman is the first to suggest that the mass disappearance may be the prophesied Rapture of the Bible, although this leader is, of course, not among those raptured—proving that he was never a true believer. As Riley, McIntire, and other Fundamentalist leaders had suggested, the "confederacy movement" knows the truth, but it has abandoned truth for political power, and its presence threatens both the political and spiritual future of Fundamentalism. By the second film, this confederation has grown to become the "world church," and by the third film it has appointed the Antichrist as its leader and is manipulating military operations and economic markets for its own ends. Only in the fourth film, after the world church has been destroyed by the Antichrist, do the Fundamentalists succeed in forming their own global fellowship.

The Two Churches

At the beginning of the series, ecumenicism is hidden in the background, but its corrosive effects can be seen in the wealth of liberal churches and the relative poverty of Fundamentalists. The first film's narrative contrasts a vibrant, denominationally independent Fundamentalist church with its large, ornate, spiritually dead counterpart. Early on, we are introduced to an earnest group of Christian young people, discussing Bible prophecy about the end of the world and the coming Rapture of true believers. Patty, who hangs around this group, is curious about the Bible's teaching, but she remains unconvinced, and the audience comes to understand why in the very next scene, where Patty sits in the pews of her liberal church. Standing behind a dark wood pulpit, surrounded by flowers and flanked by stained glass, the false teacher Reverend Turner (played by producer Russell Doughten) says,

> Commonsense shows us immediately that those differences which men of old deemed worthy of death are really dead horses. . . . To insist that the Bible is anything more than the poetic expression of those greater principles by which man lives with man is to box oneself in with a wealth of opinion and counter-opinion which really doesn't matter, because it really doesn't affect the way we are.

During the sermon, Patty is shown frowning and flipping through an open Bible on her lap. But the Fundamentalist audience would understand that the message she is hearing will not be found there. What is being preached is not from the Bible; it is a human-centered message, packing the pews while leading an unwitting congregation straight to hell. Reverend Turner is like the "professors of religion" that Finney spoke about in his *Lectures*. He is well educated and articulate. He stands in an elevated pulpit, invoking the institutionally mediated hierarchy of the established churches. He is familiar with the literature and history of the Bible, but he does not preach revival. He uses big words, but he does not adapt his speech to his audience. Repeated shots of the congregation show them looking bored or, in Patty's case, confused by the sermon. Under Reverend Turner, church has been reduced to mere ritual performance. He does not take advantage of the means of persuasion that God has provided, and he does not attempt to save the members of his congregation. He is a false teacher. His church is a false church, and we are given to understand that this church is not an isolated example. All the visual cues present this church as the norm. It is richly furnished. It is well attended. It is large and solid. When contrasted with the tiny, sparsely populated Fundamentalist church we see later in the film, the message is clear. Most churches have abandoned revivalism. The great apostasy that Fundamentalists predicted is now underway.

In the second film, after the Rapture, Reverend Turner realizes the terrible mistake he has made. Returning to Patty's old church, we now see him preaching about Bible prophecy from the book of Revelation. A shot from behind him shows that he is now speaking to a sparse handful of people scattered around the large, ornate sanctuary. Turner says, "You are so few because so many have preferred to hear the godless humanism of the great world church." Having abandoned the power and prestige of liberal confederacy, Turner becomes obsessed with Fundamentalist doctrine, and he becomes the chief educator of the series—using long lectures and complicated charts to explain to other characters (and the audience) the details of dispensationalist teachings about the end times. Yet, like Patty, he never turns his knowledge into action. He never becomes a convert, and thus he is gradually reduced to silence in the series. By the third film, he is a recluse hoarding prophecy charts in a barn, and by the final film of the series, he is living alone in a hole in the ground, eating rats—a "tormented man," as one of the characters says. Beginning in an elevated pulpit, Turner ends the series buried alive in a hole representing the eternal hell to which his lack of faith has condemned him. Unlike with Patty, however, there is no shocking death scene. Instead, the series enacts the separation to which Fundamentalist believers and the Fundamentalist church are called. Having preached the gospel to Reverend Turner, the believing characters gradually abandon him. And thus he becomes a lesson for the believing audience about the exclusivity and purity demanded of the true church. In contrast to the continually growing "world church," the Fundamentalist community is always portrayed as a small, resistant minority.

Meanwhile, every element of the ecumenical church and the state are intertwined with one another in the apocalyptic new world order represented in these films, just as Fundamentalist leaders had predicted that they would be. After her believing husband and friends are raptured away in the first film, Patty is left behind—betrayed by the false teachings of Reverend Turner and his church. As the world responds to the sudden disappearance of millions of people, the United Nations establishes its global political organization and makes a worldwide television broadcast. During the broadcast, UNITE's representative says,

> You can be sure that the Imperium, while taking absolute control over all government during this emergency, will truly represent your feelings and needs. It is because of this potential threat to our entire planet that this one-world government, the Imperium, has been formed, and each member of the world council wishes to assure those of his fellow citizens that as soon as the emergency is passed we will return to self-rule for all nations.

We cut to newspaper headlines reading: "UNITE LEADER ASSURES: NOT A 'BIG BROTHER,'" "IMPERIUM CALLS FOR TOTAL SUPPORT," and "IMPERIUM INITIATES I.D. SIGN." Then, in another broadcast, the representative continues:

> The Imperium in no way wishes to infringe upon the rights of the citizens of the world. It is just a simple necessity that each of us identify with UNITE and fully support its progress and strategy. Before the emergency, we were at each other's throats. Let unity be the positive result of our common dilemma [showing the mark of the beast on his hand]. Report today to your

> local UNITE Identification Center and show yourself a true citizen of the world.

Later, as Patty walks down the street, she sees a line of people going through the doors of an ornate stone church, which now has a sign out front reading: "UNITE I.D. CENTER." The church ceased to preach revival, and it has become a puppet of the state, imposing the will of a confederated, totalitarian government on the people.

In *A Distant Thunder*, the second film of the series, Patty and many others who have not taken the mark of the beast are captured by UNITE and imprisoned in another church. In the crowded sanctuary, one of the representatives from UNITE explains to the prisoners that they will be given one last opportunity to take the mark and escape execution. Behind him is a table, where two UNITE agents sit, ready to give out the mark. The camera pans back to show us the table and a large silver cross hanging directly above on the wall. The setup is clearly intended to mimic the Protestant communion table—an image reinforced by the yellow ribbons that hang on either side, each bearing the mark of the beast and the UNITE logo. In this scene, for the first time, the man refers to the Antichrist by name as "Brother Christopher"—"brother" and "sister" being titles that are used among certain Fundamentalist communities to denote their common fellowship in the family of Christ—and he tells the assembled prisoners that he is giving them this one final opportunity to be "saved" by the mark. One of the women warns Patty not to take the mark, saying: "They don't want you to die. They want your soul." At every level, the state occupies and mimics the form of the church, seeking to snatch souls away from Christ.

In the third film, we see that the church has also taken on the form of the state. Hiding from a government agent, David and Kathy go into a church. Like Reverend Turner's old church, it is crowded. UNITE banners hang from the wall. Outside the sanctuary is a little library alcove with bookshelves packed with books. The pastor has the mark on his forehead and stands flanked by charts and graphs. No crosses are visible. UNITE banners cover the empty choir area. The pastor is explaining to the congregation how the church can expand its market influence and profit from the military campaigns being waged by Brother Christopher.

Later Kathy tells Reverend Turner that they had "a strange experience at church." And David says, "It felt more like the board room of a major corporation." Turner takes them to his giant mural of end-times events and points to a picture of a blond woman with a revealing red top, a long, semi-transparent purple skirt, bare feet, and a crown on her head. She holds a golden goblet in her left hand and is sitting on a red, lion-like creature. Next to her are the words "Rev. 17." Turner says,

> There's your world church. When the Christians disappeared, some of the churches collapsed for lack of members, but for the rest, they just joined together in one big, sin-infested, humanistic body—the world church. In the Bible, Revelation calls her the great prostitute that commits adultery with the kings of the earth. . . . teaching people to traffic in war, in blood, in things of the flesh.

That these are references to the national and international ecumenical councils is clearly demonstrated both by the language that is used and by the visual cues linking the world church to ecumenical events.

The image of the world church in the *A Thief in the Night* films borrows heavily from imagery of the World and National Councils. For example, a widely circulated photograph from the founding convention of the National Council of Churches in 1950 shows the council's members sitting in session around a giant white cross-shaped table. Most of the members are male. Some are in vestments; others are in suits and ties. The angle of the picture positions the viewer at the back of the room and slightly above, looking down the long middle section of the cross. At the very bottom of the cross/table stands a microphone, facing out toward observers of the photograph, as though inviting them to imagine themselves speaking to, and participating in the work of, the National Council and its members. Yet all the members are facing away from the camera and the microphone, toward the head of the cross and the front of the room.[65] At the cross's head stands a white pulpit with an altar behind. A man stands hunched over the pulpit, presumably addressing the assembly. On the altar is an open Bible, flanked by flowers and candles. On the wall above the altar hangs another white cross, a miniature version of that around which the council members are gathered. To the left and right of this smaller cross are the banners of the twenty-nine Protestant and Orthodox member denominations; each banner is identical except for the denomination's name, which is set below the council's seal—a white cross imposed over an outline of the United States. Hanging above the cross on the wall, at the very top of the photograph, are the words "This Nation Under God."

In this photograph, the council members are shown linked, not by language or doctrine, but by a wordless symbol. Like the silver cross hanging over the heads of the UNITE agents offering up the mark of the beast in *A Distant Thunder*, the empty white cross functions as a repeated void that can endlessly embody the varied dreams of all the council's members, without demanding onerous allegiance to a common interpretation of its meaning. Yet, while seemingly open to diverse interpretations of doctrine, the council does demand allegiance of another type. Each distinct denomination has submitted to the practical and political authority of the National Council. The identical banners that flank the altar look like Roman imperial standards—an image that, for Fundamentalists, would invoke both doctrinal fears of the Roman Catholic Church and political fears of a future reborn Roman Empire that is often associated with the Antichrist and the seven-year tribulation in dispensationalist apocalyptic narratives. Writing for the National Association of Evangelicals, in an article accompanied by this photograph of the convention, Verne P. Kaub describes the event as "Romish Pageantry."[66] On each banner, the name and identity of the church is physically subordinated to the National Council. The white cross, representing the authority of the council unbridled by good doctrine, is imposed upon the United States. Kaub describes the leaders of the National Council taking their seats around the giant cross-shaped table by saying that they "made the Sign of the Cross," an odd phrase that indicates, again, both the Catholic nature of the proceedings and layout and the empty character of the cross, whose sign imposes religious order without limits—covering and even eliminating the American nation in the process. As Robert Ellwood says, "Pictures from the Cleveland gathering, revealing processional crosses and banners, together with Eastern Orthodox prelates in their rich vestments, suggested how far the new 'superchurch' had moved from true Protestantism."[67]

Kaub further articulates the council's political threat to national sovereignty, noting that an American flag, a Christian flag, and a United Nations flag hung in front of each balcony section. These flags, which are not visible in the photograph, are, in the context of twentieth-century apocalyptic narratives, perhaps the most explicit sign of the council's dangerous corruption. After all, as the *A Thief in the Night* series demonstrates, it is often the United Nations that establishes the world government in apocalyptic narratives. When Kathy and David visit the world church, we see that all religious symbols have been replaced by UNITE banners. Having achieved religious and political domination, the ecumenical church of *Image of the Beast* has no longer any need to make "the Sign of the Cross," but can instead openly revel in power and profit, war and "things of the flesh." In this context, the declaration of the National Council, "This Nation Under God," would only serve to reaffirm the fears of Fundamentalist communities concerned with the council's power and influence. While claiming the nation for God and Christ, the council seemed instead to be rallying an empty deity and an empty cross to support a political movement aimed at quashing Fundamentalist resistance and creating a national superchurch—bringing the American nation under a god of council authority.

In the end, the apocalyptic story goes, this god will reveal its true face, abandoning all pretense of representing the God of Fundamentalist believers. In *Image of the Beast,* the "High Priest" of the Antichrist speaks to an assembled gathering and says, "I am a voice crying in the wilderness. Make straight the pathways of your heart. Make them straight to Brother Christopher."[68] He speaks of the drought and disease brought on by "the dark god of Jesus Christ." And he urges the listeners to "resist him." The practical and tolerant Christianity of the liberal Reverend Turner becomes the malevolent and dictatorial anti-Christianity of the Antichrist. While ostensibly being told about a literal future from which Fundamentalist believers will escape, the audience is, at the same time, being warned about their allegiances in the present. Liberalism, the narrative reveals, will not remain liberal, and tolerance is only a mask that conceals a violent opposition to the Fundamentalist church. These films represent not a pacifying narrative of escapist inevitability, but an activating call, allegorically linked not to a distant, existential evil, but to an immediate perceived threat to Fundamentalist believers and communities in the present.

Media and the Network Church

As we have seen in the previous chapters, political activism has always been a troubling problem for Fundamentalist believers. On the one hand, they are called to live in the world, pay their taxes, do their work well, and so forth. On the other hand, politics is a corrupt and seductive realm, and believers who get caught up in it might forget their heavenly calling to preach the gospel and convert unbelievers for the kingdom of God. In justifying political activism, therefore, Fundamentalist narratives are always careful to demonstrate how the activities of the state are affecting the spiritual lives and callings of those within the Fundamentalist community. As scholars like Frykholm have noted, Fundamentalist believers tend not to advocate for issues like responsible environmental management,[69] although this is not merely because Fundamentalists believe the world will be ending soon. Arguably more significant in Fundamentalist narratives is the perceived danger posed by a national or international confederacy strong enough to mandate strict environmental standards. Fundamentalist fears of strong federalism have become intertwined with conservative and anti-Communist fears of strong government, and the risks of enabling a new world order seem inevitably greater than the risks posed by environmental degradation. For Fundamentalist audiences, films like these demonstrate that a state with too much power will try to first mimic and then take over the church, eliminating Fundamentalist freedom and hope for revival in the process.

What then is the solution for Fundamentalist believers? Before the Rapture, in *A Thief in the Night*, we are introduced to the independent Fundamentalist "First Church of the Open Bible." In contrast to Reverend Turner's ornate, liberal edifice, First Church is plain and undecorated. Instead of flowers, rich wood, and stained glass, a simple cross hangs on the white wall behind Pastor Balmer, who quotes the Bible and preaches about the coming Rapture: "We can conclude that we are living now in the end times. The days in which we live are seeing many prophecies being fulfilled that we have never seen fulfilled before, and surely this serves to remind all of us that the time is short at best, and if we would be followers of Jesus Christ, we must join his band now." The emphasis on a "band" of believers contrasts with the institutional stagnation of the liberal church, where the truth of God is no longer being preached. Pastor Balmer implicitly contrasts ecumenical stability with Fundamentalist marginality. But where Reverend Turner dismisses the marginal as "dead horses," Pastor Balmer stresses the mobility and readiness that marginality confers on the Fundamentalist faithful. Not bound to denominations, dependent on councils, or slowed by state bureaucracy, the band of true believers, like Christ's tiny band of disciples, are free to preach the Gospel and prepare for the imminent return of Christ.

In one sense, apocalyptic stories offer an idealized version of Fundamentalist identity and communication in the world. Even as the social order is collapsing in these films and the world is falling into chaos, public speech becomes (from the Fundamentalist believer's perspective at least) remarkably unfiltered and clear. At the beginning of *A Distant Thunder*, Patty listens to the radio in her car—driving through a chaotic, post-Rapture city—as a news reporter interviews "the pastor of a suburban church, Dr. Allan Reed." The interviewer asks Dr. Reed, "What caused this holocaust?" and mentions that some religious leaders have spoken of a "Rapture" while most deny this. The interviewer asks Dr. Reed's opinion of the Rapture, and Dr. Reed gives a detailed explanation of the dispensational doctrine of the Rapture and quotes from 1 Thessalonians 4:17. He then explains that he has become a Christian as a result of witnessing the Rapture. Later in the film, Patty and her friends read from a newspaper about two men "preaching repent, Jesus is coming" in Jerusalem. The article says, "The character of their ministry is described as similar to Moses and Elijah." It goes on to attribute to these prophets "spectacular conversions of many thousands of Jewish young men in a brief period of time," and says, "These Jewish disciples are being trained for a worldwide evangelistic effort." A little later, a television newscast shows a nuclear explosion in Uganda and also quotes religious leaders about Bible prophecy. The newscaster says, "Again the Bible haunts us with passages that used to sit on dusty shelves, now becoming screaming headlines."

In part, of course, this kind of language is a not-so-subtle attempt by the screenwriter to squeeze more exposition into the script. Facing the unenviable task of explaining the complicated dispensational system, most apocalyptic novelists and filmmakers use any available excuse to bring out the charts and explain how the immediate drama fits with the apocalyptic narrative. On the other hand, by communicating these words through mainstream media, the Fundamentalist audience is offered a dramatic example of what media could be, and this ideal only intensifies the contrast with the censorships of the world church and the Antichrist upon Fundamentalist believers later in the series. Such a conception of media and technology also fits well with what Quentin Schultze describes as an evangelical belief in the promise of media technology to empower and sanctify believers' communication as a means for transmitting gospel messages and extending the believing community—a belief rooted, Schultze argues, in a particularly Protestant ideal of direct transmission between God and humanity.[70]

Of all the films in Thompson's series, 1981's *Image of the Beast* focuses most heavily on the ecumenical and state censorship of Fundamentalist speech. When Reverend Turner shows David and Kathy his huge chart of the Tribulation period, he tells them that the authorities do not know that he has it. Communication of the truth is being suppressed. Even more extensively, the main focus of this film is on how the Antichrist has turned computer technology into an instrument for corruption. At the very beginning of the film, Kathy and her husband are shown buying a book called *The Computer Prophecies*. Later, after her husband has been raptured, Kathy reads the book and realizes that computer barcodes were a precursor to the mark of the beast—an idea popularized by Mary Stewart Relfe in her 1981 book *When Your Money Fails*. In another scene, Reverend Turner tells Kathy that the computer is "the new golden calf," and he gives some indication that even the Antichrist is a kind of computer: "a computer that speaks and convinces people that it thinks. Hundreds of millions of people will worship that inanimate object. And it's in the temple." Indeed, the few times we see "Brother Christopher," he is very different from the attractive, charismatic figures described in books like *The Late Great Planet Earth* and seen in apocalyptic films like *The Omega Code*.[71] In Thompson's films, the audience only sees the Antichrist up close one time, and then he/it is behaving like a stereotypical robot—moving his head from side to side and speaking in monotone—sitting on a golden throne in the rebuilt Jewish temple in Jerusalem. Although there is, as far as I am aware, nothing in dispensational doctrine to indicate that the Antichrist is anything but human, Thompson's fictional approach prioritizes the relationship between the Antichrist and concealment. Other apocalyptic films and novels focus on the seductive power of oratory in their depictions of the Antichrist. Thompson focuses on the power of speech to mold and shape reality—hiding truth behind media. Because the world government controls all communication through their mastery of technology, Thompson indicates, they can control how much people know and what secrets they cannot see.

However, even as the audience is given an Orwellian vision of computer surveillance, media control, and technological domination, there remains room for resistance. David's ability to create a counterfeit mark, using computer technology, indicates that Fundamentalists can make use of the enemy's technological resources to fight back. And by the fourth movie, technology is unquestionably promoted as a tool for Fundamentalist organization and resistance. The idea of a decentralized, computer-based broadcaster offers a possibility for believers to communicate with one another and build global networks for organizing with each other and spreading the gospel. That this fictional vision of computer-based communication coincided with the early period of explosive growth in online Usenet communication is surely not coincidental.[72] The image of the earth from space—an image that only appears in the final film—emphasizes its fragility, particularly in the context of nuclear weapons. But in the context of broadcasting and computer networking, it also emphasizes its shrinking size. At the beginning of the 1980s, communication technology was making the earth smaller and more manageable for the revivalist. With global satellites and computers, the possibility of a truly global fellowship of believers seems possible, and this, in turn, is linked to the hope of Christ's return at the end of the film. The Second Coming is not displayed in the *A Thief in the Night* series, but it remains the hope on the edge of Fundamentalist consciousness, mediated through the technology of revival, traveling like broadcast signals and the words of Scripture through the stars.

Conclusion

Apocalyptic narratives offer the hope of literal escape and rescue, but more importantly they allegorically place Fundamentalist believers, communities, and values at the center of contemporary political and social events. They create, for believers, counterpublic frames through which spiritual identity and political activism are linked, and in which the struggle for salvation is conflated with often-violent resistance to ecumenical tolerance and ideological battles against Communists and feminists, academics and liberals, and all the other agents and would-be agents of the Antichrist. Integrating grim literalism and allegorical imagination, apocalyptic narratives offer significant resources in the constitution and motivation of political community around the ideal of the Fundamentalist church. Such narratives open the definition of the church and expand the possibilities for public engagement; however, they do so at the cost of institutional stability. The "church" that emerges at the end of the *A Thief in the Night* series is a church stripped of walls and doors and sermons and rituals—stripped indeed of everything that is recognizably a church. As Crawford Gribben argues, "Recent prophecy novels take evangelicals beyond their notoriously low views of ecclesiology into a situation where the church itself can hardly be said to exist."[73] Certainly this is the case for the *A Thief in the Night* films, whose narrative extends the Fundamentalist critique of ecumenical councils and denominational hierarchy into a broad repudiation of the institutional church itself.

Apocalyptic narratives are set in the future, but, as Melani McAlister argues, they are "very much about the present."[74] More than revivalist scare tactics or escapist fantasies, they are intertwined with disputes about the status and role of the Fundamentalist church and identity in the political and cultural world. However, the perspectives on apocalypticism and allegory that I have offered here do nothing to dispel Buber's critique, at the beginning of this chapter, that apocalyptic narratives do not require, encourage, or even allow jeremiadic speech, self-critique, or repentance from the apocalyptic community. Individuals express self-doubt only so long as they remain outside the Fundamentalist church. Once a convert, the Fundamentalist believer is secure in his or her rightness, and this perspectival blindness continues to raise legitimate concerns about the conflation of apocalyptic narratives with present-day politics. Allegory can be and has been appropriated, as Robert Hariman argues, in a way that "displaces democratic politics, sanitizes difference, and collapses all history into the syntax of an omnipresent present."[75] Apocalyptic narratives often idealize violence, perpetuate existing social categories, and do little or nothing to question social inequities within and beyond the Fundamentalist community. In fact, discomfort with or outright antipathy toward nonbelievers, advocates for strong government, Jews, Catholics, foreigners, and women are evident throughout these narratives. For example, Patty, in the *A Thief in the Night* series, rarely questions, confronts, or acts upon male characters; she is listener, follower, and, ultimately, victim. In the first film, she sits on the floor at the feet of her husband and a male pastor while they discuss the Bible. At the midpoint of the series, she is violently disposed of so that a male figure can take over the role of church-building protagonist in the last two films.[76] Apocalyptic narratives present political action as guerilla warfare and challenge notions of compromise and cooperation as literally damnable fence sitting. In her analysis of the *Left Behind* novels, Kristy

Maddux says, "If there are only two groups of people in the world—good and evil—and if evil is the tragic, irreversible, and essential nature of some people's souls, then the only possible mode of engagement with evil is aggression."[77] Just as apocalyptic events can be read as allegorical figures for present-day believers, present-day events can be and are read as allegories of apocalypse, and political disagreements are reinterpreted as precursors to violent suppression that demand uncompromising and even militaristic responses from the faithful against their enemies.

It is hardly surprising that, as Gribben notes, the diminished respect for the institutional church in more recent apocalyptic narratives seems to have been accompanied by growing tolerance for factionalism and extremes of violence.[78] The Fundamentalist church at the end of the *A Thief in the Night* series is separated from its own history and from the collected wisdom and contestation of centuries, and it is cast upon the post-apocalyptic landscape with nothing but a cacophony of voices on the airwaves to guide its members. Yet this rejection of institutionalism is presented to the audience as the sure foundation for a new kind of institution, the establishment of a network of believers—each independent, but all collectively accountable to the same Bible and the same doctrine. At the end of the series, it is not a cacophony of individuals, but a technologically gathered community of the faithful who sings the hymn and brings about the destruction of both church and state to advance God's kingdom.

Chapter Five

The Superchurch Reimagined

⌘

> Historians will probably look back on the decade of the 70's as the beginning of the large church movement.
>
> —Jerry Falwell, Elmer Towns, *Church Aflame*, 1971

To be Fundamentalist is to be marginal. It is to adopt and enact one's own marginalization in society. It is to assume a position of outsider. It is to invoke counterpublic speech against public norms. Yet it is also to lay claim to an imagined higher standard than that which society currently upholds. It is, as we discussed in the last chapter, to envision a world in which Fundamentalist speech is normative. It is to speak for a public that the Fundamentalist community imagines but cannot, itself, enact. Therefore, we have seen, within Fundamentalism, a continual and productive tension between marginal and majority discourses.

It is widely assumed that this tension was disrupted in the late 1970s.

In 1976, a Gallup survey reported that a third of respondents identified as "born again," and 31 percent believed the Bible was "literally" true[1]—leading first George Gallup Jr. and then *Newsweek* magazine to declare 1976 "The Year of the Evangelical."[2] That same year witnessed the election of Jimmy Carter, the first "born again" president. And the confluence of spiritual and political issues brought about through events like the war in Vietnam and the Nixon administration's Watergate scandal was highlighted by the publication of former Nixon operative Charles Colson's spiritual autobiography *Born Again*. The result of these events, Susan Harding argues,

> was to reveal a hitherto "hidden Protestant Majority" that was already in some sense manifesting itself in high political places. As fundamentalists, pentecostals, charismatics, and even evangelicals, these theologically conservative Protestants had until the late 1970s seen themselves as marginals, if not enclaves or scattered remnants, relative to a perceived liberal Protestant mainstream. Once they saw themselves, and were seen, as related to one another and, taken together, as the Protestant majority, their marginal days were numbered.[3]

It is often claimed that the late 1970s marked the end of Fundamentalist marginalization—a reemergence of the Fundamentalist into the public sphere. Yet we might well be suspicious of such a blanket assertion. In adopting the language of a "Moral Majority," Fundamentalist leaders like Jerry Falwell were not abandoning marginal rhetoric. They were doing precisely what Fundamentalists had done throughout the century. As William Bell Riley had claimed to represent a majority of true believers against the crushing force of the Interchurch World Movement, Falwell claimed to speak for a majority oppressed by state-sanctioned "secular humanism." The majority he invoked was not merely, as Harding argues, "a public relations stunt," but a rhetorical construct reflecting ongoing tensions among Fundamentalists over the proper way to understand the believing community and its role in the world.[4] The politics of the Moral Majority originated in a doctrinal language of church growth and superaggresive evangelism, which reimagined the local church as a potential "superchurch" and as the means by which Fundamentalist believers could finally achieve balance between the desire for public influence and the isolating demands of enacted marginalization.

A City upon a Mountain

Almost every superchurch and megachurch tells a story of miraculous growth from impossibly humble beginnings. Robert Schuller started the Garden Grove Community Church (aka the Crystal Cathedral) in a California drive-in parking lot in 1955. Bill Hybels opened his 23,000-member Willow Creek Community Church in an Illinois movie theater in 1975. And, so the story goes, in the summer of 1956, in the former home of the Donald Duck Bottling Company in Lynchburg, Virginia, a group of thirty-five adults gathered to listen to the preaching of a twenty-two-year-old Baptist Bible College graduate named Jerry Falwell at a place that would come to be known as the Thomas Road Baptist Church.[5] Young but ambitious, Falwell launched radio and television ministries within weeks of starting his new church, and the local congregation expanded rapidly as the listening audience grew.[6] Within four years, the church's Easter service brought in over 1,000 people, and in 1964, they moved into a newly completed 1,000-seat auditorium.[7] By 1967, Thomas Road Baptist had established its own K–12 school, Lynchburg Christian Academy.[8] In 1971, with the help of Elmer Towns, Falwell established Lynchburg Baptist College, which was renamed Liberty University in 1985.[9] At the same time, Towns and Falwell claimed, Thomas Road had grown to 10,000 members and an average weekly attendance of more than 5,000.[10] Such growth, they insisted, was a sign of God's blessing and the faithfulness of the church in gathering and training leaders and evangelists who could "capture" their community.

Falwell was the central figure in these narratives of extraordinary growth, and the expansion of the church was interpreted as a validation of his personal faith and ministry. He was not simply part of the church or even the leader of the church; he was invoked as a kind of embodiment of the church, its mission, and its identity. As Towns wrote:

> Jerry Falwell is evangelism through the Thomas Road Baptist Church, a gigantic congregation where fifty to one hundred respond weekly to the invitation and receive Christ. Jerry Falwell is evangelism through "The Old-Time Gospel Hour," broadcasting the gospel weekly through the electronic miracle of television over 456 stations. Jerry Falwell is camp evangelism through Treasure Island, where over two thousand children come for a week every summer, many receiving Jesus Christ. Jerry Falwell is evangelism through Elim Home, where men under the curse of alcohol come free of

> charge to receive spiritual therapy and renewal. Jerry Falwell is evangelism through Hope Aglow Ministries, where the gospel is preached to convicts in prison throughout the east coast. Jerry Falwell is evangelism through the Lynchburg Christian schools, giving quality Christian education to children and teen-agers in their formative years. Jerry Falwell is evangelism through the Lynchburg Baptist College, training and motivating young men to build churches throughout America, similar to the Thomas Road Baptist Church. Jerry Falwell is evangelism through the printed page, The Old-Time Gospel Hour Press, distributing five million brochures and pamphlets last year and *The Old-Time Gospel Hour News*, a monthly newspaper reaching 540,000 homes. Jerry Falwell is evangelism through pastors' conferences, stimulating pastors to build superaggressive local churches similar to the Lynchburg congregation.[11]

In this strangely worded passage, Jerry Falwell functions as a metaphor for the mission of the church. It is hard not to picture the famous frontispiece of Thomas Hobbes's *Leviathan*—where the sovereign leader towers above a city, his body composed of his subjects. In the same way, Falwell is described as embodying the church and the mission of Thomas Road. The ministries of the church emanate from his words and actions. He is their essence, and they, in turn, are validations of his work and his being.

Towns said of Falwell, "Since the church is dependent upon his leadership, a two-million-dollar policy insures his life, with triple indemnity."[12] The security of the church rested in its leader. Thomas Road was imagined as a discursive and economic vehicle for Falwell's ministry around the world. In 1971, the church purchased a $225,000 private jet to accommodate Falwell's speaking schedule; the next year, they purchased another jet for $600,000.[13] "In our day of rapid transportation," Towns explained, "Jerry Falwell uses every means possible to spread the gospel."[14] In turn, the growth of Thomas Road Baptist Church was offered as proof of God's blessing on Falwell's wider ministry. It was important that narratives of growth not appear mechanistic. Falwell could not claim too much credit for the success of the church or his ministry. He needed to appear at once bold before his church and his community and humble before God. Again, like the Hobbesian sovereign, Falwell occupied the position of a prophetic figure in the narratives of Thomas Road Baptist Church, a uniquely positioned servant of God whose charge it was to rule the people and convey God's message to the world. In this context, growth was a sign of that close relationship between the prophet and God.

Part of this relationship required aggression and assertiveness in demanding God's blessing. In the fiftieth-anniversary tribute to Thomas Road, the author says that Falwell "dared to claim a city and a mountain for God."[15] Falwell did not simply ask God to build a church; he called it into existence through his interactions with God. The mountain, meanwhile, is both a description of the physical terrain of Lynchburg, Virginia, and a metaphor for unique, prophetic displays of God's power and blessing. Mountains indicate a special vantage point. They enable broader views of the world below while also bringing the one who ascends the mountain closer to God. To ascend the mountain also implies a special calling. In the Torah, God commanded the Israelites not to approach or touch the mountain, warning that those who approached without permission would die. Only the anointed leader was allowed to approach. To claim a mountain, as is ascribed to Falwell, is to claim the mantle of prophet, and from that position to speak the authoritative words of God to the people. It was on a mountain that God gave the law to Moses; it was on a mountain that Jesus preached to the multitudes; and it was on a mountain that the resurrected Christ addressed his disciples for the last time, speaking the words that Falwell claimed for his own church's mission. The mountain also enhances one's visibility, allowing the rest of the world to see; it was on a mountain that Christ was crucified, and in apocalyptic narratives it is on a mountain that he will return. Similarly, it was from a hilltop that the "city" spoken of by Jesus and John Winthrop would cast its light—a reference that Falwell explicitly invoked in his 1971 sermon "The Church at Antioch."[16] Finally, the mountain indicates a stable foundation, a place prepared by God. During the 1940s Carl McIntire and other Fundamentalist leaders attacked the ecumenical movement as a "Tower of Babel" that tried to build its own mountain to God. In contrast, Falwell—a true prophetic leader—could claim a city and a mountain that God had already provided and use it to spread the light of the Christian gospel and build God's kingdom around the world.

In the early 1970s, this mountain empire was still relatively unknown to outsiders, but within a few years it would become one of the most famous and notorious churches in the country. Its membership increased by more than 200 percent over the next decade, and it would come to play a major role in the constitution of a movement called "neo-Fundamentalism" and the religio-political organization that called itself the Moral Majority. Neo-Fundamentalism is the term commonly used for the movement advocated by Falwell and a few others, which tried to retain separation from the world, while attempting, as George Marsden says, "to bring fundamentalists back toward the centers of American life, especially through political action."[17] This last phrase, in particular, is often misunderstood. Neo-Fundamentalist political action did not emerge as a post hoc justification for the national agenda of the Moral Majority or any of the other similar groups that were established in the late 1970s.[18] Rather it emerged as a response to a series of tensions that had been building among Fundamentalist communities for several decades.

The first and most obvious indication of these tensions was the creation of two, conflicting, Fundamentalist associations in the early 1940s. The American Council of Christian Churches (ACCC) was established in 1941, and the National Association of Evangelicals (NAE) was established in 1942—both organizations that we discussed briefly in the previous chapter. The ACCC was founded by Carl McIntire, who put an explicitly, even radically, separatist stamp on the organization. The NAE, in contrast, was organized by a group of Fundamentalist believers—including J. Elwin Wright, Harold Ockenga, Carl F. H. Henry, and James DeForest Murch—whose goal was to achieve a reasoned and "positive" balance between what they saw as the radical ecumenicism of the then Federal Council of Churches on the one hand and the radical separatism of McIntire on the other. Distancing themselves from the term "Fundamentalist," the members of the NAE called themselves "new evangelicals"—a term adopted by Ockenga, who argued that the evangelicalism represented by the NAE was a return to the original spirit of the Christian New Testament, where believers were called to influence culture, rather than separating from it.[19]

As indicated by the name, Falwell's neo-Fundamentalism reflected an additional layer of tension within separatist Fundamentalism. Where the latter retained a strongly defensive posture that associated militancy with purity, Falwell was part of a loose association of Fundamentalist leaders who sought to retain separatist identity while turning militancy outward, expanding the circle of Fundamentalist influence through aggressive revivalism. This association, in turn, was rooted in a narrative of superaggressive church growth that brought together networks of pastors and independent Fundamentalist churches around the country, opening the way for the national organization that would come to be called the Moral Majority.

The Local Superchurch

In 1971, Falwell delivered a sermon titled "The Church at Antioch" for a group of Fundamentalist church leaders. In this sermon, Falwell began by contrasting two kinds of churches—a pattern that should now be familiar from previous chapters. On the one hand there was a disembodied church—invisible and universal, ecumenical and intangible.[20] This kind of church tries to encompass the whole world but has no identifiable members at home.[21] It was, however, not identified with any particular organization. Unlike, for example, William Bell Riley's attacks on the confederacy movement, Falwell's critiques about the universal church did not immediately reference the National Council of Churches, suggest an apocalyptic "world church," or speak against any particular denomination. Indeed, his critiques could have extended equally to liberal and Fundamentalist institutions, and they might, in fact, be better understood as directed against the militant separatism that had become representative of the latter. The problem with this universal church, Falwell indicated, was not so much its goals as its inability to define or achieve them. It was idealistic but impotent and incapable of advancing a transformative identity. Such critiques were not new. Writing in 1913, William Bell Riley argued that modernist theologians imagined the kingdom of God as a beautiful but ethereal, indeterminate, and unpopulated place, while Riley asked his readers to imagine a kingdom crowded with details—people, music, mansions and tables, hills and valleys.[22] Similarly, in contrast to his vague descriptions of the universal church, Falwell's "local church" was aggressive—indeed superaggressive—militaristic, forceful, and hypermasculine, promoting revivals and building a strong, visible, textured community through which to transform the world.

Falwell described a situation in which each Fundamentalist church would work to "saturate" its immediate community with the gospel message. As more people were persuaded, the local church would grow, and as it grew, even more people would be available to saturate the community. At the same time, he argued, these superchurches would be able to collect the money and resources sufficient to establish radio and television ministries and support missionary efforts around the world. The end result would be a vast network of powerful local churches, each of which would not only dominate its immediate community, but operate as a "worldwide mission center" to remotely reach the nations of the world.

In order to rhetorically reconstruct and justify this superaggressive, independent church as a model for Fundamentalist expansion, Falwell's sermon transcended church history, conflating the Fundamentalist church with an idealized church of the New Testament—a move that allowed him to get beyond differences of denomination and doctrine and recover an ideal of face-to-face communication between believers. The device was similar to that used in the *A Thief in the Night* series discussed in the previous chapter, except that whereas those films moved forward to erase the problems of church history by, literally, erasing all the true believers and starting over, Falwell moved backward to transcend that history, making the church of the first century entirely contemporaneous with that of the twentieth. In describing the need for Fundamentalist association, leaders like Riley and McIntire had spoken of a return to the Protestant Reformation. Falwell, in contrast, went much further back, and his invocation of the first-century church, though not fully explicated in this sermon, offered his audience possibilities for framing both "church growth" and, later, the "new religious right" in interdenominational terms.

Growth

Falwell argued that the New Testament book of Acts—which tells the story of the earliest Christian communities—was primarily about local churches that grew and spread through aggressive evangelism. He said,

> It all began in an Upper Room. One hundred-twenty men and women met together and prayed in obedience to the command of Christ. After ten days, in answer to God's promise, the Spirit of God was outpoured. On that day of Pentecost, 3,000 more were saved, baptized, and added to that local assembly. Three thousand added to 120 made 3,120. And then God added to that 3,120-member congregation. Soon the number came to 5,000 men

> besides the women and children. That's a pretty good church when you have 5,000 members. Later they multiplied, and eventually history and tradition tell us that, before the persecution came, the church at Jerusalem numbered in excess of 100,000. Now remember, half of a city of 200,000 were professing Christians.[23]

Two things are particularly notable in this passage. The first is Falwell's heavy reliance on statistical proof. The basis of this proof was his reinterpretation of the term "church" as it appears in the New Testament. In Acts 2:47—one of a number of passages from which Falwell assembled his numbers—the King James Version reads: "The Lord added to the church daily such as should be saved." Most commentators, including both the original and revised Scofield Bibles, identify this "church" as the universal community of true believers, but, having already dismissed the universal church and declared that "The Book of Acts is the story of planting local churches," Falwell chose to interpret the book's references to the church through that framework. The numbers he offered, therefore, were given not, as they normally are, as evidence of Christianity's rapid spread, but as proof of the truly incredible expansion of a single institution, and as statistical validation of his argument that God desires every local Fundamentalist church to experience the same kind of growth. Having reinterpreted the church as the local church, the passages Falwell referenced became a source of incontrovertible, mathematical proof that it was God's desire for all Fundamentalist churches to become massive superchurch institutions. Not only did Falwell translate his claim into a divine calling, but he rhetorically situated himself and his own superchurch—the physical setting of this sermon—at the ideational center of God's plan for the church from the beginning of Christian history. Within this framework, the numbers offered both a biblical mandate for growth and a spiritual validation of Falwell, his institution, and his prophetic calling. After all, later in this sermon, Falwell claimed that Thomas Road Baptist had "9,235 in Sunday school on Sunday morning in a city of 54,000 people."[24] If a congregation of 5,000 was "pretty good," then Thomas Road was clearly well on its way to becoming a truly remarkable work of God.

In this focus on statistical measurements and numerical growth, Falwell reimagined separatist Fundamentalism through the lenses of a number of twentieth-century revivalist movements, including parachurch college ministries like Bill Bright's Campus Crusade for Christ, the revivalist "crusades" of evangelists like Billy Graham, and, perhaps most importantly, a loose cooperative calling itself the Church Growth Movement. The latter grew out of the work of a missionary named Donald McGavran and, particularly, his 1955 book *The Bridges of God*. McGavran was interested in increasing the statistical rate of conversions for foreign missionaries in the field. He argued that a more efficient and effective evangelism was essential in order to combat the "universal materialism" of the modern world. Toward that end, he encouraged missionaries to build "bridges" between their own cultures and that of the people they were trying to evangelize. This included, for example, working within the racial and social prejudices of the people they were trying to convert, rather than demanding that they change their social identities before becoming part of the "Christian community." At the heart of McGavran's argument was the claim that churches and missionary organizations needed a more flexible methodology and scientific approach to their work. Therefore, he advocated building resource centers for evangelistic organizations that could use sociological research to study "how people become Christian" in order to strategically maximize mission resources in the service of global revival.[25]

Founded by McGavran in 1964, the Institute of Church Growth sought to provide one such resource for evangelistic organizations and began collecting data for their more scientific approach to missionary work. The institute published a bimonthly newsletter, the *Church Growth Bulletin*, which included theoretical and practical articles and resources to help missionaries adopt church growth methods in the field. Originally, the Church Growth Movement was exclusively promoted as a tool for foreign missionary growth, not home church expansion. In 1965, when he became dean of the School of World Mission at Fuller Seminary, McGavran established strict entrance requirements that excluded most North American pastors. These requirements "included three years of cross-cultural experience, validated by fluency in a second language."[26] In a 1968 article for the *Church Growth Bulletin*, McGavran attacked "selfish Christians" who stayed home and built expensive churches rather than sacrificing their comfortable lives for the unconverted overseas.[27]

However, by the early 1970s, McGavran and other Church Growth leaders were embracing American church growth. Elmer Towns—who came to Thomas Road Baptist Church in 1971 as part of Falwell's efforts to establish Lynchburg Baptist College—became one of the most prolific early supporters of what came to be called the American Church Growth Movement. In fact, in 1969, Towns wrote a book called *The Ten Largest Sunday Schools and What Makes Them Grow*, which became credited as the first book to promote Church Growth methods to American churches.[28] Among the churches examined were the Akron Baptist Temple in Akron, Ohio; Highland Park Baptist Church in Chattanooga, Tennessee; Temple Baptist Church in Detroit, Michigan; First Baptist Church in Hammond, Indiana; and, of course, Thomas Road Baptist Church, which Towns described as "the youngest church among the ten largest."[29] It was also, in 1969, the smallest of the top ten, and at thirty-five, Jerry Falwell was the youngest pastor. Yet, Towns admiringly noted Falwell's aggressiveness, his commitment to evangelistic outreach, and the strength of his television ministry.

One of the most significant features of the Church Growth Movement was that its leaders placed independent churches, rather than denominational or parachurch organizations, at the center of revivalist efforts. This marked a change from ministry programs in the mid-century, which tended to make the local church a secondary player in revivalism. Ministries like Campus Crusade for Christ or the Billy Graham Crusades focused exclusively on winning converts and gave very little thought to local churches, except as critical funding sources. In all other respects, churches were too small, too inefficient, and too obsessed with doctrinal and denominational disputes to be of much use. The Church Growth Movement, in contrast, imagined a different kind of church—scientific, independent, and methodologically flexible—and it set this church at the center of a plan for spiritual, social, and (eventually) political transformation.

The Church Growth Movement provided a methodology for growth, one that Falwell endorsed and justified for his Fundamentalist audience in this sermon through his reinterpretation of the growth described in Acts. At the same time Falwell advocated this systematization of revivalism, however, he translated it outside the realm of human authority. Thus, the second thing that is notable in the passage above is the lack of agency Falwell allocated to the early believers. He described the early growth of the church as an act of God. As the believers prayed, God brought the Spirit, and the community grew. The only action ascribed to the people was prayer. God was the agential force whose work was responsible for the salvation of souls and the growth of the church. While active in prayer, the first-century believers Falwell described in this sermon seem to be, in every other respect, passive recipients of God's will.

This appears, at first, to contradict Falwell's argument that his audience should make similar growth their "prime objective." Making no reference to prayer, Falwell, in the next paragraph, called on "every local church . . . to capture its city for Christ. . . . to win the entire metropolitan area. . . . to win every individual, every soul, and every person."[30] Yet this seeming contradiction was necessary in order for Falwell to justify these methodologies to his audience. Falwell, in this sermon, was speaking as a Fundamentalist, but the Church Growth Movement was an unquestionably "new evangelical" organization. Its leaders even included charismatic Pentecostal pastors like C. Peter Wagner and John Wimber, who would go on to lead the Vineyard movement in the 1980s.[31] Most of the prominent Fundamentalist leaders refused to fellowship with charismatics and Pentecostals because they believed in special "gifts of the Spirit" that conflicted with Fundamentalist interpretations of the Bible. Also unpopular were Church Growth advocates like Billy Graham—the one-time hand-selected heir of William Bell Riley—whose willingness to accept contributions from Catholic and ecumenical churches put him at odds with Fundamentalist separatism.

In general, there were many problems with church growth for Fundamentalists. Despite the rhetoric of city temples and tabernacles, which justified growth as an extension of revival and a way to ward off ecumenical takeover, a large church was, for the most part, seen as evidence that believers had strayed from the path and abandoned the hard truths of Fundamentalist Christianity. In the *A Thief in the Night* films, as we saw in the previous chapter, large churches stood for ecumenical apostasy while small churches stood for true belief. Among separatist Fundamentalists, small size was often held to be a sign of authenticity and commitment to the truth—representing a "faithful remnant." In Fundamentalist narratives, the relationship of liberal to Fundamentalist churches was often represented as the contrast between the weak-willed multitude and the dedicated band of believers. Thus the Fundamentalist leader and radical anti-Communist proselytizer Billy James Hargis equated large churches with apostasy, arguing that they repudiated Fundamentalist rigor and promoted what he called "a glorified religious honky-tonk."[32] It is hardly surprising, therefore, that among strict Fundamentalists, reactions to the Church Growth Movement were decidedly mixed. On the one hand, Church Growth leaders shared much in common with Fundamentalists. They believed in personal salvation. They generally believed in an inerrant, authoritative Bible.[33] They argued that liberalism and social-justice programs were dangerous distractions that could dilute revivalist efforts by making the unconverted too comfortable. On the other hand, the movement's prioritization of growth led some of its leaders to take positions at odds with Fundamentalist ideals of purity and separation, arguing, for example, that ethical issues could be approached flexibly, that churches should be nonjudgmental toward outsiders, and that the doctrine of biblical inerrancy was less important than a general adherence to the larger principles of Scripture.[34] For strict Fundamentalists, such beliefs were seen as opening ethics to a nonbiblical authority and eliminating biblical reliability. The true Fundamentalist preacher could not manipulate the truth of Scripture in order to achieve conversions, and anything that smacked of manipulation had to be rejected as antithetical to Fundamentalist identity. As the famous Fundamentalist preacher Bob Jones argued, "A witness is not responsible for the results of his testimony. . . . [The Lord] will take care of the results, but you must not compromise the testimony."[35] Fundamentalist separatism insisted on a level of institutional, as well as personal, purity that, as we have considered above, often seemed at odds with desires to witness and expand their influence as a religious, social, or political movement.

Within this context, Falwell's paradoxical language can be understood as critical to the rhetorical justification of neo-Fundamentalist superchurches. Although the city temple churches and the post-apocalyptic network were both associated with growth, their growth was limited by the ongoing necessity that they remain marginal in comparison to the apostate church and the unbelieving nation. As previously stated, Fundamentalism is only conceivable as a minority position within modernity. The idea of a Fundamentalist majority is at odds with the definitional and tropological framework through which Fundamentalist identity is validated. Falwell could not speak as a modern Fundamentalist and advocate the kind of revivalist growth that, for example, Finney described in his *Lectures*—growth that could eventually translate into a Christianized world, the kingdom of God on earth. Rather, Falwell described a church whose goal was to establish local majorities who would be able to both hold on to the fundamental truths in the midst of persecution and effectively engage in a global struggle against the enemy abroad. Transforming the language of large churches from "temples," "tabernacles," and "citadels" to "superaggressive local churches," Falwell did not abandon the macro-pessimism of premillennial Fundamentalism, but he translated it into a motivation for strong local action and media-enabled networking among believers—using the imminent return of Christ to urge his listeners to hurry up and grow. The result was an irresolvable but productive tension within Falwell's conception of growth, one that was perhaps best illustrated by his description of hopeful impossibility in superaggressive evangelism. He said,

> We [Thomas Road] have 23 percent of the town already. That means we have 80 percent to go. That means we have a good foothold. That means we have just gotten the wheels turning. The work of the Lord in any town is just as limited as your faith and your willingness to work. No matter what church you attend, you are not limited by lack of potential, by lack of sinners to reach or by too many churches to preach the gospel in your area. If you had fifty or one hundred churches in Lynchburg preaching just like this one, all of you together could not get the job done before Jesus comes.[36]

Falwell both relied upon and repudiated his statistics, using them to validate and celebrate expansion, but backing away at the moment when expansion threatened to undermine the ultimate pessimism and marginalization governing Fundamentalist identity. Victory was, in a sense, always conceivable but never realizable, and this paradox, far from suppressing action, served as its primary motivation. The Fundamentalist could not achieve dominance in any ultimate sense, but Falwell offered a neo-Fundamentalist solution that conceived of partial dominance in local terms.

Communication

To speak to outsiders, we sacrifice control. We surrender surety to another's judgment, if only for the moment, and risk change in the interaction. Of course, in most situations, the risk is minimal. I can attempt to persuade you to eat at my favorite restaurant or donate to my cause or support my political candidate without, in most cases, putting fundamental aspects of my identity at risk. However, Fundamentalist doctrine requires the believer to regularly speak to outsiders about the deepest facets of belief and being—risking not only loss of control but also loss of eternity in the process. It is a tension that Fundamentalist believers must continually negotiate—the command to speak against the risk of speech—and one that in various ways they attempt to control. Some, as we discussed in previous chapters, chose to engage in simulated speech, staging mock "debates" with outsiders through Fundamentalist publications or platforms.[37] Others rely upon preapproved scripts to guide the interaction. Campus Crusade for Christ, for example, uses a special tract called "The Four Spiritual Laws" to guide student evangelists through the witnessing experience, and students are discouraged from interjecting too much of their own voice into the exchange. Others rely on mnemonics to guide the process; illustrations with names like "The Bridge," "The Royal Road," and "The Wordless Book" are meant to help the believer maintain control and direct the interactions with outsiders. Films like *A Thief in the Night* and its sequels offer opportunities for believers to let someone else speak for them. By inviting unbelieving friends to see a movie, believers can be assured that they will hear an evangelistic message. Meanwhile, the characters in these films use common illustrations and mnemonics as they witness to one another, which are intended to help believers integrate them into their own witnessing. Still other forms of witnessing forego speech altogether; Christian products like music, T-shirts, and bumper stickers offer opportunities for a kind of silent witnessing that puts a heavy burden on the unbelieving audience to enthymematically reconstruct the text and then approach the self-marked believer with "questions," a reversal that requires the unbeliever to take the position of supplicant before speech can begin.[38]

A more complex form of control can be found in Fundamentalist broadcasting. During the 1920s and 1930s, even as the Federal Council of Churches was receiving free religious airtime and extending its influence, Fundamentalists were pioneering commercial religious radio.[39] This medium seemed to offer a way to leapfrog social alienation and take their populist religious messages directly into people's homes,[40] while simultaneously maintaining control of the message and avoiding the problems of overfriendliness with the outside world. It reconnected Fundamentalist speech with modernity. Radio preachers operated largely independently of denominational regulation, and Fundamentalists who had separated from their denominations found a new kind of community through the medium. Despite efforts by the Federal Council to restrict its range, Fundamentalist radio prospered. Radio programs like Paul Rader's *National Radio Chapel* and Charles Fuller's *Old Fashioned Revival Hour* were, as Tona Hangen argues, critical for reminding Fundamentalist believers—widely dismissed as irrelevant naysayers and ignorant country bumpkins after Scopes—that they were members of a growing, national "circle of chosen faithful."[41]

Through the language of radio, Fundamentalists began talking about missionary work and revivalism in very different ways. No longer were revivalists forced to travel to the people. Radio could go anywhere, and it seemed to offer limitless possibilities for revival speech. Missionary work and door-to-door witnessing were no longer the only options available to the faithful believer who wanted to extend the kingdom of God around the world. Ministers encouraged donations from "partners" in the gospel who, by contributing, became part of the revivalist work. Partners gained an agential stake in ministries going on across the country and around the world while never leaving their homes. The idea of an invisible force, safely transmitting the Word of God to all people everywhere, had a powerful effect on the Fundamentalist imagination.

Yet there remained problems with broadcast media. Fundamentalists needed to control the speech situation, but they required control of reception as well. In matters of eternal consequence, the audience could not be left free to accept partially or interpret selectively. Radio and, later, television offered seemingly limitless possibilities to disseminate the message, but this message could not be controlled as easily as Fundamentalist advocates had at first imagined.[42] While seeming to enable intimate and, in the case of television, face-to-face communication, large audiences and donations did not often translate into the kind of stable converts who not only believed but also sought to engage with and convert others. Indeed, in many ways the charismatic authority of the media preacher was at odds with the authoritative call to action and involvement in the world outside the broadcast. As Max Weber argues, "Charisma is a typical anti-economic force. It repudiates any sort of involvement in the everyday routine world. It can only tolerate, with an attitude of complete emotional indifference, irregular, unsystematic, acquisitive acts."[43] Furthermore, charismatic authority derives from the emotional response of a group to the charismatic leader, and there is no clear structure or organization that guarantees community survival and continuation if the leader should cease to speak, or cease to be recognized as a genuine charismatic authority by those receiving the messages. As such, media authority is particularly unstable—being wholly rooted in the continual, repeated demand for the audience's attention. There is no stable conception of community through which the audience can define their identity, not just as receivers of information, but as producers and actors based upon that information. Even while broadcasters like Paul Rader and Charles Fuller generated large and loyal audiences in the 1930s and 1940s, Fundamentalists remained a fringe community, engaging in local contestation and mock battles with their enemies.

To put it another way, media produce charismatic leaders who draw large crowds, but by themselves they do not, as John Dewey recognized, create active and sustainable publics. To better control reception, Falwell argued, Fundamentalists needed to bring converts into not simply an abstract ideal of Christian community but a visible, local association through which new believers could become invested in the demands of Fundamentalist speech and trained to bring in their own converts. This, in turn, required Fundamentalist leaders to both speak and embody the message. As local empires created both to transmit the message of the gospel to strangers and to interpellate these stranger-converts into an ideal community of common believers, local churches relied not merely on charisma, but on an immediate, situated kind of sovereign, prophetic authority.

As with the charismatic, the prophet's value lies in the recognition and reception of the audience.[44] However, while Weber describes the prophet as simply another example of the charismatic leader, I argue, following James Darsey, that the basis of prophetic authority is different in that the prophet "speaks for another," and addresses the community as though transmitting God's voice.[45] Weber characterizes the prophet, like any genuine charismatic leader, as being a purely individual authority figure who declares: "It is written . . . , but I say unto you . . ."[46] For both Weber and Darsey, the prophet invokes the authority of divine revelation, but Darsey's prophet seems in possession of a humility (or, at least, the projection of humility) and reduction of the self to duty that Weber's prophet does not share. The difference is not one of radical reorientation, but of subtle shift. For both authors, the prophet possesses uniquely individual authority; unlike the priest, whose authority rests in a "sacred tradition," the prophet derives authority from the direct call of God.[47] However, Darsey's conception of prophecy derives from, exists within, and promotes an ideal of community and external authority that leads him to position the prophet as a figure of radical community building. The prophetic *ethos*, for Darsey, is not that of a heroic individual, but of a servant—often a reluctant and suffering servant—of the community and the radical calling. The prophet's story is one of surrender to God's will, usually driven by a prominent narrative of conversion or rebirth that highlights the prophetic calling.[48]

A prophetic *ethos* in Darsey's sense points an identifiable community toward a framework of common fundamentals through which ultimate authority can be established. While Weber's prophet speaks as a charismatic law unto himself, Darsey's prophet speaks from a position of deep respect for society's fundamentals and the injustice that troubles or challenges them. As Darsey argues, describing what he calls "radical" rhetoric, "Radicalism . . . is defined by its concern with the political roots of a society, its fundamental laws, its foundational principles, its most sacred covenants. It is common for radicals to claim to be the true keepers of the faith; they oppose their society using its own most noble expressions and aspirations."[49] Such commitments may be rational, as Darsey argues, but they are not reasonable. Prophecy speaks in the language of fundamentals; it advocates separation over identification, and qualitative rather than quantitative judgments. A pure and devoted remnant is, for the prophet, better than an uncommitted throng.[50] Yet by invoking these fundamentals and appropriating the position of servant relative to them, the prophet can grow the remnant and promote engagement that expands the possibilities of community in the world—invoking jeremiadic and apocalyptic forms in order to direct the audience from passivity to collective action.

Of course, such action and engagement threatens to at once surrender control and cede authority to unbelievers. While radio and television seem safe—modes of transmission that expose the audience to the evangelistic message while not exposing the evangelist to the audience—the kind of personal speech that Falwell suggested risks exposing believers to the world's corrupting influence.[51] Balanced precariously between the poles of separatist Fundamentalism and Church Growth methods, Falwell, in this sermon, attempted to justify aggressive local engagement as a means not of eliminating but of extending separatist community.

This engagement begins with an "outpouring" of God into the believer. As we discussed above, Falwell presented the believer as at once a passive receptacle for God's purpose and an active participant in God's plan. Conversion—the end result of the persuasive act of witnessing—remained outside the evangelistic rhetor's control. The speaker was not responsible for persuading the audience but to bring sinners to the point of openness to God's Spirit. In other words, Falwell's neo-Fundamentalism was, in a sense, a condensation of the revivalist and Puritan perspectives on language. Falwell's preacher was called to speak to sinners, but he could do so from a position of relative security. Speaking from the perspective of a religious community that had, over the previous fifty years, developed careful lines of separation with those outside the Fundamentalist faith, Falwell appeared conscious of his need to maintain boundaries. Disdaining overidentification with audience, he said, "I'm so tired of these words—*sharing*, *communication*, *relevancy*, and modern lingo." Redefined in neo-Fundamentalist terms, Falwell invoked the revivalist as a kind of rhetorician, but one whose aesthetic and emotional appeals were carefully confined by the inerrant truth of God's word. Rhetorical seduction and artistry, championed by many within the Church Growth Movement, were seen as threats to Fundamentalist stability. Therefore, Falwell assured his audience that superaggressive local churches would not abandon the "foolishness of preaching" in order to build the community.[52] He said, "It is not sharing, it is preaching. It is not dialogue, it is preaching. . . . It is not coffeehouse, conversational communication, ecumenicity—it is preaching." The preaching church, he argued, was not invisible or universal, but local. It was centered. It was stable. Yet within this stability, there remained room for variety in the service of revivalism. God, Falwell reminded his audience, "is original, God is never stereotyped. God's ways are fresh and new . . . though methods and means and ideas change with situations and locations, principles never change. God's truth, God's message, God's methods, God's messengers must all meet the same criteria." Such is the paradoxical tension of neo-Fundamentalist address. Methods must be both flexible and stable. The message is new and unchanging. The standards of speech seem to forestall the possibility of its enactment.[53]

The solution to this paradox, for Falwell, was saturation: "preaching the gospel to every available person at every available time by every available means."[54] If Fundamentalist speech could not adapt to the audience, it could, perhaps, wear the audience down. The superchurch revivalist was not called to be sympathetic or understanding; he was called to be superaggressive, militaristic, and hypermasculine.[55] Describing the missionary activity of one group of early Christians, Falwell said, "They literally went through the whole island. I mean they penetrated it. They did not just hit away at the fringe or announce their meetings in the newspaper. They went through the island. They went through it like Sherman went through Georgia. They knocked on every door. They saturated it. They filled that town with their doctrine."[56] For Falwell, the ideal evangelist embodied traits analogous to both military and sexual aggression, overwhelming his targets through speech whose doctrinal purity troubled the boundaries between speech and violence. The close association between the triumphs of evangelistic conversion—souls "won" for Jesus—and the language of sublimated sexual conquest was further emphasized in the next lines of Falwell's sermon, as he moved directly from the narrative of aggressive evangelism quoted above to a story of the first television set that came to Lynchburg. It was, he recalled to his audience, owned by a local grocer, and "He had a daughter who was not particularly attractive. I started dating her and we watched television. I kept dating her until some better prospect had a television."[57] Combining the earlier narrative and Falwell's self-description of his own sublimated sexual prowess and masculine charisma, we emerge with a rather clear picture of the neo-Fundamentalist soul winner. He is opportunistic. He takes what he wants and what will benefit him most. He does not waste time wooing and seducing his targets. He attacks. He invades. He penetrates. If "Jerry Falwell is evangelism," then this seems to be the kind of evangelistic speech embodied in the rhetoric of the Fundamentalist superchurch. Such speech does not, to say the least, invite conversation, and it rarely leaves the evangelist vulnerable. Indeed, if anything, such speech is always on the side of violence and violation in its continual demand for conversions as conquests.

Falwell appropriated some of the elements of the Church Growth Movement, but he reframed them within an aggressive, militaristic Fundamentalist demand. In doing this, he was not wholly original. He borrowed from a number of Fundamentalist leaders, but in particular, his tone was influenced by the writings of Jack Hyles, the northern Indiana pastor of the First Baptist Church of Hammond. In 1959, Jack Hyles took over the already large First Baptist Church and turned it into a "Christian empire"—severing the church's denominational affiliation and instituting an aggressive evangelistic campaign. Hyles was never comfortable as a national figure, and he never attained the national prominence or notoriety of Fundamentalist leaders like Falwell or Bob Jones III, but he nevertheless became, as one journalist said, "the undisputed kingpin and premier ideologist" of the neo-Fundamentalist movement. Books like *How to Boost Your Church Attendance* (1958) and *Let's Go Soul Winning* (1962) became primers for Fundamentalist preachers and spurred a new kind of growth—oriented around a narrative of the superchurch as an aggressive, independent, and expansive congregation.[58]

In *How to Boost Your Church Attendance*, Hyles introduced many of the arguments that Falwell drew upon in his 1971 sermon, primarily that the goal of the church was to train "soul winners" for Jesus.[59] A person could not serve God, Hyles argued, without becoming an evangelist. Also, like Falwell, when Hyles addressed his readers and demanded that they become soul winners, he spoke as a warrior-prophet, constituting the audience as soldiers in a battle with an enemy for territory. Called by their minister, soul winners would understand themselves to be receiving a commission directly from God to do battle with the devil for the eternal souls of their friends and neighbors, or, as Falwell put it in his sermon, "going out to charge hell with a bucket of water."[60] The focus on souls rather than people emphasized the purely dichotomous relationship that Fundamentalist believers needed to adopt toward those outside the believing community. A person did not matter. A body was unimportant. The only thing that mattered to Hyles, as to Falwell, was the state of the soul. This, in part, helps to explain the toleration of disturbingly violent metaphors for evangelism in Fundamentalist superchurch rhetoric. The evangelist/soldier/aggressor confronts, comforts, and invades bodies and minds in a single-minded effort to penetrate and conquer souls. As Susan Harding says, "In a way, witnessing is pure fundamentalist ritual, shorn of almost all distractions. It is the plainest, most concentrated method for revealing and transmitting the Word of God, one in which language is intensified, focused, and virtually shot at the unwashed listener."[61] Such concentration focuses the community. The soul winner was elevated to a heroic status in Hyles's work. He argued that soul winners should be praised publicly from the pulpit. He argued that the best soul winners should be the leaders of Sunday school classes and Bible studies. He argued that, at all points in the church, social pressure should be brought to bear on all believers in the community to aggressively seek out and win souls for Christ.[62]

To be effective, however, Hyles argued that the soul-winning soldier must be strategic, and in this, he also anticipated much of the language that would later be popularized by the Church Growth Movement and translated by Falwell and others. The soul winner, Hyles argued, would win souls through appearance as well as speech. Everything that the evangelist did might be the difference between winning and losing the eternal battle. Therefore, Hyles had some special words on hygiene and appearance. An effective soul winner, he argued, should be neat and presentable: "It is a definite asset for a soul winner to be careful to bathe often, to avoid body odor."[63] Although the unsaved soul was always to be the soul winner's focus, that soul, this side of eternity, was inseparable from the body. Far from the disconnected speaker in an elevated pulpit, the Fundamentalist soul winner must shake the hands and smell the breath of the unsaved masses, just as they must shake and smell his. Hyles also encouraged soul winners to be discrete—carrying small "Testaments" rather than large Bibles that might "give you away." He called his audience to change tactics often and avoid repetition when seeking to win a soul, and in this effort, the large church offered unique benefits for strategic and effective soul winning. Hyles encouraged evangelists to take along different partners from the church to each soul-winning visit so that the unbeliever could meet new people and hear different versions of the message.[64]

Jack Hyles's early work was significant in that it pointed the way forward for the other Fundamentalist leaders who followed. Although not himself significant to national politics or involved in national initiatives, Hyles became a national figure. In 1975, *Time* magazine published an article titled, simply, "Superchurch," describing First Baptist of Hammond's massive Sunday school program, which on March 16, 1975, set a one-day Sunday school attendance record of 30,560 people.[65] By mixing Fundamentalist separation and strategic evangelism through his own ethos as divinely ordained prophetic speaker and anointer of soldiers for God's army, Hyles not only anticipated the work of the Church Growth Movement in the 1960s and 1970s, he appropriated the language and strategies of expansion in ways that could be made palatable to Fundamentalist exclusivity and separatism. The ideals of revivalist communication, as translated through prophetic figures like Hyles and Falwell, imagined a space within which Fundamentalist community could grow and remain separate at the same time, expanding aggressively but incrementally into the community, the nation, and "the ends of the earth."

Dominion

The goal of superchurch Fundamentalism was the expansion of the true church in the last days before the Rapture and the return of Christ. It is telling of the paradox animating neo-Fundamentalist rhetoric that the 1973 paperback edition of *Capturing a Town for Christ* featured on its back cover a promotion for both Falwell's *Old Time Gospel Hour* and Hal Lindsey's *The Late Great Planet Earth*. The claim to be living at "the end of the age" was invoked by neo-Fundamentalist leaders as a call to action. Total separation was not consistent with the belief that Christ might return any moment. Referencing a verse from Acts, Falwell said,

> Every Bible-believing, Bible-preaching, soul-winning church ought to attempt to win the entire metropolitan area to Christ. . . . We ought to try to win every individual, every soul, and every person, beginning at Jerusalem (our Lynchburg), then Judea (the surrounding county), and then Samaria (the state of Virginia for us), and ultimately the uttermost parts of the earth (worldwide missions).[66]

By transposing the place names of the New Testament onto the landscape of his immediate audience, Falwell again made the biblical text wholly contemporaneous with the present and invested the biblical call with both spiritual and political significance. Revival speech, as we have discussed before, is not conceived as the mere persuasion of individuals, but as the creation and expansion of new communities, and for the neo-Fundamentalists, such expansion was often presented in aggressive, violent, and militaristic terms. Revival was war in Falwell's description—a last battle against the forces of hell and sin for the souls of humanity in the final days of planet earth.

Elements of this war were evident in Falwell's sermon. He predicted that the first sign of a faithful, superaggressive church is that it will face "*persecution*" from those outside—from other believers who do not share "the vision," and from nonbelievers who want to stop the expansion of the church. He said, "It costs to put up local churches like this one [Thomas Road]; you can mark it down, blood, sweat, tears, heartaches, heartbreaks have gone behind this work."[67] The invocation of Winston Churchill's blood, sweat, and tears from his speech to the British troops at the beginning of the Second World War only reinforced the conflation of spiritual, political, and military identities that Falwell performed in this sermon. Indeed, the Fundamentalist superchurch was constituted as a kind of nation within the nation in Falwell's rhetoric. Rather than defining Fundamentalism in doctrinal terms, Falwell invoked the language of political and militaristic nationalism in his description of the church and its expansive mission. As he said at one point, "The reason God's people are not winning souls is because we are not training them. The Communists are training their forces."[68] This productive non sequitur enthymematically conflated the goals of the true church and the true nation. The Christian soldier was reconceived as both a spiritual and a political warrior. In threatening the nation, the Communist posed an immediate spiritual threat to the church, and thus the evangelist, not the soldier, was the first and best line of defense against the Communist forces seeking to destroy the true religio-political identity of the American nation. Just as the soldier must do battle to expand or defend the nation, the superchurch member was to do battle to expand or defend the local church in all areas of social, spiritual, economic, and political life. In his analysis of Falwell's responses to public criticism following his famous tirade against gays, lesbians, feminists, abortionists, and the ACLU on the September 13, 2001, episode of Pat Robertson's *The 700 Club*, Bruce Lincoln argues that the apologies and other discourses Falwell issued rhetorically divided the nation into two factions, one which was good and "isomorphic with 'the Church'" and the other which "while indisputably part of the nation . . . poses mortal dangers to it."[69] This should come as no surprise. Narratives of a divided church and nation have been critical features of Fundamentalism since the movement's origins, and they significantly influenced Falwell's religious and political rhetoric since well before the emergence of the Moral Majority. In his sermons and political writings, Falwell consistently invoked a "Christian nation" within the American nation, and while the goals of these nations might often cohere, any conflict left open the possibility for the soldier of Christ to enter the political realm, defending the kingdom of God against national threats of religious or political apostasy.[70]

Within this conflated nationalism, evidence of spiritual struggle could be identified in the political realm. Falwell, for example, described the "persecution" that Thomas Road endured from local authorities. When people complained about the church's aggressive bus ministry, which was going into neighboring towns and taking people to Lynchburg, they "got the state troopers and town officers against us."[71] In a neighboring town, one of the Thomas Road drivers was ticketed for having the wrong color bus, and Falwell's response was to announce it on the radio, letting the police know that he would have five buses in town the next Sunday. He said, "We got another ticket this past Sunday. We are going to save them up for souvenirs. But we are going to keep running buses. . . . When you are doing the work the way it ought to be done, brother, there will be persecutions, harassments, and ridicule—that's part of the price."[72] By referencing persecution, Falwell invoked his Fundamentalist identity, enacting the marginalization of the true church even while championing the extraordinary growth and influence of his own local church. The Fundamentalist superchurch could capture the empire but not claim it. It could invoke a majority so long as that majority remained marginalized and disempowered in the present—an impossible majority whose conquest, though assured, could never be realized. At critical points in the sermon, therefore, Falwell turned from championing aggression to adopting a fortress mentality. As in accounts of the city temples and tabernacles in the earlier part of the century, superchurches offered protection for Fundamentalist purity from outside forces. A smaller church might have had to buckle to state authority and stop running their buses for fear of the mounting fines. In contrast, Falwell boasted that his church was saving tickets up as souvenirs. They could not be intimidated or silenced, he implied, by the power of the state arrayed against the nation of believers. They were effectively shielded from that kind of local power by the size and influence of their institution.

Ironically, in 1973, the same year that this sermon was published in book form, Falwell's ministry nearly ran aground on government power that it could not so easily intimidate. That year, the Securities and Exchange Commission sued Thomas Road Baptist Church, citing fraud in its sales of church bonds to investors across the country. The suit exposed that the church's financial records were woefully inaccurate and out of date—the only oversight of Falwell's budget coming from a part-time volunteer—and although Falwell and the church were both cleared of the fraud charges, the federal judge placed the church finances under an "advisory committee" of local business leaders who were charged with eliminating the institution's unsecured debt.[73] Falwell described the incident as a battle of David versus Goliath. There was always a bigger authority ready to persecute the faithful superchurch of God.

This response to local and later national government officials helps in part to explain the expansion of superchurch Fundamentalists onto the national political stage in the 1970s. At least as late as the mid-1960s, Falwell, like many other Fundamentalist leaders, was still speaking out against believers and churches who reduced their soul winning to take an active role in politics.[74] The superchurch, however, was different. The justification for superaggressive, neo-Fundamentalist church growth was that these churches could saturate and conquer their local communities, imposing Fundamentalist standards on all areas of social, spiritual, and political life. As superchurches like Thomas Road expanded into more and more areas of media and adopted a perspective of local conquest transforming local communities, more aspects of these communities became linked to Fundamentalist identity, and threats that hampered the local conquest of superaggresive churches became identified as threats to both the true church and true nation. In his "Church at Antioch" sermon, for example, Falwell argued that a city transformed by the gospel would be able to hold back liquor trafficking.[75] Spiritual transformation, it was assumed, would produce political effects—a position that closely mirrors that taken by Finney in the nineteenth century. If, as Falwell claimed, a superchurch could convert enough people, it could control the spiritual and political life of the local community. Yet this kind of local authority would also set the Christian nation and the American nation on a collision course with one another. What if federal authorities were to seize church assets and "persecute" its members? What if federal authorities were to impose national standards on textbooks, busing, economics, and abortion? What if, in other words, the local power of the church could be usurped by higher powers that were not themselves susceptible to the saturation and intimidation efforts of superaggressive local churches? As federal authorities challenged the ability of neo-Fundamentalists to capture and conquer their local towns for Christ, the anti-confederacy, anti-federalism rhetoric, which had been so long a part of Fundamentalist identity, moved once more to the forefront. Only now, it was "secular humanist" and not ecumenical authorities who posed the greatest threat to Fundamentalist speech and action. This tension between local conquest and national oppression helps to illuminate the rhetorical processes by which secular humanism replaced ecumenicism as the dominant countersymbol within neo-Fundamentalist discourse—processes linked to the conflation of church and nation in the morality language of conservative Protestants.

Writing in his 1980 book *Listen America!*, arguably his clearest defense of the Moral Majority, Falwell claimed that the United States was being attacked on two fronts—the political and the moral—and that these fronts were intimately linked to one another. On the one hand, Communism threatened American survival, and the destruction of the church was its first priority.[76] On the other hand, secular humanism threatened the American soul—having become the nation's new established religion, supported by political leaders and mandated by the federal courts. Falwell implied that because Fundamentalism was not an "established" (i.e., institutional or denominational) religion, it was the preferred religion—the personal godliness—under which American government was intended to operate. In contrast, he argued, because established religion was antithetical to the constitutional doctrine of disestablishment, preferential treatment toward secular humanism was unconstitutional and antithetical to American governance.[77] Falwell argued that Fundamentalist believers, drawing their authority from an inerrant Bible, needed to come together to confront this new confederacy movement. He argued that secular humanism was replacing Christ with human goodness, and truth with relativism. Thus, it would lead to abortion, homosexuality, pornography, feminism, rock music, and other social sins, which threatened the corruption of local families and local towns and ultimately the destruction of American identity. He argued that secular humanism would lead to Communism, a fact to which American political leaders were blind because of their spiritual unbelief. Politics and religion were, as in the sermon we have been examining, intertwined with one another. Also as exemplified in the sermon, Falwell called on American believers to make the idealized America of the past wholly contemporaneous with the American present, creating a true America of faith and family, morality and free enterprise, which imagined the always-impossible return of the local church to the ideological center of American life.

The same language of crisis that infected Falwell's justification for superaggressive evangelism infected his justification for the Moral Majority as well. On the one hand, Falwell identified himself as a "fundamental, independent, separatist Baptist" in *Listen America!* And he claimed to understand the need to protect the purity of the Fundamentalist church. On the other hand, he argued that "When the entire issue of Christian survival is at stake, we must be willing to band together on at least the major moral issues of the day."[78] The idealism of a moniker like the "Moral Majority" was continually undercut by pronouncements of apocalyptic oppression and marginalization.

We can now better understand how the arguments of neo-Fundamentalist church growth, which validated the work of ministers like Hyles and Falwell and reimagined Fundamentalist separatism as a motivation for aggressive local expansion, also laid a discursive foundation for organizations like the Moral Majority and provided the groundwork for a reimagining of the conservative Fundamentalist as political aggressor—a narrative with which we are intimately familiar in the present day. In *Listen America!*, Falwell argued that the Moral Majority was not a political party, nor a religious organization or a platform for censorship and the elimination of civil liberties; instead it was a representation of "moral" unity, coming together "against the tide of permissiveness and moral decay that is crushing in on our society from every side."[79] While the Fundamentalist could not accommodate the world, he could imagine a remade world in his own image, and all of this could be done with the justification that it would expand the increasingly desperate work of revival in the last days. Falwell argued that biblical authority gave Fundamentalists the right to critique the moral failings of society and propose alternative laws. Therefore, for example, Falwell argued that believers must oppose the welfare state, saying, "A whole generation of Americans has grown up brainwashed by television and textbooks to believe that it is the responsibility of government to take resources from some and bestow them on others. This idea certainly was alien to the Founding Fathers of our country." He assured readers that while the standard of living might decline for some, they "will not starve to death," and, as an example of the kind of inconvenience people might suffer with the loss of welfare, Falwell told a story about a time when he and his wife could only afford to buy their two dogs cheap dry dog food, rather than the expensive meat that was recommended for them.[80] Similarly, Falwell argued that Fundamentalist believers needed to support Israel and oppose cuts to military spending,[81] support the family and oppose feminism, support capital punishment and oppose abortion, support traditional gender roles and oppose homosexuality.

If the problem was bigger than the local community, the superaggressive institution to confront it needed to be bigger than the local church. Like a superchurch, the Moral Majority expanded Fundamentalist community, while attempting to shield believers from politically, socially, and morally corruptive influences, building a network of superchurch leaders to expand superaggressive Fundamentalism across the nation and around the world. It is thus unsurprising that the board of

Moral Majority, Inc. were all prominent pastors or leaders of early superchurch congregations. In addition to Falwell, the leadership included Tim LaHaye, a prominent writer and pastor of Scott Memorial Baptist Church; Greg Dixon, pastor of the Indianapolis Baptist Temple; Charles Stanley, Southern Baptist pastor of the First Baptist Church in Atlanta; and D. James Kennedy, pastor of Coral Ridge Presbyterian Church in Fort Lauderdale.[82] The success of the Moral Majority owed a great deal to its connection to superchurches and superchurch networks. Robert Liebman says, "From its start, Moral Majority was a movement of superchurches. Falwell, Dixon, LaHaye, Stanley, and Kennedy were builders of great churches. Many state chairmen followed their example, having started their own churches and worked aggressively to build them into great churches. Several stood at the forefront of the church growth movement."[83] This is not to say that other forces were not at work in the organization of the Moral Majority, but the prominence of these church leaders and the rhetoric of church growth should not be understated.

What I have, in part, attempted to demonstrate in this chapter is that the emergence of groups like the Moral Majority did not mark the end of Fundamentalist marginalization rhetoric, because the continual enactment of marginalization was and remains critical to Fundamentalist counterpublicity. Nor should we simply equate these groups with after-the-fact responses to issues like the Supreme Court's *Roe v. Wade* decision in 1973; or the Kanawha County, West Virginia, textbook controversy in 1974; or the Christian school tax-exemption struggles in 1978. Such battles, along with a number of others, helped to provide impetus for a national movement, but the logic and rationale for the movement predated these issues, illustrating the complex and conflicted identities underlying Fundamentalist appropriations of public speech and action. These paradoxical logics can be found most clearly represented in the justifications for superaggressive Fundamentalist churches. The shift from separatism to political activism on the national stage was not so antithetical to Fundamentalist apocalypticism or inconsistent with the ongoing invocation of marginality as it might at first appear.

In addition to providing spiritual validation and organizational models for the Moral Majority, Fundamentalist superchurches provided the networks and contacts that allowed the Moral Majority to grow its mailing list as quickly as it did, and thus make plausible to the press its claim to be at the forefront of a conservative revolution. As Liebman says,

> While the work of church-building took place throughout the country, much of its impetus came from national pastors' conferences where ministers learned the fundamentals of church growth. Falwell was a leader in the movement. A number of state chairmen made their first contacts with national Moral Majority leaders at conferences sponsored by the Thomas Road Baptist Church and Jack Hyles' First Baptist Church in Hammond, Indiana.[84]

In the last chapter, we examined how, in the apocalyptic narrative of the *A Thief in the Night* films, believers are shown gathering together not through an ecumenical body, but through a network of local bodies, brought together, through technology, by a common need to confront the enemy they could not battle alone. A similar rhetorical strategy was at work in the justification and expansion of the Moral Majority, as local churches, built up through a strategy of superaggressive evangelism, were encouraged to come together and imagine themselves as a new and different kind of ecumenical network—representing an impossible majority—in order to confront the twin evils of political (Communist) and religious (secular humanist) oppression that threatened the spiritual and political identity of the true America.

Conclusion

Not all Fundamentalists embraced Falwell's superchurch arguments. Indeed, critiques of Fundamentalist superchurches and the Moral Majority often sounded a good deal like earlier condemnations of the ecumenical movement. Critics claimed that superchurches and superchurch politics were too big, too pervasive. They watered down the fundamentals of the faith, they challenged the authority of local church leaders, and they participated in the secular humanism they claimed to defend believers against.[85] For some separatist Fundamentalists, Falwell's superaggressive evangelism went too far in accommodating the culture, and many more were offended by the Moral Majority, which boasted of Mormon, Catholic, and Jewish conservatives among its ranks. For many of the new evangelicals, meanwhile, Falwell's rural Fundamentalism seemed crude, unaccommodating, and incapable of the compromises necessary for political and cultural success on the national stage.

At the height of its influence, the fact that the Moral Majority was so well advertised, gathered its mailing lists so rapidly, and used such divisive and provocative language in its publications and mailings led many to buy into the narrative and assume that the organization was, as it claimed, largely responsible for the success of the Reagan campaign and the resurgence of anti-federal and anti-Communist rhetoric in the 1980s. Naturally, in the years since then, a kind of backlash has occurred, with scholars arguing, not unreasonably, that the Moral Majority was more hype than substance, and that Fundamentalist uniformity is a problematic claim.[86] As Susan Harding argues,

> Aside from the aggressively entrepreneurial quality of especially the superchurches, the surrounding institutional and oratorical contexts of the churches were decentralized and diversely responsive to new conditions. Bible-believing Christianity functioned without a pope, without a Rome, without centralized, hierarchical, and costly denominational bureaucracies, and without a unifying written doctrinal statement. Instead, it was managed by loose, fragmentary pastoral networks or weak denominational structures and a huge host of parachurch organizations. . . . heterogeneity not homogeneity, hybridity not purity, fluidity not fixity, characterized the movement at every level.[87]

This is a fair assessment. The grandiose claims—and even more grandiose name—of Falwell's movement concealed the fact that it was only sporadically united and never represented anything like a majority. However, this is to some degree beside the point. Located within the paradoxical framework of Falwell's neo-Fundamentalism—an identity he continued to associate with throughout the 1980s[88]—we can identify the Moral Majority as an organization that both imagined and continually forestalled victory, constituting an unrealizable majority, a nonpolitical movement, as Falwell argued, continually forced to defend itself against the anti-democratic and humanist judiciary and the powerful political elite bent on persecuting the ordinary men and women of moral America.[89] Like the superchurch, the Moral Majority named a paradox in American Fundamentalism—the desire for expansion against the desire for control.

Chapter Six

The Limits of Accommodation

⌘

> I don't know how many people believe me when I say this, but I never set out to build a big church.
>
> —Bill Hybels, *Rediscovering Church*, 1995

Driving north toward Willow Creek Community Church, one passes out of the city—stores and strip malls fading into well-maintained industrial parks and suburban neighborhoods. Willow Creek does not stand out from its surroundings. Despite the acres of asphalt parking lots, the church building—a complex of interconnected additions—feels secluded, set apart in a "natural" environment, with well-maintained lawns and trees and a beautiful pond. Except for the line of cars pulling in on a Sunday morning, it resembles all the other business and industrial parks in the area, set well back from the street, shielded from the outside world. The building complex is haphazard, but not distractingly so; the corporate architectural styles of three decades fade gently into one another, united by a common façade of dark brick. No single detail calls out or draws attention to itself. No steeple or spire dominates the architectural landscape. Compared with churches like Robert Schuller's star-shaped Crystal Cathedral in Southern California, with its 10,000 panes of glass and 234-foot "Prayer Spire"—or the late D. James Kennedy's Coral Ridge Presbyterian Church in Fort Lauderdale, Florida, whose 303-foot bell tower was at one time believed to be the tallest of its kind in the United States—Bill Hybels's Willow Creek Community Church in South Barrington, Illinois, is an architectural nonentity.[1] What is likely the most discussed, cited, and analyzed American church of the past thirty years gives no outward indication of its superstar status. Like Finney's ideal revivalist, stepping down from the high pulpit and adapting his speech to the expectations of the common hearer, Willow Creek embodies a retreat from grand style and a reorientation to the ordinary—albeit white, suburban, and upper-middle-class—contours of the landscape it inhabits.

To write about Willow Creek, one is almost obligated to discuss its size. And it is a massive religious institution—approximately 23,000 weekly attendees spread across seven church "campuses," a 7,200-seat state-of-the-art auditorium, and total assets of more than $160 million.[2] Yet such statistics—for all the shock and awe they generate—actually tell us very little. Willow Creek is not, as the previous chapters have demonstrated, the first big church, nor is it by any means the largest. Similarly, although its marketing methods have been a source of continual fascination for both church and corporate leaders who want to replicate its successes, these analyses have the effect of simply conflating Willow Creek with any other corporate entity, without significantly explaining the doctrinal and discursive framework within which this marketing-like methodology is framed and justified. In other words, they may go a long way toward explaining how Willow Creek functions as an organization, but they do not explain its significant and controversial role within the contemporary Christian Fundamentalist narrative. To understand the significance of Willow Creek, we should approach it not as a "mega"-institution nor in the context of a marketing methodology, but as a notable example of a broader shift, or split, within spiritual and political Fundamentalism writ large—a shift from what I have been calling counterpublic to public imagination.

Silence, Violence, and Accommodation

Counterpublic speech, as we discussed in the first chapter, challenges the presumptions and blindness of normative public deliberation without, in Erik Doxtader's terms, losing "faith" in the value or the potential of the public itself.[3] For all their differences, the various institutions and narratives we have examined in the previous chapters participated in a common narrative of separation between the Fundamentalist church and a powerful, threatening Other—variously embodied in the figures of an ecumenical confederacy, a world church, and a secular humanist establishment. Much like the post-apocalyptic believers in the *A Thief in the Night* films, who are isolated from and persecuted by society for refusing to take the mark of the beast, modern Fundamentalists are defined—and define themselves—by their unwillingness to compromise or risk the fundamentals of belief and practice through communication with outsiders. Yet this marginalization does not lead to a simple abandonment of society or a wholesale rejection of the possibility of discourse and deliberation. As Camille Lewis argues, Fundamentalist believers, despite their separatism, must always retain the ability to be seen by and speak to the Other.[4] Or, as self-identifying Fundamentalist historian David Beale has argued, Fundamentalists expect Christ to find few true believers when he returns to earth, yet they still "pray for revival," expecting not a national transformation of spiritual and discursive norms, but "an old-fashioned renewal" involving "local churches, campuses, and communities."[5] Despite a rhetorical commitment to separation and doctrinal purity that seems to preclude any form of interaction with the society from which they are marginalized and against which they marginalize themselves, Fundamentalists never wholly abandoned narratives of expectation that sacralized speech and revivalist appeals might affect change, however limited, in the unbelieving world. Fundamentalism thus remains invested in the public, committed to engaging those outside and challenging, as Doxtader says, "the dominant conventions of public deliberation."[6] It was and is, in this sense, a community invested in counterpublic speech.

Those Fundamentalist communities that cease to challenge public norms cease also to function as marginalized or resistant. They become, in other words, something other than Fundamentalist. Those who retain marginalized identities or perspectives and yet abandon hope for change within discourse inevitably turn either to silence—isolating themselves or their members from society—or to violence against a system that cannot be spoken to or saved. As we have seen in the previous two chapters, a language of violence inhabits Fundamentalist apocalyptic and evangelistic narratives; yet so long as speech is available and the hope for revival, however modestly, retained, the risk of physical violence usurping speech is thankfully mitigated. Of course, violence need not be physical to be real. Groups like the Kansas-based Westboro Baptist Church, for example—who protest the funerals of American soldiers and other similar events holding signs with messages like "God Hates Fags" and "Thank God for IEDs"—use language not as a means to deliberate or persuade, but as a form of discursive violence and radical indictment of the very possibility of public deliberation. Neither the isolated nor the violent participate in counterpublic speech, since they have effectively abandoned the "public" side of the equation. Some of the religious movements associated with "fundamentalism" writ large fall into one of these categories, but they have not been the focus of this book. My interest, instead, has been with movements and associations that, while separated and self-isolated from the public in significant respects nonetheless retain a desire to persuade and convert unbelievers through speech that leads them into spiritual, and often political, forms of counterpublic address and action.

On the other hand, not all modes of counterpublicity are created, or remain, equal in their "counter"-orientation to the public. Certainly, there are marginal differences of approach and orientation within social movements, as we have seen in the examination of Fundamentalist communities so far. What I am considering in this chapter, however, is the kind of internal fracturing that takes place when members within a movement turn from "counter"-speech to speech that accepts and even valorizes discursive norms of public deliberation even while possibly still attempting to transform the cultural and political norms of society. In other words, asking: what are the effects when participants in counterpublic speech choose to appropriate rather than challenge the dominant discursive conventions of public life?

Within counterpublic theory, there is relatively little attention paid to this question, which is critical for understanding not only the political and rhetorical history of Christian Fundamentalist movements in the United States, but also the potentiality of counterpublic discourses to act as agents of discursive transformation in the world. By conflating counterpublicity with subaltern social movements or marginalized identities, there is a tendency to treat counterpublics as though they were wholly unified and transparent demands upon the state or dominant public. A counterpublic is often treated very much like a person who has been, for whatever reason, excluded, and who makes various specific appeals—whether discursive or performative—to a unified and dominant public on behalf of that exclusion. Thus, feminists are one counterpublic, queers are another, and Fundamentalists a third. It is this perspective, for example, that leads Melanie Loehwing and Jeff Motter to argue that counterpublics offer less space for resistance than does the Habermasian Public Sphere, because they are limited to identity groups making appeals for legitimacy to the state.[7] In contrast, if, as I suggested in the first chapter, counterpublics are only constituted through discourse—enacted in particular ways and for particular purposes—then there is no reason to expect that a community appropriating counterpublic speech should remain united in its demands or its makeup. Indeed, there is significant value to be gained in understanding the processes by which those who adopt the language of counterpublicity might also seek to reassert a public voice, located within, rather than outside and in critique of, public norms.

Willow Creek offers an example of what happens when Fundamentalists choose to speak, in Bill Hybels's terms, as "normal people living normal lives"—that is, to participate in, rather than separating from, the dominant norms of public speech and deliberation, speaking as a public rather than a counterpublic community.[8] This is a process I refer to as "accommodation." To accommodate is to disrupt and redefine the fundamental antagonism against which counterpublic discourses come to be organized. While such redefinition offers communities new avenues for engagement, appeal, and persuasion with those outside, it also creates new forms of fragmentation and exclusion between those who will accommodate and those who will not.

Assuming that counterpublicity is an operation within discourse, it should be expected that these categories would not remain fixed or absolute. Indeed, a kind of accommodation occurs every time the Fundamentalist intelligibly addresses the Other. Yet, Fundamentalist discourse, as we explored in the previous chapter, seeks to elide in various ways the risks of accommodation. In the case of Jerry Falwell's neo-Fundamentalist rhetoric, this involved recasting the Fundamentalist interlocutor in hypermasculine, militaristic, and sexually aggressive terms—metaphors that minimize the role of the evangelist as listener or participant in discursive norms and emphasize a kind of discourse that is at once intimate and wholly impersonal. The Fundamentalist minimalizes the role of accommodation in revivalist speech by claiming that all souls—unlike minds or bodies—are equal in their orientation toward either God or the devil and thus can be approached equally, without unnecessary regard for the feelings, personal lives, or social well-being of the unconverted targets. The only need for accommodation on behalf of the Fundamentalist derives from the devil's eagerness to distract sinners from the pure, transcendent truth of God's word. Thus Fundamentalist soul winners are called upon to brush their teeth and change their clothes not to increase their own ethos as speakers, but to minimize distractions and keep the souls of the unconverted open and vulnerable to the penetrating message of the Christian gospel.

In contrast, the deliberate and prolonged decision to accommodate oneself to those outside—to speak normally—involves a kind of self-critique and even separation within a social movement, which in turn challenges the ability of separatist and accommodative members to work cooperatively. Separatist Fundamentalists and so-called "new evangelical" believers rarely associate with each other, even though they share both a common mission to convert unbelievers, and frequently, a similarly conservative political orientation. Fundamentalists often contrast the strength of their separatist communities with the weakness of evangelical accommodation. As one Fundamentalist author said, "The new Evangelicalism advocates *toleration* of error. It is following the downward path of *accommodation* to error, *cooperation* with error, *contamination* by error, and ultimate *capitulation* to error."[9] Accommodation is linked to the abandonment of fundamentals for a weak-willed submission to public norms. As evangelicals move closer to error, it is implied that they move further from the unifying doctrines that are the standard for effective Fundamentalist cohesion and resistance.

A Place of Safety

The Fundamentalist emphasis on aggressive expansion and political domination, which we explored in the previous chapter, continue to be reflected in the organization and architecture of contemporary Fundamentalist superchurches like First Baptist Church of Hammond,

Indiana, and Thomas Road Baptist Church. Where the architecture of megachurches like Willow Creek often integrate with and blend into their environment—seeming to shrink from, rather than embracing, the size—Fundamentalist superchurches are often designed to physically dominate their surroundings, functioning as symbols of continuing conquest to the outside world and of protection to believers.

Completed in 2004, the current main building of First Baptist of Hammond, for example, is a massive square monolith of red brick, rising high above its working-class neighborhood with a white steeple that is easily visible for half a mile. Many of the stores, offices, and abandoned buildings that surround the church are part of its expanding ministry complex. The size and relative newness of the main building, set in the midst of an old and crumbling urban landscape, stand as testaments to the power and dominance of the church in its community. The fact that, over the years, First Baptist has bought up so much of its immediate neighborhood only enhances this testimony. As an embodiment of superaggressive growth and evangelism, the church provides a place of safety and security from the world, a haven from real-life experiences. Inside the 7,500-seat auditorium, people are dressed in their Sunday best—women in calf- or ankle-length skirts or dresses, men in coats and ties. Soft hymns play in the background. The façade at the front of the sanctuary resembles a massive portico, with white pillars and a peaked roof. A large wooden cross hangs in the center of the façade, and two large screens hang on either side.

Despite the trappings of modern technology, congregation members at First Baptist are constantly reminded of the call to separation throughout the service. The distinctive roles and functions of Fundamentalism are built into the very fabric of the experience. Those who visit this church are not entering a place that caters to outsiders. Unlike evangelical megachurches, First Baptist of Hammond makes no special effort to accommodate its visitors. Guests are constantly being hailed or repelled by the familiarity or strangeness of the experience. Even the language of the church distinguishes it from daily life and the rest of the world. Before the sermon, an elder rose to lead the congregation in a reading from the Bible. Before he started to read, the man exclaimed: "I love my King James Bible!" To which a number of people in the congregation responded by clapping and shouting, "Amen!" Then the reading proceeded "responsively," with the leader and the congregation reading alternate verses. The church has no standard Bibles and the text of the reading was not printed anywhere. It was clearly presumed that everyone had brought his or her own Bible and was reading from the same old translation. Indeed, every first-time visitor to the church receives his or her own copy of a King James Bible as a welcoming gift, reinforcing the ideal that there is not only one word of God but one version of God's word that is acceptable in this community. During his sermon, "Brother" Jack Schaap offered suggestions to young men who are preparing to get married. On their honeymoon, he told them, "Get that good old King James Bible out" (more shouts of "Amen!" from the congregation) and be "the high priest of your family."[10] The message simultaneously invoked Fundamentalist gender roles and the significance of a Bible language not accommodated to modern readers.[11] Despite being one of the largest churches in the United States, First Baptist is very different from an evangelical megachurch like Willow Creek. The difference is not so much size (both claim massive congregations) or socioeconomic status—though that clearly factors into the particular rhetorical possibilities of each congregation—as it is a profoundly different approach to outsiders and to public norms of speech and deliberation.

Like First Baptist, Thomas Road Baptist Church is a place that emphasizes safety and separation for its members while refusing to accommodate its speech to the discursive norms and expectations of outsiders. One of the pastors, delivering an illustration during an evening sermon, seemed to sum up in some ways the ongoing attitude of the church toward those outside the Fundamentalist community. He said:

> Our house is protected by God. It's also protected by an alarm system. And above my dresser it's protected by a Smith and Wesson .44 Magnum. See? So I have triple-protection. I think God needs my help. I tell my children, at nighttime, when it's dark, "If you come in my house, let us know who it is." I'm one of those guys that will go bang-bang-bang-bang-bang-bang-"Who is it?" and then go see who it was.[12]

The story serves at least three purposes. On the one hand, it offers a kind of social camaraderie. Members of the community understand the humor of the story because they understand the controversy surrounding it. It clearly demarcates boundaries of socioeconomic and political difference. It calls out to some outsiders that they are welcome, while letting others know that they are unlikely to fit in here. Second, the story emphasizes the continuation of separatist militancy. This pastor is not interested in dialogue or diversity; he is not relativistic or reserved. This is not, in short, an example of friendly or accommodative evangelicalism. Third, while warning outsiders, the story offers comfort to those on the inside. This is a safe church, the pastor reassures his congregation. It takes safety seriously, and every contingency has been accounted for. The superaggressive church can remain Fundamentalist because it is secure. Its physical size and political influence offer stability and legitimacy from which to mobilize spiritual and social activism. Yet this security is only effective if those who might promote institutional critique, alternative perspectives, or "turning," in Martin Buber's terms, are continually warned to stay away. The larger the church, the broader its boundaries, and the more it must be protected and secured against invasion.[13] More than just a joke, therefore, the anecdote tells us about the political challenge of the superchurch to Fundamentalist separation and the struggles to maintain that separatist identity in the face of political nationalization and physical growth.

In the Fundamentalist context, speech is both extended to and held back from strangers, offering them access only if they conform to a rigid set of standards, which are, nevertheless, continually challenged by the shifting perspectives of a growing, fluid community. Michael Warner says, "There is no speech or performance addressed to a public that does not try to specify in advance, in countless highly condensed ways, the lifeworld of its circulation. . . . Public discourse says not only 'Let a public exist' but 'Let it have this character, speak this way, see the world in this way.'"[14] In order to maintain the Fundamentalist community as having, in Warner's terms, a "conflictual relation to the dominant public," Fundamentalist leaders must oppose the identity of believers to that public at every level, creating a physical and ideological space within which strangers can be addressed while purity is tenuously maintained.[15] In this context, the evangelical's willingness to accommodate and even adopt public norms, radically reinventing the character of Fundamentalist identity in the process, can only be seen as a dangerous and destructive intrusion of corrosive values into the carefully balanced lifeworld of the Fundamentalist church.

Through an understanding of accommodation, it becomes evident how counterpublic speech is continually articulated not only in relation to a dominant and oppressive Other, but also through relations of counter-contestation within the community. Where scholars like Gerard

Hauser, for example, tend to focus on a dichotomy between counterpublic or populist discourses and "official public spheres" these discourses oppose, I argue that this relationship must be understood as operating within an additional complex of separations and accommodations, which address and reimagine the contours of both the community and the Other from within.[16] What may appear to be a unified community or movement from the outside may well be fragmented and fraught internally by disputes over the appropriateness and limits of accommodation.

Such an understanding of counterpublics as discursively constituted goes a long way toward helping us understand the role and function of the Fundamentalist church and Fundamentalist politics. Within this framework, evangelical megachurches are more than merely religious brands—spiritual equivalents of the shopping malls and movie theaters that dot the suburban landscapes they inhabit; they are also physical manifestations of efforts within Fundamentalism to reframe Fundamentalist publicity through accommodation to the norms of public discourse, a fraught effort to reimagine Fundamentalist identity while maintaining what is most essential (fundamental) about the Fundamentalist message. Megachurches address not merely a believer or a consumer, but a public. A church like Willow Creek is significant not so much for its size or its specific methodological or marketing strategies, but because it represents a popular and controversial effort to redefine Fundamentalist counterpublicity from within and reconceptualize the Fundamentalist church as an institution whose power derives from, rather than opposes, "the dominant conventions of public deliberation." This redefinition is not original to Bill Hybels or the megachurch. Indeed, the megachurch is but one historically contingent example of a continuing process of fragmenting, patching, redefining, and refragmenting within the Fundamentalist community. The prominence of megachurches will almost certainly fade in the coming decades, just as radio, Sunday school revivals, superchurches, and televangelist ministries have faded; but by examining the rhetoric of a church like Willow Creek, particularly in comparison to the rhetoric of superchurch Fundamentalism, we can arrive at a better understanding of the contours of Fundamentalist accommodation more broadly and its effects on ideals of spiritual and political speech and action.

The Megachurch Narrative

During the 1980s and 1990s, megachurches were, as one journalist said, "the hottest thing in Protestantism,"[17] offering a visual embodiment of open and accommodative evangelical spirituality in the late twentieth century. Where Fundamentalist churches had added terms like "temple" and "tabernacle" to their names, and pastors like Falwell spoke of superaggressive soul winning, megachurches frequently appropriated the term "community," often in place of denominational referents like "Baptist" or "Presbyterian."[18] Megachurch literature both idealized and generalized the concept of community. Where Fundamentalist narratives carefully demarcated boundaries between saints and sinners, separatists and ecumenicists, moralists and humanists, megachurch language blurred—but did not erase—these boundaries, expanding the possibilities for cooperation across lines of denomination and doctrine, and even across the ultimate Fundamentalist line of conversion. Nowhere is this blurring more evident than in the widely used megachurch category of the "seeker," a term Bill Hybels claims to have coined and which refers to a kind of middle ground between the believer and the unbeliever.[19] Seekers are not converted, but neither are they opposed or antagonistic to the idea of conversion. They have reasonable questions and doubts that keep them from accepting Jesus as their savior, and it is the purpose of the church to remove the mental and emotional obstacles that keep these people from becoming fully integrated into the temporal and eternal community of believers. This is, as should be immediately evident, a significant departure from the rhetoric of soul winning promoted by ministers like Hyles and Falwell, which imagines all unconverted souls to be alike in their place outside the kingdom of God and in their need to be confronted and penetrated with the convicting truth of the evangelist. Soul-winning rhetoric defines souls as enemy property, which need to be forcibly extracted from the devil's grasp and brought into the fortress of faith. In contrast, the term "seeker" imagines that the soul is not captured or corrupt so much as it is lost and confused. The soul is not separate from, but integrated with the mind and body, and all three can be involved in the work of evangelistic persuasion. Defending the resources Willow Creek puts into technology—when it first started, half of the church's weekly budget went for media—Bill Hybels said, "The drama, video, and media touch people on an emotional level to help thaw the deep pools of spiritual longing that often lay frozen beneath the surface."[20] Conceiving the soul as fully integrated with the mind, body, and emotions, the "seeker-sensitive" evangelist trades the mantle of the soldier for that of the lover, the reasoner, or the rhetorician.

Of course, revivalism has, as we have seen, long used emotion as a device to provoke sinners to turn to Christ. From Jonathan Edwards's hellfire sermons in the eighteenth century to the violent images of the *A Thief in the Night* films, revivalists have invoked both positive and negative emotions to alternately terrify sinners out of hell and woo them into heaven. Yet revivalism always operates within a context of heightened emotions, both good and bad, and the revivalist calls upon his listeners to repent immediately. In contrast, the seeker-sensitive evangelist calls upon them to listen and consider "the claims of Christ" before making a commitment to the Christian community. By thus separating revival from the immediate demand, megachurches expand the breadth of persuasive options available to the revivalist as well as the context within which revivalism can take place, since seekers are invited to participate in a kind of modern halfway covenant, which allows them free access to explore their questions in the context of a relatively anonymous church community.

Like the Puritans' halfway covenant, the seeker-sensitive orientation has had a clear effect on the perceived size and influence of megachurches. Key to the statistical validation of the seeker-sensitive approach was a shift, during the 1970s and 1980s, in the way growth was measured—from the seating capacity of a church sanctuary or its formal membership records, to its average weekly attendance. By detaching size from both conversions and physical space, megachurches significantly expanded their perceived capacity for "growth." No longer limited by the size of the church building, megachurches could grow in ways previously inconceivable. A church with a 7,200-seat sanctuary and six satellite locations could now be a megachurch of 23,000 weekly attendees, as at Willow Creek. A 16,000-seat auditorium could be home to a church with over 40,000 attendees, as is the case at the Lakewood Church in Houston, Texas. Using the new seeker-oriented terminology, church growth advocates like John Vaughan could even lay claim to massive "superchurch centers" like the Congregação Cristã in Sao Paulo, Brazil, which in 1984, he cites as having 600,000 adult members, spread over 3,500 congregations.[21] As weekly attendance became an increasingly dominant marker of success and significance among evangelicals, the definition of "church" expanded. Mega-"churches" now included organizations that could only have described themselves as denominations a few decades ago.

Given this shift in the terminology of growth, it is hardly surprising that in the space of a very few years, megachurches seemed to explode onto the American landscape from all directions. Pentecostals, Baptists, Presbyterians, African American churches across many denominations, and a growing number of independent congregations crossed the Church Growth community's 2,000-in-weekly-attendance bar to join the ranks of the megachurches. Some of these were older, well-established congregations, many of whose leaders suppressed or abandoned their denominational ties as they worked to expand their institutions, often changing their names to remove the denominational markers. Others, like Willow Creek, were wholly independent churches, many of which had their roots in the large number of evangelical parachurch organizations that had prospered in the mid-twentieth century. It seemed clear to their promoters and proponents that God was mightily at work, and megachurches were the proof that God was honoring the seeker-sensitive approach. Scholars and journalists descended on churches like Willow Creek, trying to describe and define their methods and replicate their results. Of course, the church leaders demurred, claiming that no human methods could account for such a miraculous revival in the modern evangelical church. As Lynne Hybels wrote in 1995, "What could seem like a patterned formula [at Willow Creek] is actually a twenty-year response to the fluid, daily, unpredictable leading of God."[22] The astonishing growth of megachurches seemed to offer substantive proof of God's blessing and validation both of the Church Growth Movement and of seeker-sensitive methods.

Academic studies added credibility to these narratives of divine blessing and evangelical business acumen, while typically ignoring the changes in the terminology of growth that helped to support the narratives. In 1997, sociologist and religious-studies scholar Donald Miller famously described the megachurch as a "new paradigm" in American religion that was restructuring religious organizations and "democratizing access to the sacred."[23] Miller followed the market-model historiography of Roger Finke and Rodney Starke, arguing that the new-paradigm churches succeeded because they best met the needs of their "clientele" and thus expanded their religious "market share." Although Miller argued that "one must never minimize the *religious experience* of participants," he consistently prioritized a marketing perspective, exploring why this new paradigm was winning the battle for bodies and resources in the spiritual marketplace, while his own liberal denomination was in steady market decline.[24] After studying the methodological innovations of the megachurches, he argued that, to succeed and grow, all denominations needed to follow the new paradigm, popularizing their messages and appealing to the needs of their consumer base. Within this context, Miller described megachurches as the first wave of a "second reformation" that pointed the way to the future of spiritual expression and engagement in America. In the face of denominational decline, he argued, "the leaders of these new paradigm churches are starting new movements, unbounded by denominational bureaucracy and the restraint of tradition—except the model of first-century Christianity."[25]

These references to a "second reformation" and the first-century church should be, by now, quite familiar. The rhetoric of Fundamentalist Christianity—of which both separatist Fundamentalists and seeker-sensitive evangelicals are a part—relies upon an erasure or transcendence of history in order to restore the fundamentals of the faith to the present. Whether these fundamentals are to be found in the sixteenth-century Reformation period, as was most common when Fundamentalists struggled for denominational control and opposed ecumenical cooperation with Catholic and Orthodox congregations, or in the first-century church, as has become more common in recent years—the purpose remains the same. Believers seek to restore the purity of the gospel and the inerrant truths of the Bible, which have been corrupted by human language and institutions. As Lynne Hybels said of Willow Creek, "We didn't dream about how to be a big church. We dreamed about Acts 2. We dreamed about what it would feel like to be part of a biblically functioning community."[26] In order to validate their doctrinal and methodological innovations, Fundamentalist superchurch and megachurch leaders invoked the New Testament church as proof that they were not innovating outside of the fundamentals of the faith, but merely erasing the unnecessary innovations of the past and restoring the original ideals of Christian community. Both accommodative and resistant communities begin at the same place, claiming a common commitment to the fundamentals of faith and practice. They interpret these fundamentals in very different ways, however, and this has a significant effect on both their spiritual and political identities.

Telling Stories

The thirty-fourth anniversary celebration of Willow Creek Community Church was called "All In!" For each of its three weekend services on October 10 and 11, 2009, the main church campus in South Barrington, Illinois, played host to all of its regional campus congregations. These included, at the time, three suburban campuses, one campus that met in the famous Chicago Theater in downtown Chicago, and Casa de Luz, the Spanish-language service that began meeting at South Barrington in 2006. Each campus had its own section of the 7,200-seat auditorium; however, section assignments were merely suggested, and audience behavior during the service indicated that many people took the seating suggestions as precisely that and sat where they wanted. Individuality and free choice are, after all, values permeating Willow Creek's rhetoric. Unlike the First Baptist Church of Hammond, where uniformity in dress and behavior dominates, Willow Creek's attendees dress casually and according to personal taste—making no visible distinction between church clothes and the clothes they might wear to a movie theater or a mall. On the one hand, this has the effect of creating a more comfortable and casual church community. Where First Baptist and Thomas Road seem determined to repel outsiders, Willow Creek makes clear efforts to appeal to and attract the "seekers" in their midst. White, upper-middle-class, suburban visitors would require almost no preparation to enter this space. They can come as they are, and if the Jesus talk becomes too unsettling, there is a coffee shop just down the hall—comfortably untouched by Christian symbolism. For others, entrance into this space might not be so unmarked, but a scattering of nonwhite bodies, both in the audience and on the stage, reflects the church's articulated efforts to create a raceless (if not classless) community. On the other hand, this individualization carries weekday standards of dress and behavior into the church context. The result, as others have noted, is a kind of vaguely religious mall experience, where strangers pass one another silently in the common hallways, on their way to inhabit the stores and boutiques through which they define their individual identities.[27] Yet it is not enough to write off Willow Creek as simply the religious equivalent of the suburban mall. Much as Falwell's call for a superaggressive local church remained caught between the Fundamentalist demand to separate from the unbelieving world and the simultaneous demand to win souls for Jesus, Willow Creek seeks to negotiate a tension between the seeker-sensitive value of individual freedom and the demands of Fundamentalist community.

In his sermon for the "All In!" service, Bill Hybels attempted to discursively negotiate this tension. He began by having the congregation read together a passage from the second chapter of the book of Acts:

> They devoted themselves to the apostles' teaching and to the fellowship, to the breaking of bread and to prayer. Everyone was filled with awe, and many wonders and miraculous signs were done by the apostles. All the believers were together and had everything in common. Selling their possessions and goods, they gave to anyone as they had need. Every day, they continued to meet together in the temple courts. They broke bread in their homes and ate together with glad and sincere hearts, praising God and enjoying the favor of all the people. And the Lord added to their number daily those who were being saved.[28]

Hybels linked this narrative of the New Testament church with the story of Willow Creek's own beginnings. Describing the church's first service in the Willow Creek Movie Theater in 1975, he said, "All we wanted to see was whether or not God could do in the twentieth century what he had done already in the first century."[29] Following the familiar pattern of other Fundamentalist leaders, Hybels made the church of the past wholly contemporaneous with the church of the present. Like John Winthrop's famous symbolic transportation of the Hebrew Promised Land to the shores of Massachusetts, Hybels's sermon cleared away the dross of history between the first and twenty-first centuries and presented Willow Creek as another "city upon a hill," called by God as a beacon to the rest of the world. By declaring that the leaders of Willow Creek "wanted to see" if God could act again as he had two millennia ago, Hybels left open the implication that God had not acted that way during the intervening centuries. Thus, his language constituted Willow Creek Community Church as a unique event and its members as a unique people, chosen and called by God to transcend the failures and foibles of Christian history in order to re-create the mythical glory of the original Christian community.

Of course, Hybels is by no means unique in this transcendent approach to history, but his appropriation of the original community differs somewhat from those we have looked at previously. In the last chapter, for example, we saw how Falwell used the first-century church in the book of Acts to statistically validate superaggressive church growth and articulate a path for spiritual and political success in the future. Yet, while Falwell focused on the aggressiveness with which the first-century church expanded, and used these narratives to validate astounding predictions about the possibilities for Fundamentalist growth and conquest in the spiritual, social, and political affairs of its local community, Hybels sidestepped the issue of growth. He said that none of the people who started Willow Creek were asking God "that Willow would become a megachurch one day or that we'd be known in various places around the world." Where Falwell demanded growth, Hybels treated it as though it were incidental. Indeed, he seemed to advocate against the idealization of growth. Speaking in a three-story auditorium packed with thousands of people, Hybels chose to idealize the most intimate and personal details of his chosen text. The early believers, he said, "took meals in each other's homes and they told stories to each other . . . stories of their own redemption, stories of God's activity in their lives. And what happened in that first church was that people got knit together almost like a family." The difference between the soldier called to conquest and the family member called to a home-cooked meal is illustrative of the different rhetorical frames offered by Falwell and Hybels.

Hybels presented a vision of the Fundamentalist church as narratively constituted. Strangers tell stories and share memories of common experiences within the church community, and the result is common identity and common cause, or, as Hybels said of the first-century church, "agreement with one another regarding the fundamental affections and allegiances in their lives." While the rhetoric of separatist Fundamentalism presents the family as something predetermined, and which it is the church's duty to support and defend, megachurches like Willow Creek challenge the notion of a predetermined identity or singular collective memory.[30] The church's pastors and literature do authorize some unifying narratives—such as the Willow Creek Movie Theater—but these are few and far between. Instead, congregation members are encouraged to develop their own stories around the central themes of life in Christ and life as a "Creeker." The literature of Willow Creek is full of members recounting "my experience" with the church. Lacking the kind of predetermined doctrinal commitments and strong collective identity found in Fundamentalist superchurches like Thomas Road or the First Baptist of Hammond,

Willow Creek authorizes a stronger sense of individual autonomy while offering regular examples of what John Gillis calls "memory sites" for the constitution and maintenance of familial community.[31]

The church building reflects this. Willow Creek's internal architecture both calls great attention to itself and points beyond itself. Walking through the front door into the interior space feels like both a continuation and a technological enhancement of the world outside. The community hallway is wide, expansive, and brightly lit by massive windows. Video screens display daily announcements and updates. Internet terminals are available to check the church website. A waterfall flows between the escalators. The natural and artificial continue to interact in the church's main auditorium, where three-story windows provide a view of waterfalls and evergreen trees on either side of the stage; video screens give the audience better-than-front-row views of the music bands and speakers; and a state-of-the-art sound system provides an auditory experience that matches the best theaters and concert venues. In their essay comparing the experience of visitors at Walt Disney World and Cape Kennedy's Astronauts Memorial, Carole Blair and Neil Michel say of Disney: "The visitor's experience is rendered as absolutely dependent upon technology; without it, there is no adventure."[32] The same is true at Willow Creek. The church experience is unimaginable apart from the technology that surrounds and penetrates it on every level. The technology molds and shapes the church experience into something that cannot be copied by anything short of a competing megachurch. You want to stay home? Fine. You want to go to another church? Fine. You think you can experience God this way anywhere else? Good luck. With few permanent icons or fixtures, technology provides a mediating screen through which the audience experiences the effects of divine blessing and the challenge of divine word.

Like most other aspects of the church, the main stage is a fluid space, with no permanent pulpit or other fixtures, continually remade to match the message. For the "All In!" service, the themes of multiplicity and unity predominated. The backdrops for the stage are often complex, but for this service, everything was kept remarkably simple—four sashed curtains hung from the ceiling, with blue and purple lights illuminating them. The curtains created at once the sense of history, harmony, and passage. As history, they carried the sense of a stage curtain, reinforcing Hybels's description of the church's beginnings in a movie theater. Yet there was not a single curtain but several—all identical—and the image of harmonized multiplicity reinforced the interplay of differently colored and gendered bodies that populated the stage throughout the service, embodying Hybels's language about strangers becoming "almost like a family" as they told their stories of God's love and redemption through the mediating frame of the church.

Such language and symbols contrast sharply with the ideals of Fundamentalist separation. At First Baptist of Hammond, for example, the pastor speaks from a fixed pulpit, from which he may roam in the excitation of his oratory, but to which he will always return. Behind him, physically and symbolically limiting the excesses of narrative and of prophetic speech, sit fourteen white, male elders—embodiments of traditional authority—and behind the elders, beyond the choir, are the fixed wall and white columns of the faux portico. Despite the tent-meeting feeling evoked by its vast, horizontally fixed auditorium and echoing sound system,[33] First Baptist represents a stability that is carefully maintained through the rigid enforcement of racial, gender, doctrinal, and political norms. In contrast, Willow Creek embodies fluidity and possibility—adopting a focus on the church as a passage to the future, rather than a guardian of the past. Thus, instead of fixed white columns, the open, multicolored curtains hang down, providing not a barrier, but a passage that invites the audience to look beyond them into the dark between them. In his study of megachurch marketing, James Twitchell describes Willow Creek (and megachurches generally) as horizontally fixed, a perspective he associates with the goal of filling seats;[34] however, there is another dimension to this horizontality—the sense of an unbounded and ever-expanding future. The congregation at Willow Creek cannot see the back of the stage, and fluid markers like curtains and screens offer not a boundary or a limit so much as an invitation to contemplate what lies beyond. Similarly, the auditorium's three-story windows, looking out on waterfalls and pine trees, invite contemplation of the world outside, a vision, to be sure, that is carefully managed—the waterfalls are artificial and the trees strategically block, on one side, the acres of cars parked out front—but that nonetheless appears open and expansive. The congregation is offered an optimistic vision of its own future in which the true, yet accommodative, church is continually expanding in both size and influence, harmonizing multiplicity through the unity of its upper-middle-class, minimally doctrinal Christian message.

The themes of multiplicity and unity continue into other aspects of the service as well. For the "All In!" service, the four curtains were matched by four drum sets—one for each of the four largest campuses. As the service started, each drummer played a solo, which was then combined with the previous solo until, by the time the rest of the music started, all the drummers were playing together in perfect rhythm. Songs were captioned in both English and Spanish on the giant screens, and at different points the song leader from Casa de Luz would direct the whole congregation to sing the Spanish words. The entire service was a microcosm of the most optimistic vision of megachurch revivalism—the expressed hope that barriers of gender, ethnicity, and language will fall away as all the world turns to Jesus. The discourse of Willow Creek, like that of the Chatham Street Chapel nearly 180 years earlier, identifies the local church as the key to this spiritual and political transformation. In his books, Hybels repeatedly reiterates that "the local church is the hope of the world."[35] As he said in his sermon for the "All In!" service, "[In] the first 75 years of the twentieth century, local churches, for the most part, had given up altogether believing that people could be reconciled to God through the efforts of a local church." He argued that people who wanted to lead their friends to Christ would be more likely to send them to Billy Graham Crusades, Campus Crusade rallies, or Christian rock concerts, because "churches, for the most part, existed for the already convinced." Of course, Hybels's description was simplistic, but this claim to have rediscovered the truth and revived the fundamentals of the church is a central part of Willow Creek's ethos. Despite the language and symbols of multiplicity, Willow Creek remains rooted in, and defensive of, an ultimately homogenous perspective of Christian identity. While repudiating the term "fundamentalist,"[36] Hybels advocates the doctrines of the "early church" as read through revivalist and Fundamentalist traditions. He believes in hell, though he is not "neurotic" about it.[37] He argues that evangelism is the primary duty of the Christian believer. Indeed, if one looks up "What Willow Believes" on the church's website, one finds, albeit in shortened form, a description of belief in general agreement with the essential doctrines of separatist Fundamentalism.[38] Heterogeneity and homogeneity are continually being renegotiated and reimagined in the tension between doctrine and fluidity.

Bodies and Souls

The physical environment, the building, offers a site constructed to maximize experience over memorialization. Change is the only constant in megachurch architecture. Stage props change from week to week as sermon topics shift. No crosses or other iconography are visible.[39] Translations of the Bible change from sermon to sermon, and even quotation to quotation within a message, as needed by the speaker for the greatest effect. God's acts in history are remembered but not historicized, and it takes little effort to transport the first century into the twentieth or the twenty-first. Like its suburban landscape, the megachurch has no defining paradigm but sprawl. The old will be torn down; the new will emerge with little memory of the old beneath its foundation. What it means to be a "Creeker" will not stay the same. It will always be growing, changing, and expanding over time.

Such an expansive future opens the possibility for creative action in the service of an ever-changing narrative and identity. In his 1994 dissertation on Willow Creek, sociologist Gregory Prichard described his first visit to the church and the "impassive slack-jaw faces" of the congregation, a description resonating with Blair and Michel's argument that visitors to the Kennedy Center and Disney World "need be only passive recipients of messages."[40] Yet, the message of megachurches is not passivity, but a different form of engagement—motivating a different kind of politics. The essential tenets of Fundamentalist belief and identity are not abolished, or even significantly altered, in a megachurch like Willow Creek. Though largely divorced from the linearity and history of Fundamentalist dogma, these tenets are not abolished, but reimagined as transformative narratives, linking the church of the idealized past with the church of the future, and continually reimagining the congregation as an active and redemptive force in and through the ideal of an almost-family.

From a perspective that sees familial and communitarian identity as the product of narrative, it is unsurprising that story, not doctrine or demand, is the dominant mode of communication at Willow Creek. Throughout this sermon, Hybels used stories that brought together past and present in the service of an imagined future—stories related to what he called the "dream of bringing the Kingdom of God fully to planet earth." The stories people tell within the church are ultimately bounded by the larger stories of Christian advancement in the world—spiritually, socially, and politically. Willow Creek has become significant as a symbol of American evangelicalism because it represents not only numerical growth, but also an intense and accommodative optimism that permeates a particular branch of evangelical culture. Stories are told not at random, but within a narrative framework that renders them incremental proofs of God's advancing work in the world. While Fundamentalist rhetoric focused on metaphors of battles, remnants, elitists, and thieves, Willow Creek embodies the idealism of an American religious majority that does not have to claim secrecy, whose vision of the world will become in time not only the vision of the larger Christian community, but eventually the world's vision of itself.

It is in this optimistic spirit that Hybels called upon his congregation to commit themselves to rescuing bodies from hunger and poverty and rescuing souls from "eternal death." Hybels described the church's growing interest in "social justice" as a "mark [of] the activity of God in the first century church that many of us know is being lived with increased intensity all over the Willow family." Using stories and projecting images on the video screens, he described how Willow Creek members have given of their time and money for the poor around the world. Pictures showed Willow Creek leaders giving food to a woman from Zimbabwe, and residents of an African village standing around a new water pump that Willow Creek paid for and helped to set up. Hybels said, "Look at the faces of these kids, who now don't have to spend half their life hauling water!" The images provided proof of the reality of the service and the possibilities of future action. In a world of complex demands, the illustrated stories Hybels told made action intelligible by showing its immediate physical results in the objects distributed and the grateful people receiving them. Indicating another picture of a water system for a hospital, he exclaimed, "You provided the funds! You're all a part of this!" Image and narrative created links between the congregation and, in Hybels's words, "people you don't know, whose faces you'll never see, whose names you can't pronounce." Narratives of the New Testament are reinscribed into the identity of the contemporary community as audience members identify themselves with the stories of social justice done in their name. Unlike Fundamentalist sermons, which typically begin with the inerrant command of God and apply that command to the behavior of the people, who are continually corrected in the service of an ultimate and clearly defined moral standard that is itself beyond critique, the rhetoric of Willow Creek begins with stories of God's people and imagines these stories continuing in the lives of an ever-changing almost-family. As stories of generosity and social justice are told and retold, these concepts can indeed become inscribed in the familial identity. Change is both possible and necessary in the megachurch context, and within this context there are possibilities for extending this form of evangelicalism beyond the political issues and boundaries most commonly associated with conservative Christians.

Yet there are, of course, limitations to the extension of social justice in this context. The unknowable people in these stories and images were not, and in a very important sense could never be, part of the church family. They could not speak; they could not tell the stories that are such an important feature of inclusion within this narratively constituted community. They were ultimately unknowable, even unintelligible as fully familial subjects in the context in which they were presented. They remained objects of charity and consumption, whose stories helped to define and extend the community's identity, while they were never incorporated into that identity as anything more than receptive vessels of the gifts handed out in the name of the megachurch. Unable to see or address the congregation, their bodies were rendered visible to the audience's gaze, transported into this sophisticated technological environment for the audience's pleasure, and verbally captioned as talking points for the audience's motivation, before whom they were supposed to be awestruck and grateful for the gifts they were given. In the same way, the congregation witnessing these images was supposed to incorporate these subjects into the constitutive narratives of the church and be thus inspired to future action. Yet at all times, in the megachurch, the boundary between real action and voyeuristic gazing is relatively thin. While the Willow Creek congregation is hardly passive or slack-jawed, there are limits to the church's incorporation of, or engagement with, those outside, and these limits can become problematic when incorporated into a political framework, leading to a more thoughtful and even progressive politics of the individual while remaining poorly equipped to challenge or symbolize systemic inequality or injustice at the level of nations, states, and even local communities. In their book *Divided by Faith*, Michael Emerson and Christian Smith argue that the evangelical church market, reflected in modern megachurches, promotes racially and culturally homogenous congregations that are internally strong, but unable to adequately reach beyond themselves and form bonds with other cultural and racial groups.[41] Willow Creek's actions in relation to systemic issues tend to focus on representative examples of giving or volunteerism, which, while hardly insignificant, point to the limitations of its own concept of community and the almost-family of the church.

These tensions between observation, inclusion, and action are ever present in the megachurch experience. Unlike the Fundamentalist call, which is linked to the external force of divine command, Hybels sought to create the grounds for action through identification with the object toward whom the action was to be directed. Thus, when describing the duty of true believers to speak to and win converts, he told a story about receiving a missing-children flyer in the mail, and said, "Every person who's outside the family of God is like a missing kid to God. . . . They're not a part of his redeemed family. . . . They've been kidnapped by the forces of evil. They're heading the wrong direction in their life. They're heading to the wrong place in eternity. The heart of the Father is broken over it." By establishing God as the grieving father of kidnapped children, Hybels simultaneously invoked the church family with which he began his sermon and drew the limits of familial community. Those unable to hear the stories of faith could not become part of the family of strangers. Thus, the act of evangelism—spreading the good news of Jesus to unbelievers—was transformed from a Fundamentalist metaphor of the soldier doing battle to the megachurch metaphor of the storyteller whose stories could both renew and redeem. And the converted became both new elements of the story and proof of its concepts, through whom the narrative of familial community could continue.

There are advantages to the rhetorical approach that Hybels invoked and the megachurch symbolizes, but there are distinct disadvantages as well. What makes a church like Willow Creek flexible and open to change and transformation also makes it vulnerable to fragmentation or to charismatic leadership. Lacking the underlying doctrinal and authoritarian structure of separatist Fundamentalism, these churches are highly dependent on continual redefinition in their search for the most attractive or persuasive methodology. While they are good at growing, they are often weak critics of the religious or social systems around them—being highly dependent on their audience's affirmation. Lacking a strong perspective that can transcend their constant flow of stories, megachurch leaders tend to be much better at identifying personal problems and struggle with systemic ones. Fundamentalist rhetoric draws strong boundaries and links personal behavior to social and political evil, validating countersymbols of "culture war," "confederacy," and "secular humanism" that permeate Fundamentalist politics. Megachurch accommodation does not really abandon the idea of social evil and "Christian worldview"—a term Hybels invoked during the "All In!" sermon—but it reorients its focus to the individual, stressing individual responsibility and individual solutions within the loose and fluid framework of the almost-family.

The Politics of Family

Megachurches like Willow Creek offer a friendly and open kind of evangelicalism that seems to challenge many of the negative connotations associated with Christian Fundamentalists in the popular imagination. For example, megachurches are, as a whole, more racially integrated than other Christian institutions, and since 2003, Bill Hybels has made "racial reconciliation" a particular priority at Willow Creek—a prioritization that has significantly expanded the church's minority population, which had reached 20 percent of the congregation in 2009. Yet, as the analysis above suggests, such multiplicity has its limits. Even as they denote unbounded openness and racial reconciliation, many suburban megachurches continue to normalize white, upper-middle-class, suburban dwellers in their visual and narrative appeals. When Hybels told the assembled congregation that "any skin color, any ethnicity, any accent, any trouble in your past, we'll welcome you," his words simultaneously embodied the openness of megachurch stories and the limits of that openness, reaching out to difference while defining it as a troubled state—a state to be accepted if defined as permanent, as with ethnic and gender differences, or fixed if defined as impermanent, as when another Willow Creek pastor linked same-sex attraction with emotional disturbance and psychological disorders during a sermon in 2006.[42] Family metaphors are often linked with organic metaphors of sickness and healing in seeker-sensitive discussions of conversion and community.[43] Those outside the family are sick and deserving of pity; they are people to be acted upon, people to be welcomed and spoken to, rather than people to be approached as equals. The language of the seeker automatically assumes that the seeker seeks what "we" in the community already have, and thus persuasion becomes a unidirectional proposition. As Hannah Arendt says when describing the danger of organic metaphors in political discourse: "The sicker the patient is supposed to be, the more likely that the surgeon will have the last word."[44]

While Fundamentalist rhetoric works from predetermined categories set in historical and authoritarian terms, accommodative megachurches shift the focus of political narratives from the national, superaggressive campaigns of groups like the Moral Majority to more individualistic, grassroots solutions to political problems. While Falwell's rhetoric of conquest manifested in a specific political organization, Hybels has tended to speak with impassioned but vague calls to reduce evil in the world. In one of his books, for example, Hybels described standing at Ground Zero a few days after the terrorist attacks of September 11, 2001, and he said, "Without churches so filled with the power of God that they can't help but spill goodness and peace and love and joy into the world, depravity will win the day; evil will flood the world. But it doesn't have to be that way. Strong, growing communities of faith can turn the tide of history."[45] As with Falwell, there was a link established between the true church and American patriotic identity, but Hybels's broad language could be easily adopted across political perspectives. Aside from calls to donate money and resources to specific projects like building schools or digging wells—activities that are always framed in personal rather than political terms—Willow Creek's rhetoric does not constitute a unified politics. Issues like abortion and homosexuality are framed as difficult problems about which the individual believer must make personal decisions regarding action. Describing Willow Creek's political commitments, Hybels wrote in 1995:

> Our approach has been to teach unapologetically on social topics that the Bible addresses, including racism, poverty, injustice, abortion, homosexuality, pornography, the environment, and so on. Then we encourage our attenders to be sensitive to the individual promptings of the Holy Spirit regarding their own social and political involvement in these causes through appropriate organizations.[46]

Rather than uniting in culture war against enemies like ecumenical confederacy or secular humanism, Willow Creek advocates an ideal of the individual and the family—an ideal that quietly silences, rather than explicitly excluding, opposition. In this sense, Willow Creek is very similar to groups like James Dobson's Focus on the Family—an organization for which Hybels was once a board member.[47] However, whereas

Focus on the Family grew increasingly concerned with naming specific fundamental threats to the family—abortionists, pornographers, homosexuals, etc.—and thus grew increasingly political in its orientation (largely through spin-off organizations like Focus on the Family Action and the Family Research Council), Willow Creek has predominantly maintained a focus on individual over collective action. Thus, while it is still a mostly conservative community, it is not at all unusual to see bumper stickers for liberal candidates and causes in the church parking lot.[48] By focusing on the individual relationship to Christ, excluded from political and social context, Willow Creek advocates a hopeful optimism that true believers will make good decisions in public, without clarifying what those decisions should be.

The success of this approach is easily visible in a packed parking lot on Sunday morning, but some of its weaknesses were illustrated in a self-analysis that Willow Creek published in 2007. The study, published under the title *Reveal: Where Are You?*, used internal survey data collected by the church to demonstrate that Willow Creek members grew less satisfied with, and more disconnected from, the church as they became more "spiritually advanced."[49] Responding to this study in his "All In!" sermon, Hybels said that he and his staff agreed to make changes to the structure of Willow Creek, deciding that

> As we go into the future, the teaching at weekend services needs to be biblically based, coming right out of the text of the word of God. It needs to be high challenge, not low challenge. Not a mild dose of anything. The full industrial strength of the teaching from the word of God. Thirdly, we want it to be intellectually rigorous. We're not going to dumb it down for any reason or for anyone. In this church . . . we want to produce intelligent Christians, who think in a Christian worldview, and who can really interact with the complexities in this really complex world. Fourth, we want it to be theologically stretching. Not just hitting the easy parts of the word of God, but the doctrines that force us to think deeply and to put our roots down deeply. Next, we want the teaching to have clear application, so that we all know what to do with the word of God when we have to put in into practice on Mondays and Tuesdays and Wednesdays. And finally we want it to be accessible to people who walk in the door, who don't understand the Bible because they didn't grow up with it. It should be accessible to both rookies and veterans.

Hybels's message illustrated the tensions between individual and community values, accommodative and separatist identity, that are continually at play in megachurch communities. For separatist Fundamentalists, the foundations of religious community derive from an inerrant Bible, and their speech and actions reflect a marginalizing and separatist incivility that sets those commands above the human norms of public discourse and deliberation. In contrast, many of those who have called themselves evangelicals—from the "new evangelicals" of the 1940s to the megachurch evangelicals of Willow Creek—thrive on language of civility and openness, deriving power from the dominant discursive norms of the public culture they inhabit and often dominate. They work within public speech, accommodating themselves to its standards and thus gaining public traction and respectability. Yet, within Fundamentalism writ large, these discursive identities are always at play with one another, invoked and rejected at various times and for various purposes. Just as the Fundamentalist can play nice with others, the evangelical can invoke the fundamentals of faith and practice to exclude, as indeed all publics exclude in the process of articulating the lifeworlds they inhabit. Ultimately, public and counterpublic speech intersect with, coexist with, and continually trouble and disrupt one another in the ongoing narratives of the almost-family, the almost-public, of the megachurch.

Conclusion

In 1983, evangelical authors Gloria Gaither and Shirley Dobson—whose husband, James Dobson, founded Focus on the Family—wrote a book called *Let's Make a Memory*. The theme of the book was building family togetherness through family activities. In the first edition of the book, the photographs of the authors on the back show the Gaither family relaxing in their immaculate back yard, while the Dobson family portrait is taken in front of the Epcot dome at Disney World.[50] The idea of building a family through stories and adventures is inherent to the value of the ephemeral, techno-saturated Disney experience. And it is inherent to the rhetoric of "family values," "personal relationship," and "seeker sensitivity" that has dominated much of the post-1980s evangelical discourse as well. It is perfectly unsurprising that the Dobson family would go to Disney World, the mother ship of memory-making and storytelling. And it is hardly coincidental that megachurches—with their Disney-like, family-friendly, highly managed yet highly varied structure—rose to prominence at the same time that "family values" was becoming the dominant discourse of conservative Christian politics.

Megachurches are not devoid of meaning or action, as many of their critics claim. Indeed, if anything, the opposite is true. Meaning and community are not given or stable—not something of the historical or doctrinal past. They require constant upkeep and negotiation. Their focus is not on establishing a perpetual Moral Majority, but on negotiating complex and shifting metaphors of family, health, and community life. The general attitude of Willow Creek might, in fact, best be described as "Let's Make a Memory"—let's narrate an identity. Ideals of community, family, church, and state are transferable, mobile, and malleable in the megachurch, but that does not diminish their potential for political influence. Through the act of telling stories, the observer becomes a participant and the participant an actor.

Conclusion

⌘

Fundamentalism is, at its essence, a church movement. By this I mean, as we have explored throughout this study, that Fundamentalist counterpublicity is intimately intertwined with narratives about the survival and status of the Fundamentalist church, a universal idealization of local believing communities. This idealization, in turn, conflates political and spiritual, public and private concerns in Fundamentalist rhetoric. The church marks the boundaries and exclusions of Fundamentalist identity, yet it also builds bridges between private belief and public action. It is in defense and propagation of the Fundamentalist church and the ideal of revivalism that the local church finds its meaning in the world. These ideals prevent Fundamentalists from remaining wholly separate and being content in their enclaves, because they act as continual demands upon the believer, invoking a hoped-for but always unrealizable perfection of the world through the church.

Are Christian Fundamentalists a counterpublic? A few have argued that they are. Michael Warner includes Fundamentalists among his list of counterpublics, noting that such a designation need not always mean marginal or "subaltern" in an objective sense.[1] Christine Gardner argues that "both evangelicals and feminists can be considered 'subaltern counterpublics,' groups that have been marginalized or excluded from the public sphere."[2] I find such a claim difficult. If we define counterpublics as objectively marginalized communities, I would not identify Christian Fundamentalists as a counterpublic—particularly given the broad definition of "Fundamentalism" that I have been using in this study. That said, my primary purpose and concern in the preceding chapters has not been to define objective marginalization or determine who counts as subaltern or excluded and in what circumstances. We might well find it difficult to identify a community that has, over the past forty years, spawned massive megachurches, parachurch organizations, lobbying firms, and media empires across the country as publicly marginal and outside the structures of hegemonic power; however, we must nevertheless acknowledge that Christian Fundamentalists often act like a counterpublic. They speak like a counterpublic. As Gardner says, "Power comes from the perceived periphery."[3] Fundamentalists appropriate narratives of marginalization and disenfranchisement, and they often justify church growth and political organization as necessary responses to the dominating forces of a false church and an unbelieving state that are conspiring to destroy their freedom and undermine their vision for America. To dismiss these narratives as "false" gets us no closer to understanding or responding to them. Rather, it is only by acknowledging and probing Fundamentalism's paradoxical yet productive tensions—between federation and fellowship, destruction and restoration, majority and minority, separation and accommodation—that we can begin to craft a fuller and more nuanced response to Fundamentalist publicity and politics.

Whether Fundamentalists challenge the perceived domination of an ecumenical superchurch or bring their own forms of superchurch ecumenicism against the culture and practices of a false church and a secular state, they position themselves inside a triumphalist, paradoxical narrative of eventual but always-deferred dominion. Within this narrative, the struggles and triumphs of local churches and associations become representative of the slow but continuing progress of an imagined Fundamentalist community into the public sphere, and the consequent realigning of the public sphere to match Fundamentalist values. Narratives of a common battle between true believers and the world they inhabit give meaning and purpose to local contestation, assuring local communities that they will not always remain marginal, and that their seemingly insignificant actions are part of a larger story with transformative potential. Even the most pessimistic of premillennialist narratives envision an unbelieving world that is burned and bombed and crushed and stripped in order to prepare it for the return of Christ and the triumphant reign of the Fundamentalist church on earth. Progress toward this Fundamentalist dominion is determined by divine will, but it is driven by human agency and the effective power of revivalist speech. Revivalism is, at its essence, a belief in the possibility of conversion through persuasion. It prioritizes speech to strangers and calls upon unbelievers to embrace personal faith and the consequent realigning of one's vision, hermeneutic, and politics to that of an ever-expanding Fundamentalist community. Whether the revival takes place locally or universally, imminently or in some post-apocalyptic future, Fundamentalist narratives construct a kind of unified identity around the belief that human speech, in the service of the Christian church and Christian gospel, can and will transform both conscience and culture.

Such ideals of transformation and revival are not limited to Christian Fundamentalism. In the first chapter, I described counterpublics as privatized associations that work within discourse to establish and create public consequentiality as a means of overcoming public exclusion and producing public legitimacy. Whether or not this privatization exists in reality, it can be and is constructed through language. It requires an act of imagination in the service of an ideal community and publicity. The purpose is not merely to separate oneself from public norms; it is also to reimagine those norms in order to establish a counterpublic community within the realm of proper, normative publicity. Counterpublicity challenges notions of an easy, open, and tolerant public sphere by identifying and embodying particular moments of public isolation, while, at the same time, speaking to and performing a new ideal of what the public can be. It is in the name and service of such an ideal that members of a community imagine a better, fairer public or, at the very least, a public that is better and fairer for them. One challenges existing conditions of publicity while speaking of this better, freer, and more representative public. One invokes a different standard or ideal of society against which the current system can be measured and found lacking.

Counterpublicity prioritizes the local and the particular over the general and universal. The gaps and inconsistencies of public norms are made manifest in their inability to account for particular activities, beliefs, or communities. To speak as a counterpublic is to present oneself as abnormal, since it is in contrast to existing standards of normalcy that such speech has meaning. Yet, this collective difference does not remain stagnant, but operates in the service of a kind of new normalization. Communities that comfortably or willingly operate outside public norms may be marginal without engaging in the language of counterpublicity. The latter term implies not merely resistance to present norms, but also an effort to make or imagine a new or different set of norms within which that which is presently abnormal, marginal, and suppressed can be normalized, accepted, and triumphant. Such a perspective is not isolated from the public, nor is it intended to wholly repudiate public discourse. It is, instead, a form of resistant speech that seeks to remake and reimagine the public good. Address to strangers is not enough, nor is it enough to merely enact marginalization. Counterpublic speech is discontented speech, and it demands change in the social norms within which a community's current disenfranchisement is perceived and enacted.

At the same time, of course, such speech is not exclusively or even predominantly directed at the dominant public or the state. As I have demonstrated in the chapters above, a great proportion of counterpublic speech is internal. The texts I have offered all spoke first to a particular Fundamentalist community, speaking a language the members of the community would understand and invoking norms to which they could easily relate. Outside audiences are implied, but only obliquely in most cases. What is offered in these sermons, articles, images, and films are lessons to members of the community about the ways in which public discourse ought to be conducted, and the framework within which Fundamentalist publicity and counterpublicity is to be imagined. These are not the dominant texts through which public Fundamentalism is presented to the outside world any more than churches are the dominant media through which public Fundamentalism is displayed; but these texts, and the thousands like them, are the foundation upon which the narratives of marginalization, resistance, and revival rest. If we wish to understand the public messages produced by Fundamentalist communities, we must begin with texts like these—texts that frame the normative values through which narratives of marginalization are constructed and the transformation of public norms defined. This is not simply to argue, as others have done, that scholars of religious movements need to have a better understanding of the doctrines or rituals behind religious speech. They do, of course, but my broader point is that a full understanding of any counterpublic speech must account for the kind of internal texts, discourses, and performances through which public address and public action are given meaning. It is my hope that this book will encourage greater attention to narratives and symbols at the boundaries of public and private where marginalization is first enacted and the language of resistance formed.

Among Fundamentalists, these internal narratives tend to use local communities, local battles, and local victories as proof of both Fundamentalist marginalization in the present and the expectation of Fundamentalist dominion in the future. The prominence of local associations and churches in Fundamentalist narratives has not been sufficiently accounted for in the scholarship; however, as this study has repeatedly demonstrated, mobilization requires investment and the perception of immediate threat. Over the past four decades, Fundamentalist communities have been so effective at mobilizing political action in part because the stage of battle is the local church, the local school board, the local courthouse, or the local business. Even national issues are consistently framed in local terms. Threats are measured in the banning of local Christmas displays, the political diatribes of community college teachers, or laws that require small businesses to act contrary to their owners' religious beliefs. Victories are measured in school board elections, prayers at state legislative assemblies, and Ten Commandments displays. Fundamentalist marginalization is consistently defined and explained in local terms, and local victories become part of the ongoing, paradoxical narrative of always-deferred dominion. Fundamentalist speech connects the local church with the Fundamentalist community, and local challenges with the continually returning threat of national confederacy.

Of course, as I indicated above, critics can legitimately question Fundamentalists' claims to represent a marginalized or oppressed community. Indeed, Fundamentalists often seem to act as the oppressors, working to silence opposition and marginalize difference that does not align itself with a particularly narrow set of social, moral, and political values. Fundamentalist churches have become prominent symbols of this perceived hypocrisy. Documentary filmmakers like Heidi Ewing, Rachel Grady, and Alexandra Pelosi, for example, have emphasized the oppressive and marginalizing power of Fundamentalist ideologies, interpretations, media, and culture, and the role that institutions like superchurches and megachurches play in furthering Fundamentalist influence.[4] It seems incredible that communities with such incontestable social and political power should claim to be themselves marginalized or oppressed. Yet this is in some ways precisely the point. Fundamentalists engage in a particularly troubled and troubling kind of counterpublic speech, and yet the Fundamentalist claim to marginalization is critical to the community's rhetorical and political force. By temporarily bracketing questions about who is and who is not legitimately "marginal," my goal in this book has been to better understand the processes by which counterpublic speech is constructed and counterpublic identities are constituted. This, in turn, will help us to better understand the margins of publicity, and to better imagine the possibilities and risks associated with the negotiation and transformation of public norms.

Looking forward, I hope that this project encourages stronger analysis of the internal dynamics of counterpublic speech, and specifically, greater focus on the discursive constitution, organization, and justification of counterpublic communities. Protest events and resistance narratives that are directed outward need to be analyzed in a context that takes account of the complex internal discourses through which a counterpublic identity is continually reimagined. Also important is the recognition that counterpublic speech operates through paradox and a continual, irresolvable, and ultimately productive tension between speech and separation, marginality and majority. There is space for critical analysis not only in the moments of public display or demand, but in the moments of self-directed speech and redefinition as well.

The Persistence of Fundamentalism

In *The Public and Its Problems*, John Dewey conceived of the public and the private not as static but as fluid and historically contingent categories. This fluidity can be troubling and disruptive; it challenges notions of a stable public sphere or consistent norms of democracy and citizenship. It is also, however, a means by which democracy remains engaged with the needs of the present and relevant to new generations of citizens, voters, students, and activists. The problem of the public is not fluidity or multiplicity. The problem, and the solution, is communication. Dewey says, "The essential need, in other words, is the improvement of the methods and conditions of debate, discussion and persuasion. That is *the* problem of the public."[5] The challenge is not to reduce or circumscribe the public. We must learn to live with it and within it, but we must also learn to imagine it in new ways and in response to new challenges.

The public will shift. It will change. Indeed, it is changing. As I mentioned at the beginning of this book, new coalitions are emerging and searching for a language and a history. Those advocating deliberative reasoning and civil discourse struggle to account for coalitions like the Tea Party that have taken political root in the United States. Like Fundamentalist responses to "superchurch" ecumenicism, the Tea Party is anti-government while inspiring its own forms of counter-government association. While, for example, the Populist Party of the 1890s argued that "the power of government—in other words, of the people—should be expanded," government has become, in the rhetorical populism of the Tea Party, a countersymbol that both implicates and negates the conservative community.[6] In 1919, William Bell Riley warned that the "Confederacy Movement" would delight Germans and Bolsheviks and destroy the religious and political identity of America. In 2010, Tea Party leaders were similarly comparing the Obama administration and advocates for "Big Government" to Fascists and Communists and arguing that empowering government would destroy faith in God and the Constitution.[7] As countersymbol, "Big Government" identifies certain, productively vague, political behaviors as betrayals of an imagined prior unity between the people and the state, and it establishes, along the lines I described in chapter 3, a new communal identity rooted in resistance to, and difference from, that which has been negated.

As another example, a 2012 report by the National Intelligence Council suggests how the landscapes of religious identities and communities are changing, and how those changes might affect politics, governance, resource management, and other aspects of national and international relations in the coming decades. The report says, in part, that

> Amid [a] fluid ideological landscape, the West's conception of secular modernity will not necessarily provide the dominant underlying values of the international system. The persistence, if not growth and deepening, of religious identity, growing environmental concerns, and resource constraints, and the empowerment of individuals through new communications technologies are already providing alternative narratives for global politics. As non-Western societies continue their economic transformation, the prospect of a retrenchment along religious, ethnic, cultural, and nationalistic lines could fuel dysfunction and fragmentation within societies. Alternatively, the intersection of Western ideas with emerging states could generate—particularly over time—new hybrid ideologies that facilitate

> collaboration in an expanding number of areas, leading to increased economic output and greater consensus on global governance issues.[8]

The relationships between religious perspectives and public deliberation are often complex—not only because of differences in belief, doctrine, or ideology, but because religious identities are part of larger narratives and broader changes in the world we collectively inhabit. Many of these perspectives are not easily integrated into Western theories of the public sphere or democratic deliberation, but they cannot simply be ignored or treated as publicly inconsequential. The problem of communication remains our problem, even if our solutions will not always be Dewey's solutions, because the public and public interests are, as he recognized, fluid. Publicity is marked not by easy civility and rationality, but by ongoing, paradoxical, and ultimately irresolvable tensions between inside and outside, civility and barbarism, secular visions of neutrality and "our dreaded fundamentalists."[9]

Despite decades of pronouncements to the contrary, Fundamentalists are not going away. Fundamentalism is adapting and changing; it is different than it was in the 1920s or the 1980s, but the narratives of hoped-for revival and dreaded confederation remain active and motivating forces in American politics. Many authors attack Fundamentalist narratives without understanding their constitutive function or the paradoxical role they serve within their communities. Books like Christine Wicker's *The Fall of the Evangelical Nation: The Surprising Crisis within the Church*, for example, demonstrate that many Fundamentalist organizations were never as big or powerful as they claimed to be.[10] Despite Wicker's title, however, this is hardly a surprising revelation. Falwell claimed to represent a moral majority, but the key to understanding that movement is not simply to discover that, in fact, he did not. The claim was part of a broader imagined identity, constituting a particular public demand upon the believer within the context of a particular narrative of the Fundamentalist community. Throughout the twentieth century, Fundamentalist groups have claimed that a revival was in the works. At various times, they pointed to evidence that people were coming back to God and the truth in great numbers. They claimed that true believers would once again capture the nation, whether spiritually or politically or both. In these claims, the numbers and precisely defined boundaries of the movement were always necessarily vague. As I discussed in chapter 5 for example, a moral majority was only conceivable if leaders like Falwell included Catholics, Mormons, and Jews in its ranks—groups with which Fundamentalists were at war in other contexts. Fundamentalist periodicals would go from condemning establishment and ecumenical Protestants as apostates in one article to combining the numbers of establishment and Fundamentalist churches in another in order to provide evidence of a continuing Protestant domination over the Catholic church in America.[11] Megachurches claiming to represent a massive movement or revival often relied, as I discussed in chapter 6, on attendance numbers calculated across multiple "campus" congregations in order to make their case. Merely pointing out these facts, however, does not demonstrate that Fundamentalist communities are failing or going away. Indeed, it tells us very little, for while it has shifted and changed over the years, a collective Fundamentalist identity and discourse has remained, and its rhetorical force shows no signs of dissipating. Indeed, as Susan Harding argues, Fundamentalism inescapably integrated with, and bonded to, modern life during the last few decades of the twentieth century, and its identity has changed the "we" we thought we were.[12]

In approaching and critiquing Fundamentalism, it is difficult not to become like Fundamentalists in one's interpretive and rhetorical strategies. It is, after all, tempting to seek converts. It is tempting to look for cracks in an ideological or political edifice. It is tempting to believe that one's own position is marked by unproblematic truth or civility, and that that of the Other is clearly and unforgivably oppressive. To yield to such temptations, however, reflects a lack of understanding and a lack of willingness to listen to the Fundamentalist voice as it speaks. The actual size of a church, organization, or denomination is far less important than the effectiveness of its claim to represent the real, pure, revivalist faith against the false, the elitist, and the apostate. Megachurches claimed to stand against the destructive moralism of separatist Fundamentalism. Whatever comes next will claim to stand against the megachurches. The work of authors like Wicker, who interpret a decline in megachurch membership with a failure of Fundamentalism, only shows just how effective a few of these churches and organizations were at marketing their influence to the broader public. Megachurch claims of domination or a "second reformation" never reflected reality. Neither did the similar claims of Fundamentalist movements like Riley's or Falwell's. What was important was the way in which these movements positioned a plain, ordinary community of believers against an intellectual, economic, and political elite. Attempts by critical pastors, journalists, and academics to uncover the cracks and failures within these movements in statistical or absolutist terms have only served to legitimize the narrative of public marginalization and subordination within which and against which counterpublic speech is justified.

This book is not an attempt to glorify or idolize Fundamentalist communities or Fundamentalist speech. Indeed, as I explained in the first chapter, it is in large part because this speech is so often deeply troubling that it seemed to offer a good foundation for this analysis. Nor, however, is it my goal to demonize or diminish the critiques and demands that Fundamentalists make upon the public. There is much with which I disagree in Fundamentalist narratives and many ideas that I find disturbing, infuriating, or just plain distasteful. And yet I am also convinced that boundaries and exclusions—even fundamentalisms, if you will—are intimately intertwined with the possibility of publics and of political action. Counterpublic speech offers new visions of the public that reimagine its fundamental limits and redefine the norms of public inclusion and participation. Believing, as I do, that no perfectly just or equitable political system is possible, I understand counterpublicity to be essential for the continued functioning of modern democracy. Counterpublic speech points us toward the local and the particular, with all its messiness, ignorance, intolerance, and lack of sophistication. And yet even in an increasingly global society, it is still most often at the level of the particular that political effects are felt and political motivations stirred. Fundamentalism has been and remains a part of this messy, contentious political process, calling for the true believers to gather in defense of its speech and ideals and in offense against its enemies—demanding that its vision of the public sphere prevail.

Certainly there is much that is troubling about Fundamentalist demands and the narrative of Fundamentalist dominion—impossible though it may be. Even more disturbing are the all-too-close ties that exist between speech and violence in many Fundamentalist narratives. The point at which alternative voices are threatened or marginal communities suppressed is the point where my own tolerance stops, and there will always, in every society, be limits beyond which tolerance cannot go. However, I do not believe that Fundamentalist speech can be eliminated or that Fundamentalists en masse can be somehow converted to what Sharon Crowley has called the "desired future" of liberalism any more than the mass of liberals are likely to become Fundamentalists.[13] Nor, frankly, do I consider the often-idealized elimination of Fundamentalism a desirable state. I believe that the work of rhetorical scholarship lies not in the elimination of agonism, but in the careful and critical examination of public address reflecting contingent and *kairotic* responses to—or impositions of—exclusion, marginalization, and the like. Just as there must be limits, these limits need not be fixed or permanent. Indeed, as the somewhat progressive yet problematic politics of institutions like Willow Creek Community Church illustrate, our always imperfect attempts to eliminate exclusion often have the inadvertent results of concealing what could be better fought or discussed in the open. Willow Creek offers a friendlier and more cosmopolitan Fundamentalism than those more separatist and working-class churches like Thomas Road or First Baptist of Hammond—one that accepts, if tacitly, what Charles Taylor has called the "post-Durkheimian" state of contemporary modernity.[14] Yet this openness and individuation of belief and action conceal the limits and exclusions that define the church community and its politics. Claiming to be nonpolitical, megachurches can do both great good and great harm to the political community, and the apparently nonpolitical openness that characterizes so many of them often makes it difficult to respond either way.

Fundamentalism is a critical check on political and social niceties. It challenges discourses of tolerance, openness, and neutrality in relation to our public norms and values, continually testing boundaries. It forces those who are not Fundamentalists to think about the limits of our reason, tolerance, violence, and rhetoric. It should encourage those invested in the rhetoric of marginal communities to think in more complex ways about the strategies that Fundamentalist communities have used to gain attention—some of which can be easily appropriated by other communities and for other purposes. Fundamentalism is unquestionably disruptive, but not necessarily demonic. It is, thankfully, not the only check on political speech. But its success over the decades at mobilizing communities and articulating narratives of resistance can and should serve as a resource for others claiming marginalization, including many for whom Fundamentalism represents nothing more than an ignorant, intolerant Other. As I hope to have demonstrated, there is much to be learned from Fundamentalism, not merely as a means to defeating its arguments, but as an example of sustained critique motivating collective action in defense of an idealized *ecclesia*—a reimagined public. Such critique is often outside the realm of civility. Tea Parties and superchurches are as critical to—and perhaps even more representative of—democratic engagement as are the polite displays of civil procedure that define and delimit our political processes. Civility must not become so civil that it cannot recognize the tensions and paradoxes through which and against which both public norms and counterpublic speech are formed. Thus it is in support of a frustrating, productive, complex, and often uncivil discourse that I arrive at the end of the present work.

Ultimately, I do not envision, expect, or hope for a world in which civility replaces alternatives or the tensions go away. Assuming the dispensationalists are wrong and the world does not end tomorrow, I imagine that we will have to endure the inadequacies and incivilities of democracy awhile longer. Having spent so long with Fundamentalist texts, I am doubtful that such arguments and sentiments can be civilly integrated into public discourse and deliberation. Yet I am just as doubtful that they will go away, and thus, in all likelihood, fundamentalisms will remain disruptive. The goal I argue is not agreement or even civility—which bears its own suppressive tendencies. The goal is greater critical facility produced by greater understanding and insight into multiple and historically contingent manifestations of public and counterpublic speech, so that we might more effectively communicate and live with one another in the midst of both civil and uncivil demands. Toward that end, I hope that this book adds to our collective understanding and opens doors for more productive interaction, contestation, and communication in the future.

Notes

⌘

Introduction

1. In order to distinguish the American Protestant movements that are the primary subject of this book from more general references to "fundamentalism" in popular media and scholarship, I have chosen to capitalize the term in the former case. For a fuller discussion of the relationship between these two understandings of fundamentalism, see chapter 1. My decision follows the practice of some other authors describing Christian Fundamentalist communities (see Beale and Amstutz). I am also influenced by Michael Kazin, who similarly differentiates categories of "populism" in his analysis of populist rhetoric. See Mark R. Amstutz, *Evangelicals and American Foreign Policy* (New York: Oxford University Press, 2014), 8; David O. Beale, *In Pursuit of Purity: American Fundamentalism since 1850* (Greenville, SC: Unusual Publications, 1986); Michael Kazin, *The Populist Persuasion* (New York: Basic Books, 1995), 5.
2. See Averil Cameron, *Christianity and the Rhetoric of Empire: The Development of Christian Discourse* (Berkeley: University of California Press, 1991), 19. From its inception, Cameron argues, Christianity "placed an extraordinary premium" on speech and the word, which became intimately linked with questions of authority and authorization and, ultimately, with state and political power.

3. On public symbols, see Angela Ray, *The Lyceum and Public Culture in the Nineteenth-Century United States* (East Lansing: Michigan State University Press, 2005), 1–2.
4. See Nancy Ammerman, "North American Protestant Fundamentalism," in *Fundamentalisms Observed*, ed. Martin E. Marty and R. Scott Appleby (Chicago: University of Chicago Press, 1991), 14.
5. Kenneth Burke, *A Rhetoric of Motives* (Berkeley: University of California Press, 1969), 19–23.
6. David O. Beale, *In Pursuit of Purity: American Fundamentalism Since 1850* (Greenville, SC: Unusual Publications, 1986), 8.
7. Camille Kaminski Lewis, *Romancing the Difference: Kenneth Burke, Bob Jones University, and the Rhetoric of Religious Fundamentalism* (Waco, TX: Baylor University Press, 2007), 8–9.
8. See Matthew Moen, *The Transformation of the Christian Right* (Tuscaloosa: University of Alabama Press, 1992), 23–24.

Chapter One. The Public and Its Fundamentalists

1. John Dewey, *The Public and Its Problems* (Chicago: Sage Books, 1927), 33, 54, 67.
2. Robert Asen, "The Multiple Mr. Dewey: Multiple Publics and Permeable Borders in John Dewey's Theory of the Public Sphere," *Argumentation and Advocacy* 39 (2003): 176.
3. Dewey, *The Public and Its Problems*, 109, 114–15, 184.
4. Dewey, *The Public and Its Problems*, 67, 131, 134–35.
5. John Giggie and Diane H. Winston, *Faith in the Market: Religion and the Rise of Urban Commercial Culture* (New Brunswick, NJ: Rutgers University Press, 2002), 82.
6. Anne C. Loveland and Otis B. Wheeler, *From Meetinghouse to Megachurch: A Material and Cultural History* (Columbia: University of Missouri Press, 2003), 83, 100–104.
7. Quoted in Robert A. Ashworth, "The Fundamentalist Movement among the Baptists," *Journal of Religion* 4 (1924): 614.
8. According to George Marsden, Curtis Lee Laws, editor of the conservative Northern Baptist newspaper the *Watchman Examiner*, was the first to apply the term "fundamentalist" to this coalition in a 1920 article, defining them as "aggressive conservatives—conservatives who feel that it is their duty to contend for the faith." See George M. Marsden, *Fundamentalism and American Culture*, 2nd ed. (New York: Oxford University Press, 2006), 159, 169.

9. John Dewey and James Hayden Tufts, *Ethics* (New York: Henry Holt and Co., 1909), 146–47.
10. Charles Taylor, *Modern Social Imaginaries* (Durham, NC: Duke University Press, 2004), 4, 49.
11. Paul Ricoeur, *From Text to Action: Essays in Hermeneutics, II*, trans. Kathleen Blarney and John B. Thompson (London: Continuum, 2008), 177. See also Andreea Deciu Ritivoi, *Paul Ricoeur: Tradition and Innovation in Rhetorical Theory* (Albany: State University of New York Press, 2006), 55–63.
12. Jürgen Habermas, *The Structural Transformation of the Public Sphere: An Inquiry into a Category of Bourgeois Society*, trans. Thomas Burger and Frederick Lawrence (Cambridge, MA: MIT Press, 1989), 27.
13. See Habermas, *The Structural Transformation of the Public Sphere*, 3.
14. Habermas, *The Structural Transformation of the Public Sphere*, 27.
15. Habermas, *The Structural Transformation of the Public Sphere*, 36.
16. Jürgen Habermas, "Three Normative Models of Democracy," in *Democracy and Difference*, ed. Seyla Benhabib (Princeton, NJ: Princeton University Press, 1996), 21–30. Although he does not engage Dewey directly, Habermas, like Dewey, worries that economic and technological changes in modern states are disrupting the possibilities for an effective, "rational-critical" public. "The world fashioned by the mass media is a public sphere in appearance only," he argues, which, while seeming to multiply the possibilities for engagement, often merely encourages silent consumption and discourages response. See Habermas, *The Structural Transformation of the Public Sphere*, 27, 37, 170–71.
17. Jürgen Habermas, "On the Relations between the Secular Liberal State and Religion," in *Political Theologies: Public Religions in a Post-Secular World*, ed. Hent de Vries and Lawrence E. Sullivan (New York: Fordham University Press, 2006), 252.
18. Jürgen Habermas, "Religion in the Public Sphere," *European Journal of Philosophy* 14 (2006): 10.
19. Chantal Mouffe, "Religion, Liberal Democracy, and Citizenship," in *Political Theologies: Public Religions in a Post-Secular World*, ed. Hent de Vries and Lawrence E. Sullivan (New York: Fordham University Press, 2006), 321, 323–24.
20. Dewey, *The Public and Its Problems*, 47–53.
21. See Dewey, *The Public and Its Problems*, 51.
22. Dewey, *The Public and Its Problems*, 49.
23. Cristina Lafont, "Religion in the Public Sphere: Remarks on Habermas's Conception of Public Deliberation in Postsecular Societies," *Constellations* 14 (2007): 239–40.
24. Nicholas Wolterstorff, "The Role of Religion in Decision and Discussion of Political Issues," in *Religion in the Public Square: The Place of Religious Convictions in Political Debate* (Lanham, MD: Rowman and Littlefield, 1997), 105.

25. Dewey, *The Public and Its Problems*, 43.
26. Nancy Fraser, "Rethinking the Public Sphere: A Contribution to the Critique of Actually Existing Democracy," in *Habermas and the Public Sphere*, ed. Craig Calhoun (Cambridge, MA: MIT Press, 1992), 129.
27. Michael Warner, *Publics and Counterpublics* (New York: Zone Books, 2002), 56.
28. Daniel C. Brouwer, "Communication as Counterpublic," in *Communication As . . . Perspectives on Theory*, ed. Gregory J. Shepherd, Jeffrey St. John, and Ted Striphas (Thousand Oaks, CA: Sage, 2006), 198–99.
29. Erik Doxtader, "In the Name of Reconciliation: The Faith and Works of Counterpublicity," in *Counterpublics and the State*, ed. Robert Asen and Daniel C. Brouwer (Albany: State University of New York Press, 2001), 61.
30. Fraser, "Rethinking the Public Sphere," 123.
31. Doxtader, "In the Name of Reconciliation," 60.
32. Robert Asen, "A Discourse Theory of Citizenship," *Quarterly Journal of Speech* 90 (2004): 189–211.
33. Doxtader, "In the Name of Reconciliation," 63.
34. Warner, *Publics and Counterpublics*, 119–21.
35. For this history, see Harriet A. Harris, *Fundamentalism and Evangelicals* (Oxford: Clarendon Press, 1998); Marsden, *Fundamentalism and American Culture*; Nancy Ammerman, "North American Protestant Fundamentalism," in *Fundamentalisms Observed*, ed. Martin E. Marty and R. Scott Appleby (Chicago: University of Chicago Press, 1991), 1–65; Ernest R. Sandeen, *The Roots of Fundamentalism: British and American Millenarianism: 1800–1930* (Chicago: University of Chicago Press, 1970).
36. Marsden, *Fundamentalism and American Culture*, 62; Joel Carpenter, *Revive Us Again: The Reawakening of American Fundamentalism* (New York: Oxford University Press, 1997), 16–17.
37. In thus defining evangelicals, I appear to directly contradict the work of prominent historians of these movements such as George Marsden, who defines fundamentalism as a militant subgroup of evangelicalism. However, Marsden is using these terms differently than I am. There is no question that "evangelical" is the more ancient term—its roots extending back to the Greek New Testament—and it is also true that in the nineteenth century a majority of Protestants were called evangelicals. In this sense, Marsden is quite correct. However, I argue that contemporary American Christian evangelicals are not simply a continuation of these older categories. The American evangelicalism that emerged from the Second World War has been significantly infected by early Fundamentalist disputes and the ongoing effort to define an identity against the anti-supernaturalism of church "modernists" on the one hand and the radicalism and anti-intellectualism of self-identifying Fundamentalists on the other. See George M. Marsden,

Understanding Fundamentalism and Evangelicalism (Grand Rapids, MI: Eerdmans, 1991), 1.

38. Ammerman, "North American Protestant Fundamentalism," 8.
39. John Calvin, *Institutes of the Christian Religion*, ed. John T. McNeill, trans. Ford Lewis Battles (Philadelphia: Westminster Press, 1960), 1:2.
40. Christian Lundberg adds a valuable conception of trope and what he calls an "economy of tropes" to the understanding of publics articulated by Warner and others. See Christian Lundberg, "Enjoying God's Death: *The Passion of the Christ* and the Practices of an Evangelical Public," *Quarterly Journal of Speech* 95 (2009): 387–411.
41. Søren Kierkegaard, *The Concept of Irony: With Constant Reference to Socrates* (London: Collins, 1966), 338–39.
42. See Timothy P. Weber, "The Two-Edged Sword: The Fundamentalist Use of the Bible," in *The Bible in America: Essays in Cultural History*, ed. Nathan O. Hatch and Mark A. Noll (New York: Oxford University Press, 1982), 114–16.
43. Nancy Ammerman, *Bible Believers: Fundamentalists in the Modern World* (New Brunswick, NJ: Rutgers University Press, 1987), 132.
44. Gleason L. Archer, "Alleged Errors and Discrepancies in the Original Manuscripts of the Bible," in *Inerrancy*, ed. Norman L. Geisler (Grand Rapids, MI: Zondervan, 1980), 59.
45. J. Barton Payne, "Higher Criticism and Biblical Inerrancy," in *Inerrancy*, ed. Norman L. Geisler (Grand Rapids, MI: Zondervan, 1980), 90.
46. See Vincent P. Branick, "The Attractiveness of Fundamentalism," in *Fundamentalism Today: What Makes It So Attractive!* ed. Marla J. Selvidge (Elgin, IL: Brethren Press, 1984), 24.
47. Edwin A. Blum, "The Apostles' View of Scripture," in *Inerrancy*, ed. Norman L. Geisler (Grand Rapids, MI: Zondervan, 1980), 39.
48. Jerry Falwell, *Listen America!* (New York: Bantam Books, 1980), 54.
49. Branick, "The Attractiveness of Fundamentalism," 24; R. S. Ellwood, *One Way: The Jesus Movement and Its Meaning* (Englewood Cliffs, NJ: Prentice-Hall, 1973), 31.
50. Ammerman, *Bible Believers*, 115.
51. 1 Peter 3:15 (AV).
52. Following Marsden, Harris identifies two broad approaches to rationality and inerrancy within what I am calling Fundamentalism. The first, which is most closely associated with contemporary, self-identifying Fundamentalists, derives from the work of scholars at Princeton Theological Seminary around the turn of the twentieth century, which remained the major conservative outlier among the established seminaries during the late nineteenth and early twentieth centuries. Led by A. A. Hodge and B. B. Warfield, the so-called "Princeton School" scholars argued that only the original (and nonexistent) autographs of the Bible

are completely without error. This argument created an iron-clad barrier against skeptics; however, as Ernest Sandeen argues, it ended up producing a rigid theology that progressively responded to higher criticism by retreating into unprovable assertions. The second, less dominant approach derives from the work of the nineteenth-century Dutch theologian and politician Abraham Kuyper. For Kuyper, the proper judgment of Scripture derived not from its empirical inerrancy but from its own self-testimony, perceived through the presuppositional framework granted to the believer by the transformative work of the Holy Spirit. Although avoiding some of the fetishization of rationality associated with Hodge and Warfield, Kuyperian thought risks sublimating speech to presumed spiritual/social hierarchies, thus eliminating the grounds for consensus-building in pluralist contexts. The influence of Kuyperian thinking on popular, contemporary Fundamentalism came primarily through the work of Francis Schaeffer and through the Christian "reconstructionist" movements of R. J. Rushdoony and Gary North. Generally speaking, Kuyperians—also known as presuppositionalists—are explicitly deductive in their approach to rationality, understanding true rationality to be only available to the converted. In contrast, the Princeton School approach claims to be inductive and available to all reasonable readers, even while its conclusions, as we discussed above, are necessarily limited by particular doctrines regarding the proper hermeneutical approach to the text. See Harris, *Fundamentalism and Evangelicals*, 135–36, 207–32; Ernest R. Sandeen, "The Princeton Theology: One Source of Biblical Literalism in American Protestantism," *Church History* 31 (1962): 307–21; James Barr, *Fundamentalism* (Philadelphia: Westminster Press, 1978), 261–70; Sandeen, *The Roots of Fundamentalism*, 118–21.

53. Stewart Custer, *Tools for Preaching and Teaching the Bible*, 2nd ed. (Greenville, SC: Bob Jones University Press, 1998), 25.

54. See Marion Elizabeth Rodgers, *Mencken: The American Iconoclast* (New York: Oxford University Press, 2005), 287–88.

55. Robert Hariman, "Introduction," in *Popular Trials: Rhetoric, Mass Media, and the Law*, ed. Robert Hariman (Tuscaloosa: University of Alabama Press, 1993), 12–13.

56. Quoted in Randy Moore, "Creationism in the United States II: The Aftermath of the Scopes Trial," *American Biology Teacher* 60 (1998): 569.

57. "Vanishing Fundamentalism," *Christian Century*, June 24, 1926, 799. See also David Zietsma, "Building the Kingdom of God: Religious Discourse, National Identity, and the Good Neighbor Policy, 1930–1938," *Rhetoric and Public Affairs* 11 (2008): 182. Founded as the *Christian Oracle* in 1884, the *Christian Century* remains one of the most prominent national Protestant periodicals, and it has been, throughout its history, a strong opponent of Fundamentalism.

58. Susan F. Harding, "American Protestant Moralism and the Secular Imagination: From Temperance to the Moral Majority," *Social Research* 76 (2009): 1278, 1281, 1303.

59. For examples of this broad appropriation of the language of fundamentalism, see David Domke, *God Willing? Political Fundamentalism in the White House, the "War on Terror," and the Echoing Press* (Ann Arbor, MI: Pluto Press, 2004); M. Lane Bruner, "Rationality, Reason and the History of Thought," *Argumentation* 20 (2006): 186–87; Eric English, Stephen Llano, Gordon R. Mitchell, Catherine E. Morrison, John Rief, and Carly Woods, "Debate as a Weapon of Mass Destruction," *Communication and Critical/Cultural Studies* 4 (2007): 224–25; Henry A. Giroux, "The Crisis of Public Values in the Age of the New Media," *Critical Studies in Media Communication* 28 (2011): 9–12.
60. See Carol K. Winkler, *In the Name of Terrorism: Presidents on Political Violence in the Post–World War II Era* (New York: State University of New York Press, 2006); James Darsey, "Patricia Roberts-Miller, Demagoguery, and the Troublesome Case of Eugene Debs," *Rhetoric and Public Affairs* 9 (2006): 464.
61. Sharon Crowley, *Toward a Civil Discourse: Rhetoric and Fundamentalism* (Pittsburgh, PA: University of Pittsburgh Press, 2006), 197.
62. Earl Shorris, *The Politics of Heaven: America in Fearful Times* (New York: Norton, 2007), 71.
63. See Wendy Brown, "Subjects of Tolerance: Why We Are Civilized and They Are the Barbarians," in *Political Theologies: Public Religions in a Post-Secular World*, ed. Hent de Vries and Lawrence E. Sullivan (New York: Fordham University Press, 2006), 313.
64. Crowley, *Toward a Civil Discourse*, 56.
65. See Brown, "Subjects of Tolerance," 299, 313.
66. See Sara Diamond, *Roads to Dominion: Right-Wing Movements and Political Power in the United States* (New York: Guilford Press, 1995), 5–6.
67. Harding, "American Protestant Moralism and the Secular Imagination," 1303.
68. David Barstow, "Lighting a Fuse for Rebellion on the Right: Loose Alliance of Protestors Join under Tea Party Umbrella," *New York Times*, February 16, 2010, A16.
69. See Theda Skocpol and Vanessa Williamson, *The Tea Party and the Remaking of Republican Conservatism* (New York: Oxford University Press, 2012), 48–54; Barstow, "Lighting a Fuse for Rebellion on the Right," A16–17.
70. Ronald P. Formisano, *The Tea Party: A Brief History* (Baltimore, MD: Johns Hopkins University Press, 2012), 53–54.
71. "Senator DeMint to Brody File: Tea Party Movement Will Bring On 'Spiritual Revival,'" *The Brody File: CBN News Blogs*, April 21, 2010, http://blogs.cbn.com/thebrodyfile/archive/2010/04/21/senator-demint-to-brody-file-tea-party-movement-will-bring.aspx.
72. Jim DeMint, *The Great American Awakening: Two Years That Changed America, Washington, and Me* (Nashville, TN: B&H Publishing Group, 2011).

Chapter Two. The Fundamentals of Revival

1. Howard H. Martin, "Puritan Preachers on Preaching: Notes on American Colonial Rhetoric," *Quarterly Journal of Speech* 50 (1964): 285.
2. Everett H. Emerson, "John Udall and the Puritan Sermon," *Quarterly Journal of Speech* 44 (1958): 282–84.
3. Roy Fred Hudson, "Rhetorical Invention in Colonial New England," *Speech Monographs* 25 (1958): 215.
4. If an axiom was in doubt, the critic could support it syllogistically, but Ramus's work prioritized practical, axiomatic truth-statements and sought to limit the use of syllogism. See Perry Miller, *The New England Mind: The Seventeenth Century* (New York: Macmillan, 1939), 126–41, 151.
5. Warren Guthrie, "The Development of Rhetorical Theory in America," *Speech Monographs* 13 (1946): 16–18.
6. See John Charles Adams, "Linguistic Values and Religious Experience: An Analysis of the Clothing Metaphors in Alexander Richardson's Ramist-Puritan Lectures on Speech 'Speech is a Garment to Cloath Our Reason,'" *Quarterly Journal of Speech* 76 (1990): 63.
7. Jerald C. Brauer, "Conversion: From Puritanism to Revivalism," *Journal of Religion* 58 (1978): 241.
8. Miller, *The New England Mind: The Seventeenth Century*, 202, 288, 325–26, 359.
9. Miller, *The New England Mind: The Seventeenth Century*, 87.
10. On the relationship between heresy and resistance, see Talal Asad, "Medieval Heresy: An Anthropological View," *Social History* 11 (1986): 345–62.
11. See Harry S. Stout, *The New England Soul: Preaching and Religious Culture in Colonial New England* (New York: Oxford University Press, 1986), 58–61.
12. Sacvan Bercovitch, *The American Jeremiad* (Madison: University of Wisconsin Press, 1978), 4.
13. He makes this argument in contrast to Perry Miller, who reads jeremiads pessimistically. See Bercovitch, *The American Jeremiad*, 6–7.
14. Bercovitch, *The American Jeremiad*, 23.
15. Bercovitch, *The American Jeremiad*, 176–81.
16. John M. Murphy, "'A Time of Shame and Sorrow': Robert F. Kennedy and the American Jeremiad," *Quarterly Journal of Speech* 76 (1990): 409, 412.
17. See Michael Walzer, *The Revolution of the Saints: A Study in the Origins of Radical Politics* (Cambridge, MA: Harvard University Press, 1965), 291.
18. Perry Miller, *The New England Mind: From Colony to Province* (Cambridge, MA: Harvard University Press, 1953), 234, 283. On ignorance of the divine will opening a space for human agency, see Stephen D. O'Leary, "A Dramatistic Theory of Apocalyptic Rhetoric," *Quarterly Journal of Speech* 79 (1993): 398.

19. Following from Aristotle, Hans Blumenberg describes rhetoric as motivation to action in the absence of "definitive evidence." See Hans Blumenberg, "An Anthropological Approach to the Contemporary Significance of Rhetoric," in *After Philosophy: End or Transformation?*, ed. Kenneth Baynes, James Bohman, and Thomas McCarthy (Cambridge, MA: MIT Press, 1987), 432, 435.
20. Frank Lambert, "'Pedlar in Divinity': George Whitefield and the Great Awakening, 1737–1745," *Journal of American History* 77 (1990): 813.
21. George Marsden, *Jonathan Edwards: A Life* (New Haven, CT: Yale University Press, 2003), 209.
22. As Lambert details, it remains unclear how much influence Edwards had on the final text. See Frank Lambert, *Inventing the Great Awakening* (Princeton, NJ: Princeton University Press, 1999), 55ff.
23. Jonathan Edwards, "A Faithful Narrative of the Surprising Work of God in the Conversion of Many Hundred Souls in Northampton, and the Neighboring Towns and Villages of the County of Hampshire, in the Province of the Massachusetts-Bay in New-England," in *Works of Jonathan Edwards*, vol. 4, *The Great Awakening*, ed. C. C. Goen (1737; New Haven, CT: Yale University Press, 1972), 152.
24. Mark Vásquez, *Authority and Reform: Religious and Educational Discourses in Nineteenth-Century New England Literature* (Knoxville: University of Tennessee Press, 2003), 3.
25. For Edwards's defense of the New Light position, see Jonathan Edwards, "The Distinguishing Marks of a Work of the Spirit of God," in *Works of Jonathan Edwards*, vol. 4, *The Great Awakening*, ed. C. C. Goen (1741; New Haven, CT: Yale University Press, 1972), 241.
26. Jonathan Edwards, "Letter: To the Reverend James Robe of Kilsyth, Scotland," in *Works of Jonathan Edwards*, vol. 4, *The Great Awakening*, ed. C. C. Goen (1743; New Haven, CT: Yale University Press, 1972), 536.
27. Stout, *The New England Soul*, 208–9.
28. Randall Balmer, *Blessed Assurance: A History of Evangelicalism in America* (Boston: Beacon Press, 1999), 65.
29. Edwards died of a smallpox inoculation on March 22, 1758.
30. Nathan O. Hatch, *The Democratization of American Christianity* (New Haven, CT: Yale University Press, 1989), 4.
31. Hatch, *The Democratization of American Christianity*, 7–9; Roger Finke and Rodney Starke, *The Churching of America, 1776–2005: Winners and Losers in Our Religious Economy*, 2nd ed. (New Brunswick, NJ: Rutgers University Press, 2005), 55–57, 68–72.
32. Finke and Starke, *The Churching of America*, 74, 79; Hatch, *The Democratization of American Christianity*, 10.
33. B. W. Gorham, *Camp Meeting Manual* (Boston: H. V. Degen, 1854), 16.

34. Nan Johnson, *Nineteenth-Century Rhetoric in North America* (Carbondale: Southern Illinois University Press, 1991), 19–20.
35. Nan Johnson, *Nineteenth-Century Rhetoric in North America*, 145, 160–61.
36. Richard Whately, *Elements of Rhetoric: Comprising the Substance of the Article in the Encyclopaedia Metropolitana with Additions* (Boston: Munroe, 1852), 282.
37. See John Albert Broadus, *A Treatise on the Preparation and Delivery of Sermons*, 17th ed. (New York: Armstrong, 1891), 220.
38. For a discussion of the role of adaptation in nineteenth-century rhetoric, see Nan Johnson, "Nineteenth-Century Rhetoric," in *Encyclopedia of Rhetoric*, ed. Thomas O. Sloane (Oxford: Oxford University Press, 2001), 518–20.
39. John Bryan, *Robert Mills: America's First Architect* (New York: Princeton Architectural Press, 2001), 46–49. Unhappy with changes the congregation made to his original design, Mills rarely mentioned the Circular Church and later claimed that the 1812 Sansom Street building was the first of his auditorium-style churches (49).
40. Quoted in John Thomas Scharf and Thompson Westcott, *History of Philadelphia, 1609–1884* (Philadelphia: L. H. Everts & Co., 1884), 2: 1310.
41. Charles G. Finney, *The Memoirs of Charles G. Finney: The Complete Restored Text*, ed. Garth Rosell and Richard A. G. Dupuis (Grand Rapids, MI: Academie Books, 1989), 9.
42. See Jeanne Halgren Kilde, *When Church Became Theatre: The Transformation of Evangelical Architecture and Worship in Nineteenth-Century America* (New York: Oxford University Press, 2002), 12.
43. Hatch, *The Democratization of American Christianity*, 196–99.
44. Quoted in Susan Hayes Ward, *The History of the Broadway Tabernacle Church, from Its Organization in 1840* (New York: Trow Print, 1901), 19. Also see Finney, *The Memoirs of Charles G. Finney*, 91.
45. Finney, *The Memoirs of Charles G. Finney*, 81.
46. John Wolffe, *The Expansion of Evangelicalism: The Age of Wilberforce, More, Chalmers and Finney* (Downers Grove, IL: InterVarsity Press, 2007), 72, 77.
47. Quoted in Ephraim Perkins, "A 'Bunker Hill' Contest, A.D. 1826, Between the 'Holy Alliance' for the Establishment of Heirarchy [*sic*], and Ecclesiastical Domination Over the Human Mind, on the One Side; and the Asserters of Free Inquiry, Bible Religion, Christian Freedom, and Civil Liberty on the Other. The Rev. Charles Finney, 'Home Missionary,' and High Priest of the Expeditions of the Alliance in the Interior of New York; Head Quarters, County of Oneida," 1826; reprint, *Christian Examiner and Theological Review*, May–June 1827, 248.
48. Finney, *The Memoirs of Charles G. Finney*, 53–54, 61.
49. Finney, *The Memoirs of Charles G. Finney*, 83.
50. Charles Hambrick-Stowe, *Charles G. Finney and the Spirit of American Evangelicalism* (Grand Rapids, MI: Eerdmans, 1996), 39–40.

51. Susan Hayes Ward, *The History of the Broadway Tabernacle Church*, 21.
52. Finney, *The Memoirs of Charles G. Finney*, 354–55; Ward, *The History of the Broadway Tabernacle Church*, 23.
53. William E. Dodge, "The Origin of the Evangelist," *New York Evangelist*, January 8, 1880, 4; Finney, *The Memoirs of Charles G. Finney*, 369 n. 55.
54. Anne Loveland and Otis B. Wheeler, *From Meetinghouse to Megachurch: A Material and Cultural History* (Columbia: University of Missouri Press, 2003), 24.
55. Ward, *The History of the Broadway Tabernacle Church*, 22.
56. Lewis Tappan, "History of the Free Churches in the City of New York," appendix to Andrew Reed and James Matheson, *A Narrative of the Visit to the American Churches by the Deputation from the Congregational Union of England and Wales* (London: Jackson and Walford, 1835), 2: 505.
57. Finney, *The Memoirs of Charles G. Finney*, 296 n. 70.
58. Tappan, "History of the Free Churches in the City of New York," 504–5.
59. Finney, *The Memoirs of Charles G. Finney*, 354.
60. Tappan, "History of the Free Churches in the City of New York," 506; Loveland and Wheeler, *From Meetinghouse to Megachurch*, 24–28. The chapel reportedly held more than 3,000 people during some public events. See "Editorial," *New-Hampshire Statesman and State Journal*, May 25, 1833.
61. Hambrick-Stowe, *Charles G. Finney and the Spirit of American Evangelicalism*, 135.
62. Finney, *The Memoirs of Charles G. Finney*, 357–58.
63. Finney, *The Memoirs of Charles G. Finney*, 359; Kathryn T. Long, "'Turning . . . Piety into Hard Cash': The Marketing of Nineteenth-Century Revivalism," in *God and Mammon: Protestants, Money, and the Market, 1790–1860*, ed. Mark A. Noll (Oxford: Oxford University Press, 2002), 239.
64. The Third Free Church had been established on December 9, 1832. After the third and fourth free churches, conflicts with other ministers and lay leaders over the free pews and the strident abolitionism of many free-church members hampered the Tappans' efforts. The fifth and sixth planned free churches never materialized. When Finney's Broadway Tabernacle was established in 1836, it was designated the Seventh Free Church. See Tappan, "History of the Free Churches in the City of New York," 505–7; Finney, *The Memoirs of Charles G. Finney*, 361 n. 25. On the role of the Broadway Tabernacle in abolitionist and death-penalty debates in the late 1830s and early 1840s, see Stephen John Hartnett, *Executing Democracy*, vol. 2, *Capital Punishment and the Remaking of America, 1835–1843* (East Lansing: Michigan State University Press, 2012), 131–34.
65. Kilde, *When Church Became Theatre*, 34.
66. Kilde, *When Church Became Theatre*, 34–41.
67. Ellen Eslinger, *Citizens of Zion: The Social Origins of Camp Meeting Revivalism* (Knoxville: University of Tennessee Press, 1999), xi.

68. Eslinger, *Citizens of Zion*, xx–xxi.
69. Kilde, *When Church Became Theatre*, 87, 113–15, 197–98.
70. M. Christine Boyer, *The City of Collective Memory: Its Historical Imagery and Architectural Entertainments* (Cambridge, MA: MIT Press, 1994), 74.
71. Kilde, *When Church Became Theatre*, 34.
72. "Anniversary of the American Bible Society," *New-York Spectator*, May 15, 1832; "American Tract Society," *New-York Spectator*, May 9, 1833; "American Education Society," *New-York Spectator*, May 15, 1832; "American Seaman's Friend Society," *New-York Spectator*, May 9, 1833; *New-York Spectator*, October 8, 1832; "American Board of Missions," *Daily National Intelligencer* (Washington, DC), October 15, 1832; "American Sunday School Union," *New-York Spectator*, April 22, 1833; "Sacred Music," *New-York Spectator*, April 29, 1833; "Deaf & Dumb," *New-York Spectator*, May 13, 1833; "Manual Labor Institutions," *Vermont Chronicle*, December 7, 1832; "American Temperance Society," *New-York Spectator*, May 9, 1833; E. Wright Jr., "Letter from Professor Wright," *The Liberator* (Boston, MA), June 29, 1833; "Moral: Rev. J. R. M'Dowell." *The Liberator* (Boston, MA), January 12, 1833, 8.
73. Kilde, *When Church Became Theatre*, 230 n. 52.
74. "Rev. C. G. Finney," *Ohio Observer*, November 27, 1834, col. C. See also Daniel Walker Howe, *What Hath God Wrought: The Transformation of America, 1815–1848* (New York: Oxford University Press, 2007), 174.
75. "Female Anti-Slavery Society of Chatham Street Chapel," *The Emancipator and Journal of Public Morals*, April 15, 1834.
76. "Courier and Enquirer," *The Emancipator and Journal of Public Morals*, July 1, 1834.
77. "Chatham-Street Chapel," *New-York Spectator*, July 10, 1834.
78. "The Fourth of July," *New-York Spectator*, July 7, 1834; "Row at the Chatham Street Chapel," *Providence Patriot, Columbian Phoenix*, July 12, 1834.
79. "Chatham-Street Chapel," *New-York Spectator*, July 10, 1834; Lewis Tappan, "Riot at Chatham-Street Chapel," *The Liberator*, July 12, 1834, 110.
80. "Another Black Riot," *United States' Telegraph*, July 11, 1834; "Another Riot at New-York," *The Liberator*, July 12, 1834, 111; "Riots in New York," *Ohio Observer*, July 24, 1834. Most sources agree that Tappan and his family were absent at the time of the vandalism. See also Tyler Anbinder, *Five Points: The 19th-Century New York City Neighborhood That Invented Tap Dance, Stole Elections, and Became the World's Most Notorious Slum* (New York: Free Press, 2001), 9–10.
81. "Riots and Continued Disturbances of the Peace," *United States' Telegraph*, July 14, 1834.
82. "Rev. C. G. Finne [*sic*]," *New-York Spectator*, July 24, 1834.

83. Finney was apparently so discouraged that he briefly considered giving up preaching and buying the farm where he and his family were staying. See Finney, *The Memoirs of Charles G. Finney*, 372 n. 67.

84. Hambrick-Stowe, *Charles G. Finney and the Spirit of American Evangelicalism*, 150.

85. Kurt W. Ritter, "American Political Rhetoric and the Jeremiad Tradition: Presidential Nomination Acceptance Addresses, 1960–1976," *Central States Speech Journal* 31, no. 3 (1980): 158.

86. Habakkuk 3:2 (AV).

87. Charles Finney, *Lectures on Revivals of Religion*, 6th ed. (New York: Leavitt Lord, 1835), 9.

88. Finney, *Lectures on Revivals of Religion*, 12.

89. Finney, *Lectures on Revivals of Religion*, 23.

90. See Edwin S. Gaustad, *The Great Awakening in New England* (New York: Harper, 1957), 48.

91. There are some signs here of the perfectionist doctrines that Finney took up a few years later. See Finney, *Lectures on Revivals of Religion*, 10.

92. Finney, *Lectures on Revivals of Religion*, 57–59, 93.

93. Aristotle, *On Rhetoric: A Theory of Civic Discourse*, trans. George A. Kennedy (New York: Oxford University Press, 1991), 1378a, 121.

94. Finney, *Lectures on Revivals of Religion*, 253.

95. Finney, *Lectures on Revivals of Religion*, 11.

96. Finney, *Lectures on Revivals of Religion*, 109, 133, 158, 418.

97. Finney, *Lectures on Revivals of Religion*, 24, 57, 74.

98. Finney, *Lectures on Revivals of Religion*, 23–24, 240–41, 301.

99. "Three Chapters on Religion: Chapter II: Class of the Fundamentalists," *Catholic Telegraph*, May 7, 1842, 145.

100. "Three Chapters on Religion: Introduction, Chapter I: Class of Indifference," *Catholic Telegraph*, April 30, 1842, 137.

101. Finney, *Lectures on Revivals of Religion*, 12–13, 16, 18, 26, 98.

102. Finney, *Lectures on Revivals of Religion*, 15, 23, 275.

103. Finney, *Lectures on Revivals of Religion*, 274.

104. Finney, *Lectures on Revivals of Religion*, 138.

105. See James H. Moorhead, "Apocalypticism in Mainstream Protestantism, 1800 to Present," in *The Encyclopedia of Apocalypticism*, vol. 3, *Apocalypticism in the Modern Period and the Contemporary Age*, ed. Stephen J. Stein (New York: Continuum, 2001), 73–76.

106. Finney, *The Memoirs of Charles G. Finney*, 373 n. 71.

107. See Richard Carwardine, *Evangelicals and Politics in Antebellum America* (New Haven, CT: Yale University Press, 1993), 294.
108. Robert Baird, *Religion in America: or an Account of the Origin, Relation to the State, and Present Condition of the Evangelical Churches in the United States: With Notices of the Unevangelical Denominations* (New York: Harper & Brothers, 1844), 267. See also Carwardine, *Evangelicals and Politics in Antebellum America*, 2–5.
109. Baird, *Religion in America*, 202, 214. Baird specifically names Catholics, Unitarians, and Universalists as heretical Christian communities.

Chapter Three. Countersymbols and Confederacy

1. See W. B. Riley, "The World Premillennial Conference vs. the Coming Confederacy," *School and Church*, January–March 1919, 92–93.
2. "Report of World Conference on the Fundamentals of the Faith," *School and Church*, July-September 1919, 170; W. B. Riley, "The Christian Fundamentals Movement, Its Battles, Its Achievements, Its Certain Victory," *Christian Fundamentals in School and Church*, October-December 1922, 4–14; William Vance Trollinger Jr., *God's Empire: William Bell Riley and Midwestern Fundamentalism* (Madison: University of Wisconsin Press, 1990), 55.
3. See W. B. Riley, *The Menace of Modernism* (New York: Christian Alliance, 1917); J. Gresham Machen, *Christianity and Liberalism* (1923; reprint, Grand Rapids, MI: Wm. B. Eerdmans, 1983), 2.
4. Nancy D. Wadsworth, "Ambivalent Miracles: The Possibilities and Limits of Evangelical Racial Reconciliation Politics," in *Faith and Race in American Political Life*, ed. Robin Dale Jacobsen and Nancy D. Wadsworth (Charlottesville: University of Virginia Press, 2012), 253.
5. See George C. Rable, *God's Almost Chosen Peoples: A Religious History of the American Civil War* (Chapel Hill: University of North Carolina Press, 2010), 122–26, 134–35.
6. Rable, *God's Almost Chosen Peoples*, 244, 246.
7. Molly Oshatz, *Slavery and Sin: The Fight against Slavery and the Rise of Liberal Protestantism* (New York: Oxford University Press, 2012), 4.
8. See Ferenc Morton Szasz, *The Divided Mind of Protestant America, 1880–1930* (Tuscaloosa: University of Alabama Press, 1982), 19–20.
9. See Szasz, *The Divided Mind of Protestant America*, 11–13; John R. Commons, "The Churches and Political Reforms," in *Christianity Practically Applied: The Discussions of the International Christian Conference* (New York: Baker and Taylor, 1894), 214.

10. Josiah Strong, *Our Country: Its Possible Future and Its Present Crisis* (New York: Baker and Taylor, 1891), 248; Quoted in "Supplement" in John R. Mott, *The Evangelization of the World in This Generation* (New York: Student Volunteer Movement for Foreign Missions, 1901), 217. See also George W. Northrup, "Address of the President," in *American Baptist Missionary Union: Seventy-Seventh Annual Report with the Proceedings of the Annual Meeting Held in Cincinnati, Ohio* (Boston: Missionary Rooms, 1891), 7.
11. Strong, *Our Country*, 45.
12. Matthew Frye Jacobson, *Barbarian Virtues: The United States Encounters Foreign Peoples at Home and Abroad, 1876–1917* (New York: Hill and Wang, 2000), 67–73.
13. Strong, *Our Country*, 56.
14. Charles Finney, *Lectures on Revivals of Religion*, 6th ed. (New York: Leavitt Lord, 1835), 293.
15. Austin Phelps, "Introduction," in Josiah Strong, *Our Country: Its Possible Future and Its Present Crisis* (New York: Baker and Taylor, 1891), 14.
16. Although the concept that colonists to America were a called and chosen people extends back at least as far as John Winthrop's 1630 sermon "A Model of Christian Charity," the "American dream" would be most famously named in James Truslow Adams's 1931 work *The Epic of America*.
17. According to Szasz, by 1906, New York had 112 institutional churches, Chicago had approximately twenty-five, and other big cities had at least one. See Szasz, *The Divided Mind of Protestant America*, 49–50.
18. "Institutional Churches," in *The New Encyclopedia of Social Reform*, ed. William D. P. Bliss, Rudolph M. Binder, and Edward Page Gaston (London: Funk and Wagnalls, 1909), 629. The pastor quoted is Charles Albert Dickinson, pastor of the Berkeley Temple in Boston, Massachusetts.
19. See Lyle Schaller, *The Seven-Day-a-Week Church* (Nashville, TN: Abingdon Press, 1992).
20. Walter Rauschenbusch, *A Theology for the Social Gospel* (New York: Macmillan Co., 1922), 165–66.
21. Strong, *Our Country*, 92.
22. See Martin E. Marty, *Modern American Religion*, vol. 1, *The Irony of It All, 1893–1919* (Chicago: University of Chicago Press, 1986), 164, 273.
23. Robert A. Schneider, "Voice of Many Waters: Church Federation in the Twentieth Century," in *Between the Times: The Travail of the Protestant Establishment in America, 1900–1960*, ed. William R. Hutchison (Cambridge: Cambridge University Press, 1989), 95.
24. See Harry F. Ward, *The Social Creed of the Churches* (New York: Abingdon Press, 1914); Charles S. McFarland, "The Social Program of the Federal Council of the Churches of Christ in America," *Proceedings of the Academy of Political Science*

in the City of New York 2 (1912): 175; Worth Tippy, "Social Work of the Federal Council of Churches," *Journal of Social Forces* 1 (1922): 36–38.

25. See William R. Hutchison, "Protestantism as Establishment," in *Between the Times: The Travail of the Protestant Establishment in America, 1900–1960*, ed. William R. Hutchison (Cambridge: Cambridge University Press, 1989), 5; John F. Piper, "The American Churches in World War I," *Journal of the American Academy of Religion* 38 (1970): 147–55.
26. On Rockefeller's role in the Interchurch World Movement, see Charles E. Harvey, "John D. Rockefeller, Jr. and the Interchurch World Movement of 1919–1920: A Different Angle on the Ecumenical Movement," *Church History* 51 (1982): 198–209.
27. Szasz, *The Divided Mind of Protestant America*, 89.
28. "Southern Presbyterians and the Interchurch Movement," *Herald and Presbyter* 91 (1920): 4–5.
29. See W. B. Riley, "The Great Divide or Christ and the Present Crisis," *School and Church*, July–September 1919, 190.
30. Machen, *Christianity and Liberalism*, 171.
31. Doris A. Graber, *Verbal Behavior and Politics* (Urbana: University of Illinois Press, 1976), 289.
32. J. G. A. Pocock, *Politics, Language, and Time: Essays on Political Thought and History* (Chicago: University of Chicago Press, 1989), 280.
33. David Zarefsky, *President Johnson's War on Poverty: Rhetoric and History* (Tuscaloosa: University of Alabama Press, 1986), 10–11.
34. See David Zarefsky, "Rhetorical Interpretations of the American Civil War," *Quarterly Journal of Speech* 81 (1995): 108.
35. Paul J. Achter, "TV, Technology, and McCarthyism: Crafting the Democratic Renaissance in an Age of Fear," *Quarterly Journal of Speech* 90 (2004): 314–15. On the association of condensation symbols and synecdoche, see, for example, Martín Carcasson, "Ending Welfare as We Know It: President Clinton and the Rhetorical Transformation of the Anti-Welfare Culture," *Rhetoric and Public Affairs* 9 (2007): 658.
36. Christian Lundberg, "Enjoying God's Death: *The Passion of the Christ* and the Practices of an Evangelical Public," *Quarterly Journal of Speech* 95 (2009): 389. See also Christian Lundberg, *Lacan in Public: Psychoanalysis and the Science of Rhetoric* (Tuscaloosa: University of Alabama Press, 2012), 27–29.
37. Joshua Gunn, "Maranatha," *Quarterly Journal of Speech* 98 (2012): 374.
38. Michael Calvin McGee, "The 'Ideograph': A Link between Rhetoric and Ideology," *Quarterly Journal of Speech* 66 (1980): 1–16.
39. McGee, "The 'Ideograph,'" 8. In this passage, McGee is engaging with José Ortega y Gasset, *Man and People*, trans. William R. Trask (New York: Norton, 1957).
40. McGee, "The 'Ideograph,'" 15.

41. See, for example, Trevor Parry-Giles, "Ideology and Poetics in Public Issue Construction: Thatcherism, Civil Liberties, and 'Terrorism' in Northern Ireland," *Communication Quarterly* 43 (1995): 182–96; Carol Winkler, *In the Name of Terrorism: Presidents on Political Violence in the Post–World War II Era* (Albany: State University of New York Press, 2006), 95; Richard Jackson, Marie Breen Smith, and Jeroen Gunning, "Critical Terrorism Studies: Framing a New Research Agenda," in *Critical Terrorism Studies: A New Research Agenda* (New York: Routledge, 2009), 228; Eric Connelly, "State Secrets and Redaction: The Interaction between Silence and Ideographs," *Western Journal of Communication* 76 (2012): 236–49.
42. See McGee, "The 'Ideograph,'" 15.
43. Michael Warner, *Publics and Counterpublics* (New York: Zone Books, 2002), 56.
44. This is not, of course, to imply that resistant communities cannot become hegemonic and create their own ideologies (and ideographs). Indeed, American Fundamentalism, as considered in this study, might be considered an excellent example of this movement from resistant to hegemonic discourses.
45. I have in mind W. J. T. Mitchell's description of landscape as a "cultural medium" that both naturalizes contingent social constructions and interpellates its audience into a determinate relationship with this naturalized social world. See W. J. T. Mitchell, "Introduction," in *Landscape and Power*, ed. W. J. T. Mitchell (Chicago: University of Chicago Press, 2002), 2.
46. Leland M. Griffin, "The Rhetoric of Historical Movements," *Quarterly Journal of Speech* 38 (1952): 186.
47. Leland M. Griffin, "A Dramatistic Theory of the Rhetoric of Movements," in *Landmark Essays on Kenneth Burke*, ed. Barry Brummett (Davis, CA: Hermagoras Press, 1993), 207. See also Kenneth Burke, *Language as Symbolic Action: Essays on Life, Literature, and Method* (Berkeley: University of California Press, 1966), 9–13, 16.
48. Reprinted in "Appendix A: The 1878 Niagara Creed," in David O. Beale, *In Pursuit of Purity: American Fundamentalism since 1850* (Greenville, SC: Unusual Publications, 1986), 375–79. On the influence of the Creed, see Beale, *In Pursuit of Purity*, 24–25.
49. Henry George Liddell and Robert Scott, *A Greek-English Lexicon* (Oxford: Clarendon Press, 1996), 218–19. Stephen Wilson provides a representative list of additional Greek sources in which apostasy is used as the term for political revolt or rebellion. See Stephen G. Wilson, *Leaving the Fold: Apostates and Defectors in Antiquity* (Minneapolis: Fortress Press, 2004), 14 n. 10.
50. Wilson, *Leaving the Fold*, 3.
51. John M. G. Barclay, "Paul among Diaspora Jews: Anomaly or Apostate?," *Journal for the Study of the New Testament* 60 (1995): 111–12.
52. Wilson, *Leaving the Fold*, 12.

53. H. G. Kippenberg, "Apostasy," *Encyclopedia of Religion* (Detroit: Thompson Gale, 2005), 432. On the corruption of common language as a key element in the critique of apostasy, see Giorgio Agamben's discussion of Irenaeus's treatise *Against Heresies*; Giorgio Agamben, *The Kingdom and the Glory: For a Theological Genealogy of Economy and Government* (Stanford, CA: Stanford University Press, 2011), 31–34.
54. Irenaeus, "Selections from the Work against Heresies," in *Early Christian Fathers*, ed. Cyril C. Richardson (Philadelphia: Westminster Press, 1953), 368.
55. Robert N. Bellah, "Civil Religion in America," *Daedalus* 96 (1967): 14.
56. Michael J. Lee, "The Conservative Canon and Its Uses," *Rhetoric and Public Affairs* 15 (2012): 12.
57. C. I. Scofield, *The Scofield Reference Bible* (New York: Oxford University Press, 1909), 1280 n. 1. Scofield also distinguishes apostasy from other forms of non-orthodox belief or behavior, in a way that Irenaeus does not: "Apostasy differs therefore from error concerning truth, which may be the result of ignorance (Acts xix. 1–6), or heresy, which may be due to the snare of Satan (2 Tim. ii. 25, 26), both of which may consist with true faith" (1280–81 n. 1).
58. Scofield, *The Scofield Reference Bible*, 969 n. 1, 970–71 n. 2.
59. George M. Marsden, *Fundamentalism and American Culture*, 2nd ed. (New York: Oxford University Press, 2006), 118–19; Richard W. Flory, "The Fundamentals," in *Encyclopedia of Fundamentalism*, ed. Brenda E. Brasher (New York: Routledge, 2001), 186.
60. Philip Mauro, "Modern Philosophy," in *The Fundamentals* (Chicago: Testimony Publishing, 1910–15), 2: 86, 100.
61. See Harriet A. Harris, *Fundamentalism and Evangelicals* (Oxford: Clarendon Press, 1998), 27–28; Marsden, *Fundamentalism and American Culture*, 118–19; Ernest R. Sandeen, *The Roots of Fundamentalism: British and American Millenarianism, 1800–1930* (Chicago: University of Chicago Press, 1970), 206–7.
62. Seven denominations—whose members are sometimes referred to as "established" or, later, "mainline" churches—dominated the Protestant landscape in the first part of the twentieth century. These were: Congregationalists, Episcopalians, Presbyterians, Methodists, (Northern) Baptists, Disciples of Christ, and United Lutherans. Generally speaking, this list refers only to the white branches of these denominations. See Hutchison, "Protestantism as Establishment," 4.
63. Riley, "The World Premillennial Conference," 91. See also Szasz, *The Divided Mind of Protestant America*, 89.
64. See Herbert Booth, *The Christian Confederacy* (Chicago: Goodspeed Press, 1915), 10; Riley, *The Menace of Modernism*, 156.
65. Riley, "The World Premillennial Conference," 92.
66. Riley, "The World Premillennial Conference," 94.
67. Riley, "The World Premillennial Conference," 95.

68. Riley, "The World Premillennial Conference," 95.
69. "Report of World Conference on the Fundamentals of the Faith," 176.
70. *Polyptoton* is the ancient figure in which the root of a word migrates into different parts of speech, often in the same text. See Jeanne Fahnestock, *Rhetorical Figures in Science* (New York: Oxford University Press, 1999), 170–71; Jeanne Fahnestock, *Rhetorical Style: The Uses of Language in Persuasion* (New York: Oxford University Press, 2011), 131.
71. See Maurice Charland, "Constitutive Rhetoric: The Case of the *Peuple Québécois*," *Quarterly Journal of Speech* 73 (1987): 134, 138.
72. Riley, "The Great Divide or Christ and the Present Crisis," 183–84.
73. Riley, "The Great Divide," 186.
74. 1 Cor. 1:27 (AV).
75. W. B. Riley, "The Gospel for War Times," in *Light on Prophecy: A Coordinated, Constructive Teaching, Being the Proceedings and Addresses at the Philadelphia Prophetic Conference, May 28–30* (New York: Christian Herald, 1918), 332–33, 337.
76. Riley, "The Great Divide or Christ and the Present Crisis," 187.
77. Riley, "The Great Divide," 190.
78. Riley, "The Great Divide," 184.
79. Phaedra C. Pezzullo, "Resisting 'National Breast Cancer Awareness Month': The Rhetoric of Counterpublics and Their Cultural Performances," *Quarterly Journal of Speech* 89 (2003): 347.
80. W. S. Bradshaw, "The Inter-Church World Movement," *School and Church*, January–March 1920, 289.
81. Trollinger, *God's Empire*, 115.
82. See James H. Madison, "Reformers and the Rural Church, 1900–1950," *Journal of American History* 73 (1986): 646–47; Trollinger, *God's Empire*, 114–17.
83. Bradshaw, "The Inter-Church World Movement," 290.
84. See "The Institutional Church," *Christian Fundamentals in School and Church*, January-March 1921, 36; Bradshaw, "The Inter-Church World Movement," 288.
85. See "From Baptist Temple News We Reprint the Virginia Declaration," *School and Church*, April-June 1920, 329–30. On the Northern Baptists' "New World Movement," see also Robert A. Ashworth, "The Fundamentalist Movement among the Baptists," *Journal of Religion* 4 (1924): 611–31.
86. W. B. Riley, "Dr. W. B. Riley Endorses the Fort Wayne Gospel Temple, Its Pastor, and Tabernacle Movement," *Fort Wayne Gospel Temple*, May 24, 1940, 1, 3.
87. W. B. Riley, "The Conflict of Christianity and Its Counterfeit," *Christian Fundamentals in School and Church*, July-September 1921, 10.
88. Kristy Maddux, *The Faithful Citizen: Popular Christian Media and Gendered Civic Identities* (Waco, TX: Baylor University Press, 2010), 17.

89. Markku Ruotsila, *Origins of Christian Anti-Internationalism: Conservative Evangelicals and the League of Nations* (Washington, DC: Georgetown University Press, 2008), 3.
90. Ruotsila, *Origins of Christian Anti-Internationalism*, 39–40. See also Mark Matthews, "The Doctrine of Our Lord's Return," in *Light on Prophecy: A Coordinated, Constructive Teaching, Being the Proceedings and Addresses at the Philadelphia Prophetic Conference, May 28–30* (New York: Christian Herald, 1918), 71–72.
91. W. B. Riley, "The Interchurch World Movement," *School and Church*, April-June 1920, 320. On the mid-twentieth-century Fundamentalist practice of staging mock debates with outsiders, see Joel Carpenter, *Revive Us Again: The Reawakening of American Fundamentalism* (New York: Oxford University Press, 1997), 64.

Chapter Four. The Superchurch Revealed

1. See Robert C. Fuller, *Naming the Antichrist: The History of an American Obsession* (New York: Oxford University Press, 1995), 132–33.
2. James Darsey, *The Prophetic Tradition and Radical Rhetoric in America* (New York: New York University Press, 1997), 114–15.
3. Darsey, *The Prophetic Tradition and Radical Rhetoric in America*, 118.
4. Martin Buber, "The Two Foci of the Jewish Soul," in *The Writings of Martin Buber*, ed. Will Herberg (New York: Meridian Books, 1956), 273.
5. Martin Buber, "Prophecy, Apocalyptic, and the Historical Hour," in *Pointing the Way: Collected Essays*, ed. and trans. Maurice Friedman (New York: Harper, 1963), 202–3.
6. See Barry Brummett, *Contemporary Apocalyptic Rhetoric* (New York: Praeger, 1991), 37–38.
7. On fiction recreating and structuring action, see Paul Ricoeur, "Imagination in Discourse and Action," in *Rethinking Imagination: Culture and Creativity*, ed. Gillian Robinson and John Rundell (London: Routledge, 1994), 125.
8. Stephen O'Leary, *Arguing the Apocalypse: A Theory of Millennial Rhetoric* (New York: Oxford University Press, 1994), 14, 20, 42, 57–58. In part this is a historical problem for O'Leary, whose reading strategy—which bridges two cases separated by nearly 130 years—leads him to view as philosophically similar apocalyptic narratives that have very different ideological sources and political influences.
9. Sharon Crowley, *Toward a Civil Discourse: Rhetoric and Fundamentalism* (Pittsburgh, PA: University of Pittsburgh Press, 2006), 5.
10. See, for example, Stephen O'Leary and Michael McFarland, "The Political Use of Mythic Discourse: Prophetic Interpretation in Pat Robertson's Presidential Campaign," *Quarterly Journal of Speech* 75, no. 4 (1989): 433–52; Nancy Ammerman,

"North American Protestant Fundamentalism," in *Fundamentalisms Observed*, ed. Martin E. Marty and R. Scott Appleby (Chicago: University of Chicago Press, 1991), 47; Didi Herman, *The Antigay Agenda: Orthodox Vision and the Christian Right* (Chicago: University of Chicago Press, 1997), 188–89; Angela M. Lahr, *Millennial Dreams and Apocalyptic Nightmares: The Cold War Origins of Political Evangelicalism* (New York: Oxford University Press, 2007), 11–12, 15, 39–40; Cynthia Burack, *Sin, Sex, and Democracy: Antigay Rhetoric and the Christian Right* (Albany: State University of New York Press, 2008), 20–22. In contrast, see Tom D. Daniels, Richard J. Jensen, and Allen Lichtenstein, "Resolving the Paradox in Politicized Christian Fundamentalism," *Western Journal of Speech Communication* 49 (1985): 262.

11. Crawford Gribben, *Writing the Rapture: Prophecy Fiction in Evangelical America* (New York: Oxford University Press, 2009).
12. Crowley argues that apocalyptic teachers are deliberately manipulating their apocalyptic narratives in order to legitimize Fundamentalist action. Following Susan Harding, she argues that authors like Lindsey and LaHaye, beginning in the 1980s, changed their theological writings to justify Fundamentalist activism, an analysis that is, at best, simplistic. By linking Fundamentalist politics to the ideological manipulations of a few powerful figures within the conservative Christian community, Crowley depicts apocalyptic believers as dangerously irrational and unthinking readers who blindly follow their leaders' manipulations. See Crowley, *Toward a Civil Discourse*, 111–12; Susan Friend Harding, *The Book of Jerry Falwell: Fundamentalist Language and Politics* (Princeton, NJ: Princeton University Press, 2000), 241–45.
13. Crowley, *Toward a Civil Discourse*, 6.
14. See Robert Glenn Howard, *Digital Jesus: The Making of a New Christian Fundamentalist Community on the Internet* (New York: New York University Press, 2011).
15. Darsey, *The Prophetic Tradition and Radical Rhetoric in America*, 118.
16. David L. Barr, "The Apocalypse of John as Oral Enactment," *Interpretation* 40 (1986): 243–56.
17. See O'Leary, *Arguing the Apocalypse*, 77–78.
18. Paul Ricoeur, *Time and Narrative*, trans. Kathleen McLaughlin and David Pellauer (Chicago: University of Chicago Press, 1984), 1:46.
19. Ammerman, "North American Protestant Fundamentalism," 6.
20. In some versions of these narratives, the "beast" and the "Antichrist" are different names for the same figure, while in other versions, they are different entities, working, for the most part, toward the same goal.
21. Jeanne Halgren Kilde, "How Did *Left Behind*'s Particular Vision of the End Times Develop? A Historical Look at Millenarian Thought," in *Rapture, Revelation, and*

the End Times: Exploring the Left Behind *Series*, ed. Bruce David Forbes and Jeanne Halgren Kilde (New York: Palgrave Macmillan, 2004), 52–53.

22. Randall Balmer, *Mine Eyes Have Seen the Glory: A Journey into the Evangelical Subculture in America*, 4th ed. (New York: Oxford University Press, 2006), 36.
23. Kilde, "How Did *Left Behind*'s Particular Vision of the End Times Develop?," 53–54.
24. See David O. Beale, *In Pursuit of Purity: American Fundamentalism since 1850* (Greenville, SC: Unusual Publications, 1986), 38.
25. Gribben, *Writing the Rapture*, 8.
26. Gribben, *Writing the Rapture*, 9.
27. Hal Lindsey and C. C. Carlson, *The Late Great Planet Earth* (Grand Rapids, MI: Zondervan, 1970), 42, 50–56.
28. See *Working Together through the National Council of Churches* (New York: National Council of Churches, 1957), 4–5; J. Elwin Wright, "The Federal Council Prepares the Way for Coming World Church," *United Evangelical Action*, March 1943; "Presbyterians Reject Federal Council Mission Membership," *United Evangelical Action*, July 1, 1943.
29. Oswald J. Smith, "Ecclesiastical Babylon," editorial, *United Evangelical Action*, June 15, 1947, 2.
30. James DeForest Murch, "Why Evangelicals Cannot Co-operate in the FCCCA," *United Evangelical Action*, September 15, 1946, 5–7.
31. See George M. Marsden, *Understanding Fundamentalism and Evangelicalism* (Grand Rapids, MI: Eerdmans, 1991), 71.
32. Carl McIntire, *Modern Tower of Babel* (Collingswood, NJ: Christian Beacon Press, 1949), xiii, 276.
33. James DeForest Murch, *The Growing Super-Church: A Critique of the National Council of Churches* (N.p.: National Association of Evangelicals, 1952), 33, 55, 67, 72.
34. A. L. Lindholm, *The Truth about Roman Catholicism and the Coming Man-Made, One-World Super-Church* (San Fernando, CA: The Gospel Truth, 1967), 75, 78.
35. G. Russell Evans, *Apathy, Apostasy and Apostles: A Study of the History and Activities of the National Council of Churches of Christ in the U.S.A. with Sidelights on Its Ally, the World Council of Churches* (New York: Vantage Press, 1973), 94.
36. H. Norton Mason, *The National Council of Churches of Christ in the U.S.A.: An Appraisal of Its Origin and Present Direction* (Victoria, TX: Foundation for Christian Theology, 1967), 27.
37. See Allan J. Lichtman, *White Protestant Nation: The Rise of the American Conservative Movement* (New York: Atlantic Monthly Press, 2008), 150.
38. Quoted in "Federal Council Hit by Fundamentalists," *New York Times*, October 31, 1948, 70.
39. McIntire, *Modern Tower of Babel*, v.

40. McIntire, *Modern Tower of Babel*, 102.

41. Billy James Hargis, *The National Council of Churches Indicts Itself on 50 Counts of Treason to God and Country!* (Tulsa, OK: Christian Crusade, 1964), 32. See also Billy James Hargis, *The Facts about Communism and Our Churches* (Tulsa, OK: Christian Crusade, 1962), 51–52, 152.

42. *How Red Is the National Council of Churches?* (Pittsburgh, PA: Laymen's Commission of the American Council of Christian Churches, 1966).

43. "For the Defense," *Time* magazine, July 14, 1961, 38.

44. See Hargis, *The National Council of Churches Indicts Itself*, 31. In ascribing responsibility for Pearl Harbor, Hargis identifies the National Council as a direct continuation of the Federal Council that existed in 1941.

45. Billy James Hargis and Bill Sampson, *The Cross and the Sickle . . . Superchurch* (Tulsa, OK: Crusader Books, 1982), 1.

46. McIntire, *Modern Tower of Babel*, v.

47. James DeForest Murch, "The Spirit of the Antichrist," *United Evangelical Action*, December 1, 1945, 12.

48. Lindsey and Carlson, *The Late Great Planet Earth*, 130–32.

49. Heather Hendershot, *Shaking the World for Jesus: Media and Conservative Evangelical Culture* (Chicago: University of Chicago Press, 2004), 184, 188.

50. See Glenn W. Shuck, *Marks of the Beast: The Left Behind Novels and the Struggle for Evangelical Identity* (New York: New York University Press, 2005), 6–7.

51. Because of the venues in which it was shown, precise viewership numbers are impossible, but as Randall Balmer reported in 1989, executive producer Russell Doughten estimated that the film had been seen by approximately one hundred million people, a figure that did not account for multiple viewings. As Balmer says, "Even if you slash that number in half to account for hyperbole, fifty million is still a staggering figure, a viewership that would be the envy of many Hollywood producers." See Balmer, *Mine Eyes Have Seen the Glory*, 62.

52. Balmer, *Mine Eyes Have Seen the Glory*, 64.

53. Hendershot, *Shaking the World for Jesus*, 187.

54. Marilyn Manson and Neil Strauss, *The Long Hard Road out of Hell* (New York: ReganBooks, 1998), 19.

55. Amy Johnson Frykholm, *Rapture Culture:* Left Behind *in Evangelical America* (New York: Oxford University Press, 2004), 4–5. In his book on prophecy fiction, Crawford Gribben also recalls seeing the film as a teenager, although he merely notes it as a commonly shared memory among his family members. See Gribben, *Writing the Rapture*, ix.

56. Hendershot, *Shaking the World for Jesus*, 187–88.

57. Paraphrasing Mark 13:36 (New Living Translation).

58. The passage describing the beast and the mark comes from Revelation 13:11–18.

59. *A Thief in the Night*, dir. Donald W. Thompson (Des Moines, IA: Mark IV Pictures, 1972).

60. *A Distant Thunder*, dir. Donald W. Thompson (Des Moines, IA: Mark IV Pictures, 1977).

61. Christian O. Lundberg, "Evangelical Economies of Violence and the Politics of Imaginary Publics," PhD diss., Northwestern University, 2006, 343.

62. *Image of the Beast*, dir. Donald W. Thompson (Des Moines, IA: Mark IV Pictures, 1981).

63. *The Prodigal Planet*, dir. Donald W. Thompson (Des Moines, IA: Mark IV Pictures, 1983). The passage is from Matthew 7:25 (New International Version).

64. See Hargis, *The Facts About Communism and Our Churches*, 117–18; Lahr, *Millennial Dreams and Apocalyptic Nightmares*, 44–45.

65. *Working Together Through the National Council of Churches* (New York: National Council of Churches, 1957), 5. In one copy of the photograph, one older man stares directly at the camera, as though daring viewers to disrupt the proceedings, while all the rest look away. See Nathan H. VanderWerf, *The Times Were Very Full: A Perspective on the First 25 Years of the National Council of the Churches of Christ in the United States of America, 1950–1975* (New York: National Council of the Churches of Christ in the United States of America, 1976), 19.

66. Verne P. Kaub, "Super-Church Is Born," *United Evangelical Action*, January 1, 1951, 3–4, 6, 8. This article features a copy of the photograph, although the bottom half of the image is cut off just below the crossbeam of the table/cross, which is thus only identifiable as a cross through Kaub's description.

67. Robert S. Ellwood, *1950: Crossroads of American Religious Life* (Louisville, KY: Westminster John Knox Press, 2000), 186.

68. Cf. Matthew 3:3.

69. Amy Johnson Frykholm, "What Social and Political Messages Appear in the *Left Behind* Books? A Literary Discussion of Millenarian Fiction," in *Rapture, Revelation, and the End Times: Exploring the* Left Behind *Series*, ed. Bruce David Forbes and Jeanne Halgren Kilde (New York: Palgrave Macmillan, 2004): 176.

70. Quentin J. Schultze, *Christianity and the Mass Media in America: Toward a Democratic Accommodation* (East Lansing: Michigan State University Press, 2003), 1–2, 10–16.

71. *The Omega Code*, dir. Robert Marcarelli (Providence Entertainment, 1999).

72. See Howard, *Digital Jesus*, 49.

73. Gribben, *Writing the Rapture*, 162.

74. Melani McAlister, "Prophecy, Politics and the Popular: The *Left Behind* Series and Christian Fundamentalism's New World Order," *South Atlantic Quarterly* 102 (2003): 782.

75. Robert Hariman, "Allegory and Democratic Public Culture in the Postmodern Era," *Philosophy and Rhetoric* 35 (2002): 289.

76. On the declining leadership roles offered to women in mid-century Fundamentalism, see Joel Carpenter, *Revive Us Again: The Reawakening of American Fundamentalism* (New York: Oxford University Press, 1997), 68.
77. Kristy Maddux, *The Faithful Citizen: Popular Christian Media and Gendered Civic Identities* (Waco, TX: Baylor University Press, 2010), 116.
78. Gribben, *Writing the Rapture*, 162–64.

Chapter Five. The Superchurch Reimagined

1. Referenced in R. Stephen Warner, "Theoretical Barriers to the Understanding of Evangelical Christianity," *Sociological Analysis* 40 (1979): 2–3.
2. See Lyman A. Kellstedt, John C. Green, James L. Guth, and Corwin E. Smidt, "Religious Voting Blocs in the 1992 Election: The Year of the Evangelical?," *Sociology of Religion* 55 (1994): 309 n. 1.
3. Susan Friend Harding, *The Book of Jerry Falwell: Fundamentalist Language and Politics* (Princeton, NJ: Princeton University Press, 2000), 19–20.
4. Harding, *The Book of Jerry Falwell*, 20.
5. The first service was held in the Mountain View Elementary School, where Jerry Falwell had been a student, and they moved to the bottling plant soon after. See Ruth McClellan, *An Incredible Journey: Thomas Road Baptist Church and 50 Years of Miracles* (Lynchburg, VA: Liberty University, 2006), 24–25; Jonathan Falwell, *InnovateChurch* (Nashville, TN: B&H Books, 2008), 265–66.
6. McClellan, *An Incredible Journey*, 40.
7. McClellan, *An Incredible Journey*, 98, 108.
8. The school was renamed Liberty Christian Academy in 2005. See McClellan, *An Incredible Journey*, 54.
9. McClellan, *An Incredible Journey*, 56–57.
10. Jerry Falwell and Elmer Towns, *Church Aflame* (Nashville, TN: Impact Books, 1971), 15.
11. Elmer Towns and Jerry Falwell, *Capturing a Town for Christ* (Old Tappan, NJ: Fleming H. Revell, 1973), 87.
12. Towns and Falwell, *Capturing a Town for Christ*, 98–99.
13. Towns and Falwell, *Capturing a Town for Christ*, 40.
14. Towns and Falwell, *Capturing a Town for Christ*, 41.
15. McClellan, *An Incredible Journey*, 22.
16. Jerry Falwell, "The Church at Antioch," in *Capturing a Town for Christ*, by Elmer Towns and Jerry Falwell (Old Tappan, NJ: Fleming H. Revell, 1973), 113.

17. George M. Marsden, *Understanding Fundamentalism and Evangelicalism* (Grand Rapids, MI: Eerdmans, 1991), 76.
18. A number of Fundamentalist and evangelical groups developed during the late 1970s, including the National Christian Action Council, the Religious Roundtable, and the Christian Voice; but of these, Falwell's Moral Majority became the most prominent and influential. See Matthew Moen, *The Transformation of the Christian Right* (Tuscaloosa: University of Alabama Press, 1992), 16–19, 26; Robert C. Liebman, "Mobilizing the Moral Majority," in *The New Christian Right: Mobilization and Legitimation*, ed. Robert C. Liebman and Robert Wuthnow (New York: Aldine Publishing Company, 1983), 49–50.
19. See Harriet A. Harris, *Fundamentalism and Evangelicals* (Oxford: Clarendon Press, 1998), 39.
20. Falwell, "The Church at Antioch," 112.
21. Falwell, "The Church at Antioch," 124.
22. See William Bell Riley, *The Evolution of the Kingdom* (New York: Chas. C. Cook, 1913), 19–20.
23. Falwell, "The Church at Antioch," 113.
24. Falwell, "The Church at Antioch," 119–20.
25. Donald McGavran, *The Bridges of God: A Study in the Strategy of Missions* (New York: Friendship Press, 1955), 2–3, 10, 15.
26. Gary L. McIntosh, "Introduction: Why Church Growth Can't Be Ignored," in *Evaluating the Church Growth Movement*, ed. Gary L. McIntosh (Grand Rapids, MI: Zondervan, 2004), 16.
27. *Church Growth Bulletin*, November 1968, 45.
28. McIntosh, "Introduction," 24.
29. Elmer L. Towns, *The Ten Largest Sunday Schools and What Makes Them Grow* (Grand Rapids, MI: Baker Book House, 1969), 99. Most of the churches had been established in the late nineteenth century or during the 1930s–1940s, although, as was the case with First Baptist of Hammond, for example, many had not experienced their growth spurts until much later.
30. Falwell, "The Church at Antioch," 113.
31. Donald E. Miller, *Reinventing American Protestantism* (Berkeley: University of California Press, 1999), 46.
32. Billy James Hargis, *The National Council of Churches Indicts Itself on 50 Counts of Treason to God and Country!* (Tulsa, OK: Christian Crusade, 1964), 3–4.
33. *Church Growth Bulletin*, May 1966, 4.
34. See Lesslie Newbigin, in *Church Growth Bulletin*, September 1966, 10; *Church Growth Bulletin*, January 1968, 2–3; Ralph D. Winter, "Polygamy: Rules and Practices," *Church Growth Bulletin*, March 1969, 63.

35. Bob Jones, *All Fullness Dwells* (Greenville, SC: Bob Jones University Press, 1942), 116.
36. Falwell, "The Church at Antioch," 120.
37. Joel Carpenter, *Revive Us Again: The Reawakening of American Fundamentalism* (Oxford: Oxford University Press, 1997), 64.
38. See Heather Hendershot, *Shaking the World for Jesus: Media and Conservative Evangelical Culture* (Chicago: University of Chicago Press, 2004), 50.
39. Allan J. Lichtman, *White Protestant Nation: The Rise of the American Conservative Movement* (New York: Atlantic Monthly Press, 2008), 28. In 1926, when the National Broadcasting Corporation (NBC) became the first radio network, they decided that they would not sell airtime to religious groups, but would instead donate time to Catholic, Jewish, and Protestant broadcasters. In selecting Protestant broadcasters, NBC developed a very close relationship with the Federal Council of Churches, and the Council's Department of National Religious Radio became the dominant voice for selecting Protestant broadcasters and messages on the national airwaves. See Tona J. Hangen, *Redeeming the Dial: Radio, Religion, and Popular Culture in America* (Chapel Hill: University of North Carolina Press, 2002), 23–24.
40. Carpenter, *Revive Us Again*, 130–31. See also Steve Bruce, *Pray TV: Televangelism in America* (London: Routledge, 1990), 25.
41. Hangen, *Redeeming the Dial*, 49. By the early 1940s, Charles Fuller's *Old Fashioned Revival Hour* had the largest audience of any program in the United States. See Marsden, *Understanding Fundamentalism and Evangelicalism*, 68.
42. See Bruce, *Pray TV*, 40, 121, 168.
43. Max Weber, *The Theory of Social and Economic Organization*, ed. Talcott Parsons (1947; New York: Free Press, 1964), 362.
44. James Darsey, *The Prophetic Tradition and Radical Rhetoric in America* (New York: New York University Press, 1997), 33.
45. Darsey, *The Prophetic Tradition*, 16.
46. Weber, *The Theory of Social and Economic Organization*, 361.
47. Darsey, *The Prophetic Tradition*, 31–32.
48. Darsey, *The Prophetic Tradition*, 28–29.
49. Darsey, *The Prophetic Tradition*, 9.
50. Darsey, *The Prophetic Tradition*, 21–22.
51. See Nancy Ammerman, *Bible Believers: Fundamentalists in the Modern World* (New Brunswick, NJ: Rutgers University Press, 1987), 95.
52. Falwell is referencing 1 Corinthians 1:27, which says (AV), "But God hath chosen the foolish things of the world to confound the wise; and God hath chosen the weak things of the world to confound the things which are mighty." This passage was also referenced by William Bell Riley (see chapter 2).

53. Falwell, "The Church at Antioch," 112, 116–17, 124.
54. Falwell, "The Church at Antioch," 114.
55. Although Falwell speaks *about* female evangelists, he rarely speaks *to* them, which seems to validate Susan Harding's claim that Falwell's rhetoric—and that of the Moral Majority generally—is "spoken from a specifically male point of view." See Harding, *The Book of Jerry Falwell*, 155.
56. Falwell, "The Church at Antioch," 125.
57. Falwell, "The Church at Antioch," 125–26.
58. Bruce Buursma, "'Superchurch' Thrives on Fundamentalism," *Chicago Tribune*, November 6, 1983, C3.
59. The idea of "soul winning" derives from a passage in the Hebrew Bible—"he that winneth souls is wise" (Proverbs 11:30, AV)—but the phrase does not seem to have become common parlance until the mid-nineteenth century.
60. Falwell, "The Church at Antioch," 119.
61. Harding, *The Book of Jerry Falwell*, 37.
62. Jack Hyles, *How to Boost Your Church Attendance* (Grand Rapids, MI: Zondervan, 1958), 15–17.
63. Hyles, *How to Boost Your Church Attendance*, 26.
64. Hyles, *How to Boost Your Church Attendance*, 18, 28.
65. "Superchurch," *Time* magazine, December 1, 1975, 67.
66. Falwell, "The Church at Antioch," 113. The verse Falwell references is Acts 1:8 (AV), in which Jesus says to his disciples: "But ye shall receive power, after that the Holy Ghost is come upon you: and ye shall be witnesses unto me both in Jerusalem, and in all Judea, and in Samaria, and unto the uttermost part of the earth."
67. Falwell, "The Church at Antioch," 117.
68. Falwell, "The Church at Antioch," 122.
69. Bruce Lincoln, *Holy Terrors: Thinking about Religion after September 11* (Chicago: University of Chicago Press, 2003), 48–49.
70. See Jerry Falwell, *Listen America!* (New York: Bantam Books, 1980), 25.
71. Falwell, "The Church at Antioch," 118.
72. Falwell, "The Church at Antioch," 118–19.
73. See Harding, *The Book of Jerry Falwell*, 116–17; Dirk Smillie, *Falwell Inc.: Inside a Religious, Political, Educational, and Business Empire* (New York: St. Martin's Press, 2008), 79–81.
74. See J. Brooks Flippen, *Jimmy Carter, the Politics of Family, and the Rise of the Religious Right* (Athens: University of Georgia Press, 2011), 4.
75. Falwell, "The Church at Antioch," 114.
76. Falwell, *Listen America!*, 75.

77. Falwell, *Listen America!*, 46, 56.
78. Falwell, *Listen America!*, 224–25.
79. Falwell, *Listen America!*, 6.
80. Falwell, *Listen America!*, 11–12, 67.
81. Falwell, *Listen America!*, 84–98.
82. Liebman, "Mobilizing the Moral Majority," 58–60.
83. Liebman, "Mobilizing the Moral Majority," 66.
84. Liebman, "Mobilizing the Moral Majority," 67.
85. See Gabriel Fackre, *The Religious Right and Christian Faith* (Grand Rapids, MI: Eerdmans, 1982), 105–6; Erwin W. Lutzer, *Pastor to Pastor: Tackling the Problems of Ministry* (Grand Rapids, MI: Kregel, 1998), 16, 48–49.
86. See, for example, Clyde Wilcox, *God's Warriors: The Christian Right in Twentieth-Century America* (Baltimore, MD: Johns Hopkins University Press, 1992), xiii–xiv.
87. Harding, *The Book of Jerry Falwell*, 273–74.
88. See Jerry Falwell, "Foreword," in *Fundamentalism Today: What Makes It So Attractive!*, ed. Marla J. Selvidge (Elgin, IL: Brethren Press, 1984).
89. Jerry Falwell, "Future-Word: An Agenda for the Eighties," in *The Fundamentalist Phenomenon: The Resurgence of Conservative Christianity*, ed. Ed Dobson, Ed Hindson, and Jerry Falwell (Garden City, NY: Doubleday, 1981).

Chapter Six. The Limits of Accommodation

1. Anne C. Loveland and Otis B. Wheeler, *From Meetinghouse to Megachurch: A Material and Cultural History* (Columbia: University of Missouri Press, 2003), 154, 177.
2. Willow Creek is a member of the Evangelical Council for Financial Accountability, an accreditation agency that works with Christian nonprofit organizations. Recent financial data is available at: http://www.ecfa.org and http://www.willowcreek.org/giving.
3. See Erik Doxtader, "The Rhetorical Question of Human Rights—A Preface," *Quarterly Journal of Speech* 96 (2010): 359.
4. Camille Kaminski Lewis, *Romancing the Difference: Kenneth Burke, Bob Jones University, and the Rhetoric of Religious Fundamentalism* (Waco, TX: Baylor University Press, 2007), 9.
5. David O. Beale, *In Pursuit of Purity: American Fundamentalism since 1850* (Greenville, SC: Unusual Publications, 1986), 10–11.

6. Erik Doxtader, "In the Name of Reconciliation: The Faith and Works of Counterpublicity," in Counterpublics and the State, ed. Robert Asen and Daniel C. Brouwer (Albany: State University of New York Press, 2001), 63.
7. Melanie Loehwing and Jeff Motter, "Publics, Counterpublics, and the Promise of Democracy," *Philosophy and Rhetoric* 42 (2009): 220–41.
8. See, for example, Bill Hybels, *Just Walk across the Room: Simple Steps Pointing People to Faith* (Grand Rapids, MI: Zondervan, 2006), 127. Hybels urges believers to avoid what he calls the "Weird God Story" when speaking to nonbelievers and instead focus on the normal and human over the miraculous.
9. Charles Jahleel Woodbridge, *The New Evangelicalism* (1969), quoted in *The Fundamentalist Phenomenon: The Resurgence of Conservative Christianity*, ed. Ed Dobson, Jerry Falwell, and Edward E. Hindson (Garden City, NY: Doubleday, 1981), 152.
10. Based on sermon notes from March 22, 2009.
11. In March 2013, Jack Schaap was sentenced to twelve years in federal prison for "transporting a minor with intent to engage in criminal sexual activity." See "Fired NW Indiana Megachurch Pastor Sentenced to 12 Years in Prison for Sex with Girl, 17," Associated Press, March 20, 2013, http://global.factiva.com; Andy Grimm, "Former Pastor Gets 12 Years," *Chicago Tribune*, sec. 1, p. 13.
12. Charlie Davidson, "What God Wants with Your Life," audio sermon, Thomas Road Baptist Church, December 16, 2007.
13. On the relationship between expansion and security, see Talal Asad, "Medieval Heresy: An Anthropological View," *Social History* 11 (1986): 355–56.
14. Michael Warner, *Publics and Counterpublics* (New York: Zone Books, 2002), 114.
15. Warner, *Publics and Counterpublics*, 118.
16. Gerard A. Hauser, "Prisoners of Conscience and the Counterpublic Sphere of Prison Writing," in *Counterpublics and the State*, ed. Robert Asen and Daniel C. Brouwer (Albany: State University of New York Press, 2001), 36–37.
17. R. Gustav Niebuhr, "Mighty Fortresses: Megachurches Strive to Be All Things to All Parishioners," *Wall Street Journal*, May 13, 1991, A1.
18. See Kimon Howland Sargeant, *Seeker Churches: Promoting Traditional Religion in a Nontraditional Way* (New Brunswick, NJ: Rutgers University Press, 2000), 28.
19. Lynne Hybels and Bill Hybels, *Rediscovering Church: The Story and Vision of Willow Creek Community Church* (Grand Rapids, MI: Zondervan, 1995), 16. Although Hybels did not invent the term, he did, certainly, popularize it within the context of church growth and megachurch evangelism.
20. Hybels and Hybels, *Rediscovering Church*, 67, 174.
21. John N. Vaughan, *The World's Twenty Largest Churches* (Grand Rapids, MI: Baker Book House, 1984), 19.
22. Hybels and Hybels, *Rediscovering Church*, 53.

23. Donald E. Miller, *Reinventing American Protestantism: Christianity in the New Millennium* (Berkeley: University of California Press, 1997), 1.
24. Miller, *Reinventing American Protestantism*, 3–4. For recent work by Finke and Starke, see Roger Finke and Rodney Starke, *The Churching of America, 1776–2005: Winners and Losers in Our Religious Economy*, 2nd ed. (New Brunswick, NJ: Rutgers University Press, 2005).
25. Miller, *Reinventing American Protestantism*, 11.
26. Hybels and Hybels, *Rediscovering Church*, 50.
27. See, for example, Sargeant, *Seeker Churches*, 106–9; Ruth A. Tucker, *Left Behind in a Megachurch World: How God Works through Ordinary Churches* (Grand Rapids, MI: Baker Books, 2006), 88.
28. Acts 2:42–47 (New International Version).
29. All quotations from the sermon are based on notes taken at the event. At the time of this writing, a version of the sermon is also available online at http://media.willowcreek.org/weekend/all-in-anniversary-celebration.
30. On the notion of collective memory, see, for example, John Bodnar, *Remaking America: Public Memory, Commemoration, and Patriotism in the Twentieth Century* (Princeton, NJ: Princeton University Press, 1992), 11–20, 245.
31. John R. Gillis, "Memory and Identity: The History of a Relationship," in *Commemorations: The Politics of National Identity*, ed. John R. Gillis (Princeton, NJ: Princeton University Press, 1994), 15.
32. Carole Blair and Neil Michel, "Commemorating in the Theme Park Zone: Reading the Astronauts Memorial," in *At the Intersection: Cultural Studies and Rhetorical Studies*, ed. Thomas Rosteck (New York: Guilford Press, 1999), 55.
33. Despite its 7,500 seats, the First Baptist auditorium is only two stories tall, and thus it spreads in all directions, unlike the three-story-high, vertically oriented auditorium of Willow Creek.
34. James B. Twitchell, *Branded Nation: The Marketing of Megachurch, College Inc., and Museumworld* (New York: Simon & Schuster, 2004), 82.
35. See, for example, Bill Hybels, Kevin G. Harney, and Sherry Harney, *Colossians* (Grand Rapids, MI: Zondervan, 1999), 23; Bill Hybels, *Courageous Leadership* (Grand Rapids, MI: Zondervan, 2002), 15.
36. Hybels and Hybels, *Rediscovering Church*, 92.
37. Bill Hybels, *Honest to God? Becoming an Authentic Christian* (Grand Rapids, MI: Zondervan, 1990), 123.
38. "What Willow Believes," http://www.willowcreek.org.
39. On the church's use of religious iconography, see Stewart M. Hoover, "The Cross at Willow Creek: Seeker Religion and the Contemporary Marketplace," in *Religion and Popular Culture*, ed. Bruce David Forbes and Jeffrey H. Mahan (Berkeley: University of California Press, 2000).

40. Gregory A. Pritchard, "The Strategy of Willow Creek Community Church: A Study in the Sociology of Religion," PhD diss., Northwestern University, 1994, 83; Blair and Michel, "Commemorating in the Theme Park Zone: Reading the Astronauts Memorial," 63. Pritchard's research was later published as G. A. Pritchard, *Willow Creek Seeker Services: Evaluating a New Way of Doing Church* (Grand Rapids, MI: Baker Books, 1996); however, the reference above was not included.
41. See Michael O. Emerson and Christian Smith, *Divided by Faith: Evangelical Religion and the Problem of Race in America* (New York: Oxford University Press, 2000), 141–50.
42. Gene Appel, "Is God . . . Homophobic?," sermon at Willow Creek Community Church, November 4, 2006.
43. See Lee Strobel, *Inside the Mind of Unchurched Harry and Mary: How to Reach Friends and Family Who Avoid God and the Church* (Grand Rapids, MI: Zondervan, 1993), 15, 23, 104.
44. Hannah Arendt, *On Violence* (Orlando, FL: Harcourt, 1969), 75.
45. Hybels, *Courageous Leadership*, 22.
46. Hybels and Hybels, *Rediscovering Church*, 212.
47. In the early 1990s, when Hybels was serving as a board member at Focus on the Family, he reportedly angered James Dobson by agreeing to serve as a "religious adviser" for the Clinton White House, and he left the board soon afterwards. See Dan Gilgoff, *The Jesus Machine: How James Dobson, Focus on the Family, and Evangelical America are Winning the Culture War* (New York: St. Martin's Press, 2007), 38–39.
48. On the conservative theology of megachurch pastors, see Sargeant, *Seeker Churches*, 20–21.
49. Greg L. Hawkins and Cally Parkinson, *Reveal: Where Are You?* (Barrington, IL: Willow Creek Resources, 2007), 45–54.
50. Gloria Gaither, Shirley Dobson, and Russ Flint, *Let's Make a Memory: Great Ideas for Building Family Traditions and Togetherness* (Waco, TX: Word Books, 1983).

Conclusion

1. Michael Warner, *Publics and Counterpublics* (New York: Zone Books, 2002), 121.
2. Christine J. Gardner, *Making Chastity Sexy: The Rhetoric of Evangelical Abstinence Campaigns* (Berkeley: University of California Press, 2011), 14.
3. Gardner, *Making Chastity Sexy*, 193.

4. See *Jesus Camp*, dir. Heidi Ewing and Rachel Grady (A&E IndieFilms, 2006); *Friends of God: A Road Trip with Alexandra Pelosi*, dir. Alexandra Pelosi (HBO, 2007).
5. John Dewey, *The Public and Its Problems* (Chicago: Sage Books, 1927), 208.
6. "Omaha Platform," in *The Encyclopedia of Social Reform*, ed. William D. P. Bliss (New York: Funk and Wagnalls Co., 1897), 955.
7. See W. B. Riley, "The Great Divide or Christ and the Present Crisis," *School and Church*, July-September 1919, 187, 190; Ronald P. Formisano, *The Tea Party: A Brief History* (Baltimore, MD: Johns Hopkins University Press, 2012), 13, 29, 35–36.
8. *Global Trends 2030: Alternative Worlds* (Washington, DC: National Intelligence Council, 2012), 12.
9. Susan F. Harding, "American Protestant Moralism and the Secular Imagination: From Temperance to the Moral Majority," *Social Research* 76 (2009): 1281. See also Wendy Brown, "Subjects of Tolerance: Why We Are Civilized and They Are the Barbarians," in *Political Theologies: Public Religions in a Post-Secular World*, ed. Hent de Vries and Lawrence E. Sullivan (New York: Fordham University Press, 2006), 298–317.
10. Christine Wicker, *The Fall of the Evangelical Nation: The Surprising Crisis inside the Church* (New York: HarperOne, 2008).
11. See "Protestantism Shows Gains in New Survey," *United Evangelical Action*, July 15, 1950, 10–11.
12. Harding, "American Protestant Moralism and the Secular Imagination," 1303.
13. Sharon Crowley, *Toward a Civil Discourse: Rhetoric and Fundamentalism* (Pittsburgh, PA: University of Pittsburgh Press, 2006), 199.
14. Charles Taylor, *A Secular Age* (Cambridge, MA: Belknap Press, 2007), 487–88.

Bibliography

⌘

Achter, Paul J. "TV, Technology, and McCarthyism: Crafting the Democratic Renaissance in an Age of Fear." *Quarterly Journal of Speech* 90 (2004): 307–26.

Adams, John Charles. "Linguistic Values and Religious Experience: An Analysis of the Clothing Metaphors in Alexander Richardson's Ramist-Puritan Lectures on Speech, 'Speech is a Garment to Cloath Our Reason.'" *Quarterly Journal of Speech* 76 (1990): 58–68.

Agamben, Giorgio. *The Kingdom and the Glory: For a Theological Genealogy of Economy and Government*. Stanford, CA: Stanford University Press, 2011.

"American Board of Missions." *Daily National Intelligencer* [Washington, DC], October 15, 1832.

"American Education Society." *New-York Spectator*, May 15, 1832.

"American Seaman's Friend Society." *New-York Spectator*, May 9, 1833.

"American Sunday School Union." *New-York Spectator*, April 22, 1833.

"American Temperance Society." *New-York Spectator*, May 9, 1833.

"American Tract Society." *New-York Spectator*, May 15, 1832.

Ammerman, Nancy. *Bible Believers: Fundamentalists in the Modern World*. New Brunswick, NJ: Rutgers University Press, 1987.

———. "North American Protestant Fundamentalism." In *Fundamentalisms Observed*, ed. Martin E. Marty and R. Scott Appleby, 1–65. Chicago: University of Chicago Press, 1991.

Amstutz, Mark R. *Evangelicals and American Foreign Policy*. New York: Oxford University Press, 2014.

Anbinder, Tyler. *Five Points: The 19th-Century New York City Neighborhood That Invented Tap Dance, Stole Elections, and Became the World's Most Notorious Slum*. New York: Free Press, 2001.

"Anniversary of the American Bible Society." *New-York Spectator*, May 15, 1832.

"Another Black Riot." *United States' Telegraph*, July 11, 1834.

"Another Riot at New-York." *The Liberator*, July 12, 1834.

Appel, Gene. "Is God . . . Homophobic?" Sermon at Willow Creek Community Church, November 4, 2006.

"Appendix A: The 1878 Niagara Creed." In *In Pursuit of Purity: American Fundamentalism since 1850*, by David O. Beale, 375–79. Greenville, SC: Unusual Publications, 1986.

Archer, Gleason L. "Alleged Errors and Discrepancies in the Original Manuscripts of the Bible." In *Inerrancy*, ed. Norman L. Geisler, 55–82. Grand Rapids, MI: Zondervan, 1980.

Arendt, Hannah. *On Violence*. Orlando, FL: Harcourt, 1969.

Aristotle. *On Rhetoric: A Theory of Civic Discourse*. Translated by George A. Kennedy. New York: Oxford University Press, 1991.

Asad, Talal. "Medieval Heresy: An Anthropological View." *Social History* 11 (1986): 345–62.

Asen, Robert. "A Discourse Theory of Citizenship." *Quarterly Journal of Speech* 90 (2004): 189–211.

———. "The Multiple Mr. Dewey: Multiple Publics and Permeable Borders in John Dewey's Theory of the Public Sphere." *Argumentation and Advocacy* 39 (2003): 174–88.

Ashworth, Robert A. "The Fundamentalist Movement among the Baptists." *Journal of Religion* 4 (1924): 611–31.

Baird, Robert. *Religion in America: or an Account of the Origin, Relation to the State, and Present Condition of the Evangelical Churches in the United States: With Notices of the Unevangelical Denominations*. New York: Harper & Brothers, 1844.

Balmer, Randall. *Blessed Assurance: A History of Evangelicalism in America*. Boston: Beacon Press, 1999.

———. *Mine Eyes Have Seen the Glory: A Journey into the Evangelical Subculture in America*. 4th ed. New York: Oxford University Press, 2006.

Barclay, John M. G. "Paul among Diaspora Jews: Anomaly or Apostate?" *Journal for the Study of the New Testament* 60 (1995): 89–120.

Barr, David L. "The Apocalypse of John as Oral Enactment." *Interpretation* 40 (1986): 243–56.

Barr, James. *Fundamentalism*. Philadelphia: Westminster Press, 1978.

Barstow, David. "Lighting a Fuse for Rebellion on the Right: Loose Alliance of Protestors Join under Tea Party Umbrella." *New York Times*, February 16, 2010.

Beale, David O. *In Pursuit of Purity: American Fundamentalism since 1850*. Greenville, SC: Unusual Publications, 1986.

Bellah, Robert N. "Civil Religion in America." *Daedalus* 96 (1967): 1–21.

Bercovitch, Sacvan. *The American Jeremiad*. Madison: University of Wisconsin Press, 1978.

Bitzer, Lloyd F. "The Rhetorical Situation." *Philosophy and Rhetoric* 1 (1968): 1–14.

Blair, Carole, and Neil Michel. "Commemorating in the Theme Park Zone: Reading the Astronauts Memorial." In *At the Intersection: Cultural Studies and Rhetorical Studies*, ed. Thomas Rosteck. New York: Guilford Press, 1999.

Blum, Edwin A. "The Apostles' View of Scripture." In *Inerrancy*, ed. Norman L. Geisler, 37–53. Grand Rapids, MI: Zondervan, 1980.

Blumenberg, Hans. "An Anthropological Approach to the Contemporary Significance of Rhetoric." In *After Philosophy: End or Transformation?*, ed. Kenneth Baynes, James Bohman, and Thomas McCarthy, 429–58. Cambridge, MA: MIT Press, 1987.

Bodnar, John. *Remaking America: Public Memory, Commemoration, and Patriotism in the Twentieth Century*. Princeton, NJ: Princeton University Press, 1992.

Booth, Herbert. *The Christian Confederacy*. Chicago: Goodspeed Press, 1915.

Boyer, M. Christine. *The City of Collective Memory: Its Historical Imagery and Architectural Entertainments*. Cambridge, MA: MIT Press, 1994.

Bradshaw, W. S. "The Inter-Church World Movement." *School and Church*, January–March 1920.

Branick, Vincent P. "The Attractiveness of Fundamentalism." In *Fundamentalism Today: What Makes It So Attractive!*, ed. Marla J. Selvidge. Elgin, IL: Brethren Press, 1984.

Brauer, Jerald C. "Conversion: From Puritanism to Revivalism." *Journal of Religion* 58 (1978): 227–43.

Broadus, John Albert. *A Treatise on the Preparation and Delivery of Sermons*. 17th ed. New York: Armstrong, 1891.

Brouwer, Daniel C. "Communication as Counterpublic." In *Communication As . . . Perspectives on Theory*, ed. Gregory J. Shepherd, Jeffrey St. John, and Ted Striphas, 195–208. Thousand Oaks, CA: Sage, 2006.

Brown, Wendy. "Subjects of Tolerance: Why We Are Civilized and They Are the Barbarians." In *Political Theologies: Public Religions in a Post-Secular World*, ed. Hent de Vries and Lawrence E. Sullivan, 298–317. New York: Fordham University Press, 2006.

Bruce, Steve. *Pray TV: Televangelism in America*. London: Routledge, 1990.

Brummett, Barry. *Contemporary Apocalyptic Rhetoric*. New York: Praeger, 1991.

Bruner, M. Lane. "Rationality, Reason and the History of Thought." *Argumentation* 20 (2006): 185–208.

Bryan, John. *Robert Mills: America's First Architect*. New York: Princeton Architectural Press, 2001.

Buber, Martin. "Prophecy, Apocalyptic, and the Historical Hour." In *Pointing the Way: Collected Essays*, ed. and trans. Maurice Friedman. New York: Harper, 1963.

———. "The Two Foci of the Jewish Soul." In *The Writings of Martin Buber*, ed. Will Herberg. New York: Meridian Books, 1956.

Burack, Cynthia. *Sin, Sex, and Democracy: Antigay Rhetoric and the Christian Right*. Albany: State University of New York Press, 2008.

Burke, Kenneth. *Language as Symbolic Action: Essays on Life, Literature, and Method*. Berkeley: University of California Press, 1966.

———. *A Rhetoric of Motives*. Berkeley: University of California Press, 1969.

Buursma, Bruce. "'Superchurch' Thrives on Fundamentalism." *Chicago Tribune*, November 6, 1983.

Calvin, John. *Institutes of the Christian Religion*. Vol. 1. Edited by John T. McNeill. Translated by Ford Lewis Battles. Philadelphia: Westminster Press, 1960.

Cameron, Averil. *Christianity and the Rhetoric of Empire: The Development of Christian Discourse*. Berkeley: University of California Press, 1991.

Carcasson, Martín. "Ending Welfare As We Know It: President Clinton and the Rhetorical Transformation of the Anti-Welfare Culture." *Rhetoric and Public Affairs* 9 (2007): 657–78.

Carpenter, Joel. *Revive Us Again: The Reawakening of American Fundamentalism*. New York: Oxford University Press, 1997.

Carwardine, Richard. *Evangelicals and Politics in Antebellum America*. New Haven, CT: Yale University Press, 1993.

Charland, Maurice. "Constitutive Rhetoric: The Case of the *Peuple Québécois*." *Quarterly Journal of Speech* 73 (1987): 133–50.

"Chatham-Street Chapel." *New-York Spectator*, July 10, 1834.

Church Growth Bulletin, January 1968.

———, November 1968.

Commons, John R. "The Churches and Political Reforms." In *Christianity Practically Applied: The Discussions of the International Christian Conference*. New York: Baker and Taylor, 1894.

Connelly, Eric. "State Secrets and Redaction: The Interaction between Silence and Ideographs." *Western Journal of Communication* 76 (2012): 236–49.

"Courier and Enquirer." *The Emancipator and Journal of Public Morals*, July 1, 1834.

Crowley, Sharon. *Toward a Civil Discourse: Rhetoric and Fundamentalism*. Pittsburgh, PA: University of Pittsburgh Press, 2006.

Custer, Stewart. *Tools for Preaching and Teaching the Bible*. 2nd ed. Greenville, SC: Bob Jones University Press, 1998.

Daniels, Tom D., Richard J. Jensen, and Allen Lichtenstein. "Resolving the Paradox in Politicized Christian Fundamentalism." *Western Journal of Speech Communication* 49 (1985): 248–66.

Darsey, James. "Patricia Roberts-Miller, Demagoguery, and the Troublesome Case of Eugene Debs." *Rhetoric and Public Affairs* 9 (2006): 463–88.

———. *The Prophetic Tradition and Radical Rhetoric in America*. New York: New York University Press, 1997.

Davidson, Charlie. "What God Wants with Your Life." Sermon at Thomas Road Baptist Church, December 16, 2007.

"Deaf & Dumb." *New-York Spectator*, May 13, 1833.

DeMint, Jim. *The Great American Awakening: Two Years That Changed America, Washington, and Me*. Nashville, TN: B&H Publishing Group, 2011.

Dewey, John. *The Public and Its Problems*. Chicago: Sage Books, 1927.

Dewey, John, and James Hayden Tufts. *Ethics*. New York: Henry Holt and Co., 1909.

Diamond, Sara. *Roads to Dominion: Right-Wing Movements and Political Power in the United States*. New York: Guilford Press, 1995.

A Distant Thunder. Directed by Donald W. Thompson. Des Moines, IA: Mark IV Pictures, 1977.

Dobson, Ed, Ed Hindson, and Jerry Falwell, eds. *The Fundamentalist Phenomenon: The Resurgence of Conservative Christianity*. Garden City, NY: Doubleday, 1981.

Dodge, William E. "The Origin of the Evangelist." *New York Evangelist*, January 8, 1880.

Domke, David. *God Willing? Political Fundamentalism in the White House, the 'War on Terror,' and the Echoing Press*. Ann Arbor, MI: Pluto Press, 2004.

Doxtader, Erik. "In the Name of Reconciliation: The Faith and Works of Counterpublicity." In *Counterpublics and the State*, ed. Robert Asen and Daniel C. Brouwer, 59–85. Albany: State University of New York Press, 2001.

———. "The Rhetorical Question of Human Rights—A Preface." *Quarterly Journal of Speech* 96 (2010): 353–79.

"Editorial." *New-Hampshire Statesman and State Journal*, May 25, 1833.

Edwards, Jonathan. "The Distinguishing Marks of a Work of the Spirit of God." 1741. Reprinted in *Works of Jonathan Edwards*, vol. 4, *The Great Awakening*, ed. C. C. Goen. New Haven, CT: Yale University Press, 1972.

———. "A Faithful Narrative of the Surprising Work of God in the Conversion of Many Hundred Souls in Northampton, and the Neighboring Towns and Villages of the County of Hampshire, in the Province of the Massachusetts-Bay in New-England." 1737. Reprinted in *Works of Jonathan Edwards*, vol. 4, *The Great Awakening*, ed. C. C. Goen. New Haven, CT: Yale University Press, 1972.

———. "Letter: To the Reverend James Robe of Kilsyth, Scotland." 1743. Reprinted in *Works of Jonathan Edwards*, vol. 4, *The Great Awakening*, ed. C. C. Goen. New Haven, CT: Yale University Press, 1972.

Ellwood, Robert S. *1950: Crossroads of American Religious Life*. Louisville, KY: Westminster John Knox Press, 2000.

———. *One Way: The Jesus Movement and Its Meaning*. Englewood Cliffs, NJ: Prentice-Hall, 1973.

Emerson, Everett H. "John Udall and the Puritan Sermon." *Quarterly Journal of Speech* 44 (1958): 282–84.

Emerson, Michael O., and Christian Smith. *Divided by Faith: Evangelical Religion and the Problem of Race in America*. New York: Oxford University Press, 2000.

English, Eric, Stephen Llano, Gordon R. Mitchell, Catherine E. Morrison, John Rief, and Carly Woods. "Debate as a Weapon of Mass Destruction." *Communication and Critical/Cultural Studies* 4 (2007): 221–25.

Eslinger, Ellen. *Citizens of Zion: The Social Origins of Camp Meeting Revivalism*. Knoxville: University of Tennessee Press, 1999.

Evangelical Council for Financial Accountability. Http://www.ecfa.org.

Evans, G. Russell. *Apathy, Apostasy and Apostles: A Study of the History and Activities of the National Council of Churches of Christ in the U.S.A. with Sidelights on Its Ally, the World Council of Churches*. New York: Vantage Press, 1973.

Fackre, Gabriel. *The Religious Right and the Christian Faith*. Grand Rapids, MI: Eerdmans, 1982.

Fahnestock, Jeanne. *Rhetorical Figures in Science*. New York: Oxford University Press, 1999.

———. *Rhetorical Style: The Uses of Language in Persuasion*. New York: Oxford University Press, 2011.

Falwell, Jerry. "The Church at Antioch." In *Capturing a Town for Christ*, by Elmer Towns and Jerry Falwell. Old Tappan, NJ: Fleming H. Revell, 1973.

———. "Foreword." In *Fundamentalism Today: What Makes It So Attractive!*, ed. Marla J. Selvidge. Elgin, IL: Brethren Press, 1984.

———. "Future-Word: An Agenda for the Eighties." In *The Fundamentalist Phenomenon: The Resurgence of Conservative Christianity*, ed. Ed Dobson, Ed Hindson, and Jerry Falwell. Garden City, NY: Doubleday, 1981.

———. *Listen America!* New York: Bantam Books, 1980.

Falwell, Jerry, and Elmer Towns. *Church Aflame*. Nashville, TN: Impact Books, 1971.

Falwell, Jonathan. *InnovateChurch*. Nashville, TN: B&H Books, 2008.

"Federal Council Hit by Fundamentalists." *New York Times*, October 31, 1948.

"Female Anti-Slavery Society of Chatham Street Chapel." *The Emancipator and Journal of Public Morals*, April 15, 1834.

Finke, Roger, and Rodney Starke. *The Churching of America, 1776–2005: Winners and Losers in Our Religious Economy*. 2nd ed. New Brunswick, NJ: Rutgers University Press, 2005.

Finney, Charles. *Lectures on Revivals of Religion*. 6th ed. New York: Leavitt Lord, 1835.

———. *The Memoirs of Charles G. Finney: The Complete Restored Text*, ed. Garth Rosell and Richard A. G. Dupuis. Grand Rapids, MI: Academie Books, 1989.

"Fired NW Indiana Megachurch Pastor Sentenced to 12 Years in Prison for Sex with Girl, 17." Associated Press, March 20, 2013. Http://global.factiva.com.

Flippen, J. Brooks. *Jimmy Carter, the Politics of Family, and the Rise of the Religious Right*. Athens: University of Georgia Press, 2011.

Flory, Richard W. "The Fundamentals." In *Encyclopedia of Fundamentalism*, ed. Brenda E. Brasher. New York: Routledge, 2001.

Formisano, Ronald P. *The Tea Party: A Brief History*. Baltimore, MD: Johns Hopkins University Press, 2012.

"For the Defense." *Time* magazine, July 14, 1961.

"The Fourth of July." *New-York Spectator*, July 7, 1834.

Fraser, Nancy. "Rethinking the Public Sphere: A Contribution to the Critique of Actually Existing Democracy." In *Habermas and the Public Sphere*, ed. Craig Calhoun. Cambridge, MA: MIT Press, 1992.

Friends of God: A Road Trip with Alexandra Pelosi. Directed by Alexandra Pelosi. HBO, 2007.

"From Baptist Temple News We Reprint the Virginia Declaration." *School and Church*, April–June 1920.

Frykholm, Amy Johnson. *Rapture Culture:* Left Behind *in Evangelical America*. New York: Oxford University Press, 2004.

———. "What Social and Political Messages Appear in the *Left Behind* Books? A Literary Discussion of Millenarian Fiction." In *Rapture, Revelation, and the End Times: Exploring the* Left Behind *Series*, ed. Bruce David Forbes and Jeanne Halgren Kilde. New York: Palgrave Macmillan, 2004.

Fuller, Robert C. *Naming the Antichrist: The History of an American Obsession*. New York: Oxford University Press, 1995.

Gaither, Gloria, Shirley Dobson, and Russ Flint. *Let's Make a Memory: Great Ideas for Building Family Traditions and Togetherness*. Waco, TX: Word Books, 1983.

Gardner, Christine J. *Making Chastity Sexy: The Rhetoric of Evangelical Abstinence Campaigns*. Berkeley: University of California Press, 2011.

Gaustad, Edwin S. *The Great Awakening in New England*. New York: Harper, 1957.

Giggie, John, and Diane H. Winston. *Faith in the Market: Religion and the Rise of Urban Commercial Culture*. New Brunswick, NJ: Rutgers University Press, 2002.

Gilgoff, Dan. *The Jesus Machine: How James Dobson, Focus on the Family, and Evangelical America are Winning the Culture War*. New York: St. Martin's Press, 2007.

Gillis, John R. "Memory and Identity: The History of a Relationship." In *Commemorations: The Politics of National Identity*, ed. John R. Gillis. Princeton, NJ: Princeton University Press, 1994.

Giroux, Henry A. "The Crisis of Public Values in the Age of the New Media." *Critical Studies in Media Communication* 28 (2011): 8–29.

Global Trends 2030: Alternative Worlds. Washington, DC: National Intelligence Council, 2012.

Gorham, B. W. *Camp Meeting Manual*. Boston: H. V. Degen, 1854.

Graber, Doris A. *Verbal Behavior and Politics*. Urbana: University of Illinois Press, 1976.

Gribben, Crawford. *Writing the Rapture: Prophecy Fiction in Evangelical America*. New York: Oxford University Press, 2009.

Griffin, Leland M. "A Dramatistic Theory of the Rhetoric of Movements." In *Landmark Essays on Kenneth Burke*, ed. Barry Brummett. Davis, CA: Hermagoras Press, 1993.

———. "The Rhetoric of Historical Movements." *Quarterly Journal of Speech* 38 (1952): 184–88.

Grimm, Andy. "Former Pastor Gets 12 Years." *Chicago Tribune*, March 21, 2013, sec. 1, p. 13.

Gunn, Joshua. "Maranatha." *Quarterly Journal of Speech* 98 (2012): 359–85.

Guthrie, Warren. "The Development of Rhetorical Theory in America." *Speech Monographs* 13 (1946): 14–22.

Habermas, Jürgen. "On the Relations between the Secular Liberal State and Religion." In *Political Theologies: Public Religions in a Post-Secular World*, ed. Hent de Vries and Lawrence E. Sullivan, 251–60. New York: Fordham University Press, 2006.

———. "Religion in the Public Sphere." *European Journal of Philosophy* 14 (2006): 1–25.

———. *The Structural Transformation of the Public Sphere: An Inquiry into a Category of Bourgeois Society*. Translated by Thomas Burger and Frederick Lawrence. Cambridge, MA: MIT Press, 1989.

———. "Three Normative Models of Democracy." In *Democracy and Difference*, ed. Seyla Benhabib, 21–30. Princeton, NJ: Princeton University Press, 1996.

Hambrick-Stowe, Charles. *Charles G. Finney and the Spirit of American Evangelicalism*. Grand Rapids, MI: Eerdmans, 1996.

Hangen, Tona J. *Redeeming the Dial: Radio, Religion, and Popular Culture in America*. Chapel Hill: University of North Carolina Press, 2002.

Harding, Susan F. "American Protestant Moralism and the Secular Imagination: From Temperance to the Moral Majority." *Social Research* 76 (2009): 1277–1306.

———. *The Book of Jerry Falwell: Fundamentalist Language and Politics*. Princeton, NJ: Princeton University Press, 2000.

Hargis, Billy James. *The Facts about Communism and Our Churches*. Tulsa, OK: Christian Crusade, 1962.

———. *The National Council of Churches Indicts Itself on 50 Counts of Treason to God and Country!* Tulsa, OK: Christian Crusade, 1964.

Hargis, Billy James, and Bill Sampson. *The Cross and the Sickle . . . Superchurch*. Tulsa, OK: Crusader Books, 1982.

Hariman, Robert. "Allegory and Democratic Public Culture in the Postmodern Era." *Philosophy and Rhetoric* 35 (2002): 267–96.

———. "Introduction." In *Popular Trials: Rhetoric, Mass Media, and the Law*, ed. Robert Hariman. Tuscaloosa: University of Alabama Press, 1993.

Harris, Harriet A. *Fundamentalism and Evangelicals*. Oxford: Clarendon Press, 1998.

Hartnett, Stephen John. *Executing Democracy*. Vol. 2, *Capital Punishment and the Remaking of America, 1835–1843*. East Lansing: Michigan State University Press, 2012.

Harvey, Charles E. "John D. Rockefeller, Jr. and the Interchurch World Movement of 1919–1920: A Different Angle on the Ecumenical Movement." *Church History* 51 (1982): 198–209.

Hatch, Nathan O. *The Democratization of American Christianity*. New Haven, CT: Yale University Press, 1989.

Hauser, Gerard A. "Prisoners of Conscience and the Counterpublic Sphere of Prison Writing." In *Counterpublics and the State*, ed. Robert Asen and Daniel C. Brouwer. Albany: State University of New York Press, 2001.

Hawkins, Greg L., and Cally Parkinson. *Reveal: Where Are You?* Barrington, IL: Willow Creek Resources, 2007.

Hendershot, Heather. *Shaking the World for Jesus: Media and Conservative Evangelical Culture*. Chicago: University of Chicago Press, 2004.

Herman, Didi. *The Antigay Agenda: Orthodox Vision and the Christian Right*. Chicago: University of Chicago Press, 1997.

Hoover, Stewart M. "The Cross at Willow Creek: Seeker Religion and the Contemporary Marketplace." In *Religion and Popular Culture*, ed. Bruce David Forbes and Jeffrey H. Mahan. Berkeley: University of California Press, 2000.

Howard, Robert Glenn. *Digital Jesus: The Making of a New Christian Fundamentalist Community on the Internet*. New York: New York University Press, 2011.

Howe, Daniel Walker. *What Hath God Wrought: The Transformation of America, 1815–1848*. New York: Oxford University Press, 2007.

How Red Is the National Council of Churches? Pittsburgh, PA: Laymen's Commission of the American Council of Christian Churches, 1966.

Hudson, Roy Fred. "Rhetorical Invention in Colonial New England." *Speech Monographs* 25 (1958): 215–21.

Hutchison, William R. "Protestantism as Establishment." In *Between the Times: The Travail of the Protestant Establishment in America, 1900–1960*, ed. William R. Hutchison. Cambridge: Cambridge University Press, 1989.

Hybels, Bill. "All In!" Sermon at Willow Creek Community Church, October 11, 2009. Http://media.willowcreek.org/weekend/all-in-anniversary-celebration.

———. *Courageous Leadership*. Grand Rapids, MI: Zondervan, 2002.

———. *Honest to God? Becoming an Authentic Christian*. Grand Rapids, MI: Zondervan, 1990.

———. *Just Walk across the Room: Simple Steps Pointing People to Faith*. Grand Rapids, MI: Zondervan, 2006.

Hybels, Bill, Kevin G. Harney, and Sherry Harney. *Colossians*. Grand Rapids, MI: Zondervan, 1999.

Hybels, Lynne, and Bill Hybels. *Rediscovering Church: The Story and Vision of Willow Creek Community Church*. Grand Rapids, MI: Zondervan, 1995.

Hyles, Jack. *How to Boost Your Church Attendance*. Grand Rapids, MI: Zondervan, 1958.

Image of the Beast. Directed by Donald W. Thompson. Des Moines, IA: Mark IV Pictures, 1981.

"The Institutional Church." *Christian Fundamentals in School and Church*, January–March 1921.

"Institutional Churches." In *The New Encyclopedia of Social Reform*, ed. William D. P. Bliss, Rudolph M. Binder, and Edward Page Gaston. London: Funk and Wagnalls, 1909.

Irenaeus. "Selections from the Work against Heresies." In *Early Christian Fathers*, ed. Cyril C. Richardson. Philadelphia, PA: Westminster Press, 1953.

Jackson, Richard, Marie Breen Smith, and Jeroen Gunning. "Critical Terrorism Studies: Framing a New Research Agenda." In *Critical Terrorism Studies: A New Research Agenda*. New York: Routledge, 2009.

Jacobson, Matthew Frye. *Barbarian Virtues: The United States Encounters Foreign Peoples at Home and Abroad, 1876–1917*. New York: Hill and Wang, 2000.

Jesus Camp. Directed by Heidi Ewing and Rachel Grady. A&E IndieFilms, 2006.

Johnson, Nan. "Nineteenth-Century Rhetoric." In *Encyclopedia of Rhetoric*, ed. Thomas O. Sloane, 518–20. Oxford: Oxford University Press, 2001.

———. *Nineteenth-Century Rhetoric in North America*. Carbondale: Southern Illinois University Press, 1991.

Jones, Bob. *All Fullness Dwells*. Greenville, SC: Bob Jones University Press, 1942.

Kaub, Verne P. "Super-Church Is Born." *United Evangelical Action,* January 1, 1951.

Kazin, Michael. *The Populist Persuasion*. New York: Basic Books, 1995.

Kellstedt, Lyman A., John C. Green, James L. Guth, and Corwin E. Smidt. "Religious Voting Blocs in the 1992 Election: The Year of the Evangelical?" *Sociology of Religion* 55 (1994): 307–26.

Kierkegaard, Søren. *The Concept of Irony: With Constant Reference to Socrates*. London: Collins, 1966.

Kilde, Jeanne Halgren. "How Did *Left Behind*'s Particular Vision of the End Times Develop? A Historical Look at Millenarian Thought." In *Rapture,*

Revelation, and the End Times: Exploring the Left Behind *Series*, ed. Bruce David Forbes and Jeanne Halgren Kilde. New York: Palgrave Macmillan, 2004.

———. *When Church Became Theatre: The Transformation of Evangelical Architecture and Worship in Nineteenth-Century America*. New York: Oxford University Press, 2002.

Kippenberg, H. G. "Apostasy." In *Encyclopedia of Religion*, ed. Lindsay Jones. Detroit, MI: Thompson Gale, 2005.

Lafont, Cristina. "Religion in the Public Sphere: Remarks on Habermas's Conception of Public Deliberation in Postsecular Societies." *Constellations* 14 (2007): 239–59.

Lahr, Angela M. *Millennial Dreams and Apocalyptic Nightmares: The Cold War Origins of Political Evangelicalism*. New York: Oxford University Press, 2007.

Lambert, Frank. *Inventing the Great Awakening*. Princeton, NJ: Princeton University Press, 1999.

———. "'Pedlar in Divinity': George Whitefield and the Great Awakening, 1737–1745." *Journal of American History* 77 (1990): 812–37.

Lee, Michael J. "The Conservative Canon and Its Uses." *Rhetoric and Public Affairs* 15 (2012): 1–39.

Lewis, Camille Kaminski. *Romancing the Difference: Kenneth Burke, Bob Jones University, and the Rhetoric of Religious Fundamentalism*. Waco, TX: Baylor University Press, 2007.

Lichtman, Allan J. *White Protestant Nation: The Rise of the American Conservative Movement*. New York: Atlantic Monthly Press, 2008.

Liddell, Henry George, and Robert Scott. *A Greek-English Lexicon*. Oxford: Clarendon Press, 1996.

Liebman, Robert C. "Mobilizing the Moral Majority." In *The New Christian Right: Mobilization and Legitimation*, ed. Robert C. Liebman and Robert Wuthnow. New York: Aldine Publishing Company, 1983.

Lincoln, Bruce. *Holy Terrors: Thinking about Religion after September 11*. Chicago: University of Chicago Press, 2003.

Lindholm, A. L. *The Truth about Roman Catholicism and the Coming Man-Made, One-World Super-Church*. San Fernando, CA: The Gospel Truth, 1967.

Lindsey, Hal, and C. C. Carlson. *The Late Great Planet Earth*. Grand Rapids, MI: Zondervan, 1970.

Loehwing, Melanie, and Jeff Motter. "Publics, Counterpublics, and the Promise of Democracy." *Philosophy and Rhetoric* 42 (2009): 220–41.

Long, Kathryn T. "'Turning . . . Piety into Hard Cash': The Marketing of Nineteenth-Century Revivalism." In *God and Mammon: Protestants, Money, and the Market, 1790–1860*, ed. Mark A. Noll. Oxford: Oxford University Press, 2002.

Loveland, Anne C., and Otis B. Wheeler. *From Meetinghouse to Megachurch: A Material and Cultural History*. Columbia: University of Missouri Press, 2003.

Lundberg, Christian. "Enjoying God's Death: *The Passion of the Christ* and the Practices of an Evangelical Public." *Quarterly Journal of Speech* 95 (2009): 387–411.

———. "Evangelical Economies of Violence and the Politics of Imaginary Publics." PhD diss., Northwestern University, 2006.

———. *Lacan in Public: Psychoanalysis and the Science of Rhetoric*. Tuscaloosa: University of Alabama Press, 2012.

Lutzer, Erwin W. *Pastor to Pastor: Tackling the Problems of Ministry*. Grand Rapids, MI: Kregel, 1998.

Machen, J. Gresham. *Christianity and Liberalism*. 1923. Reprint, Grand Rapids, MI: Eerdmans, 1983.

Maddux, Kristy. *The Faithful Citizen: Popular Christian Media and Gendered Civic Identities*. Waco, TX: Baylor University Press, 2010.

Madison, James H. "Reformers and the Rural Church, 1900–1950." *Journal of American History* 73 (1986): 645–68.

Manson, Marilyn, and Neil Strauss. *The Long Hard Road out of Hell*. New York: ReganBooks, 1998.

"Manual Labor Institutions." *Vermont Chronicle*, December 7, 1832.

Marsden, George M. *Fundamentalism and American Culture*. 2nd ed. New York: Oxford University Press, 2006.

———. *Jonathan Edwards: A Life*. New Haven, CT: Yale University Press, 2003.

———. *Understanding Fundamentalism and Evangelicalism*. Grand Rapids, MI: Eerdmans, 1991.

Martin, Howard H. "Puritan Preachers on Preaching: Notes on American Colonial Rhetoric." *Quarterly Journal of Speech* 50 (1964): 285–92.

Marty, Martin E. *Modern American Religion*. Vol. 1, *The Irony of It All, 1893–1919*. Chicago: University of Chicago Press, 1986.

Mason, H. Norton. *The National Council of Churches of Christ in the U.S.A.: An Appraisal of Its Origin and Present Direction*. Victoria, TX: Foundation for Christian Theology, 1967.

Matthews, Mark. "The Doctrine of Our Lord's Return," In *Light on Prophecy: A Coordinated, Constructive Teaching, Being the Proceedings and Addresses at the Philadelphia Prophetic Conference, May 28–30*. New York: The Christian Herald, 1918.

Mauro, Philip. "Modern Philosophy." In *The Fundamentals*, vol. 2. Chicago: Testimony Publishing, 1910–15.

McAlister, Melani. "Prophecy, Politics and the Popular: The *Left Behind* Series and Christian Fundamentalism's New World Order." *South Atlantic Quarterly* 102 (2003): 773–98.

McClellan, Ruth. *An Incredible Journey: Thomas Road Baptist Church and 50 Years of Miracles*. Lynchburg, VA: Liberty University, 2006.

McFarland, Charles S. "The Social Program of the Federal Council of the Churches of Christ in America." *Proceedings of the Academy of Political Science in the City of New York* 2 (1912): 175.

McGavran, Donald. *The Bridges of God: A Study in the Strategy of Missions*. New York: Friendship Press, 1955.

McGee, Michael Calvin. "The 'Ideograph': A Link between Rhetoric and Ideology." *Quarterly Journal of Speech* 66 (1980): 1–16.

McIntire, Carl. *Modern Tower of Babel*. Collingswood, NJ: Christian Beacon Press, 1949.

McIntosh, Gary L. "Introduction: Why Church Growth Can't Be Ignored." In *Evaluating the Church Growth Movement*, ed. Gary L. McIntosh. Grand Rapids, MI: Zondervan, 2004.

Miller, Donald E. *Reinventing American Protestantism*. Berkeley: University of California Press, 1999.

Miller, Perry. *The New England Mind: From Colony to Province*. Cambridge, MA: Harvard University Press, 1953.

———. *The New England Mind: The Seventeenth Century*. New York: Macmillan, 1939.

Mitchell, W. J. T. "Introduction." In *Landscape and Power*, ed. W. J. T. Mitchell. Chicago: University of Chicago Press, 2002.

Moen, Matthew. *The Transformation of the Christian Right*. Tuscaloosa: University of Alabama Press, 1992.

Moore, Randy. "Creationism in the United States II: The Aftermath of the Scopes Trial." *American Biology Teacher* 60 (1998): 568–77.

Moorhead, James H. "Apocalypticism in Mainstream Protestantism, 1800 to Present." In *The Encyclopedia of Apocalypticism*, vol. 3, *Apocalypticism in the Modern Period and the Contemporary Age*, ed. Stephen J. Stein. New York: Continuum, 2001.

"Moral: Rev. J. R. M'Dowell." *The Liberator*, January 12, 1833.

Mott, John R. *The Evangelization of the World in This Generation*. New York: Student Volunteer Movement for Foreign Missions, 1901.

Mouffe, Chantal. "Religion, Liberal Democracy, and Citizenship." In *Political Theologies: Public Religions in a Post-Secular World*, ed. Hent de Vries and Lawrence E. Sullivan, 318–26. New York: Fordham University Press, 2006.

Murch, James DeForest. *The Growing Super-Church: A Critique of the National Council of Churches*. N.p.: National Association of Evangelicals, 1952.

———. "The Spirit of the Antichrist." *United Evangelical Action*, December 1, 1945.

———. "Why Evangelicals Cannot Co-operate in the FCCCA." *United Evangelical Action*, September 15, 1946.

Murphy, John M. "'A Time of Shame and Sorrow': Robert F. Kennedy and the American Jeremiad." *Quarterly Journal of Speech* 76 (1990): 401–14.

Newbigin, Lesslie. *Church Growth Bulletin*, September 1966.

Niebuhr, R. Gustav. "Mighty Fortresses: Megachurches Strive to Be All Things to All Parishioners." *Wall Street Journal*, May 13, 1991.

Northrup, George W. "Address of the President." In *American Baptist Missionary Union: Seventy-Seventh Annual Report with the Proceedings of the Annual Meeting Held in Cincinnati, Ohio* (Boston: Missionary Rooms, 1891).

O'Leary, Stephen D. *Arguing the Apocalypse: A Theory of Millennial Rhetoric*. New York: Oxford University Press, 1994.

———. "A Dramatistic Theory of Apocalyptic Rhetoric." *Quarterly Journal of Speech* 79 (1993): 385–426.

O'Leary, Stephen, and Michael McFarland. "The Political Use of Mythic Discourse: Prophetic Interpretation in Pat Robertson's Presidential Campaign." *Quarterly Journal of Speech* 75 (1989): 433–52.

"Omaha Platform." In *The Encyclopedia of Social Reform*, ed. William D. P. Bliss. New York: Funk and Wagnalls Co., 1897.

The Omega Code. Directed by Robert Marcarelli. Providence Entertainment, 1999.

Ortega y Gasset, José. *Man and People*. Translated by William R. Trask. New York: Norton, 1957.

Oshatz, Molly. *Slavery and Sin: The Fight against Slavery and the Rise of Liberal Protestantism*. New York: Oxford University Press, 2012.

Parry-Giles, Trevor. "Ideology and Poetics in Public Issue Construction: Thatcherism, Civil Liberties, and 'Terrorism' in Northern Ireland." *Communication Quarterly* 43 (1995): 182–96.

Payne, J. Barton. "Higher Criticism and Biblical Inerrancy." In *Inerrancy*, ed. Norman L. Geisler, 83–113. Grand Rapids, MI: Zondervan, 1980.

Perkins, Ephraim. "A 'Bunker Hill' Contest, A.D. 1826, Between the 'Holy Alliance' for the Establishment of Heirarchy [*sic*], and Ecclesiastical

Domination Over the Human Mind, on the One Side; and the Asserters of Free Inquiry, Bible Religion, Christian Freedom, and Civil Liberty on the Other. The Rev. Charles Finney, 'Home Missionary,' and High Priest of the Expeditions of the Alliance in the Interior of New York; Head Quarters, County of Oneida." 1826. Reprint, *Christian Examiner and Theological Review*, May 1, 1827.

Pezzullo, Phaedra C. "Resisting 'National Breast Cancer Awareness Month': The Rhetoric of Counterpublics and Their Cultural Performances." *Quarterly Journal of Speech* 89 (2003): 345–65.

Phelps, Austin. "Introduction." In *Our Country: Its Possible Future and Its Present Crisis*, by Josiah Strong. New York: Baker and Taylor, 1891.

Piper, John F. "The American Churches in World War I." *Journal of the American Academy of Religion* 38 (1970): 147–55.

Pocock, J. G. A. *Politics, Language, and Time: Essays on Political Thought and History*. Chicago: University of Chicago Press, 1989.

"Presbyterians Reject Federal Council Mission Membership." *United Evangelical Action*, July 1, 1943.

Pritchard, Gregory A. *The Strategy of Willow Creek Community Church: A Study in the Sociology of Religion*. PhD diss., Northwestern University, 1994.

———. *Willow Creek Seeker Services: Evaluating a New Way of Doing Church*. Grand Rapids, MI: Baker Books, 1996.

The Prodigal Planet. Directed by Donald W. Thompson. Des Moines, IA: Mark IV Pictures, 1983.

"Protestantism Shows Gains in New Survey." *United Evangelical Action*, July 15, 1950.

Rable, George C. *God's Almost Chosen Peoples: A Religious History of the American Civil War*. Chapel Hill: University of North Carolina Press, 2010.

Rauschenbusch, Walter. *A Theology for the Social Gospel*. New York: Macmillan Co., 1922.

Ray, Angela. *The Lyceum and Public Culture in the Nineteenth-Century United States*. East Lansing: Michigan State University Press, 2005.

"Report of World Conference on the Fundamentals of the Faith." *School and Church*, July–September 1919.

"Rev. C. G. Finne [*sic*]." *New-York Spectator*, July 24, 1834.

"Rev. C. G. Finney." *Ohio Observer*, November 27, 1834.

Ricoeur, Paul. "Imagination in Discourse and Action." In *Rethinking Imagination: Culture and Creativity*, ed. Gillian Robinson and John Rundell. London: Routledge, 1994.

———. *From Text to Action: Essays in Hermeneutics, II*. Translated by Kathleen Blarney and John B. Thompson. London: Continuum, 2008.

———. *Time and Narrative*. Vol. 1. Translated by Kathleen McLaughlin and David Pellauer. Chicago: University of Chicago Press, 1984.

Riley, W. B. "The Christian Fundamentals Movement, Its Battles, Its Achievements, Its Certain Victory." *Christian Fundamentals in School and Church*, October–December 1922.

———. "The Conflict of Christianity and Its Counterfeit." *Christian Fundamentals in School and Church*, July–September 1921.

———. "Dr. W. B. Riley Endorses the Fort Wayne Gospel Temple, Its Pastor, and Tabernacle Movement." *Fort Wayne Gospel Temple*, May 24, 1940.

———. *The Evolution of the Kingdom*. New York: Chas. C. Cook, 1913.

———. "The Gospel for War Times." In *Light on Prophecy: A Coordinated, Constructive Teaching, Being the Proceedings and Addresses at the Philadelphia Prophetic Conference, May 28–30*. New York: Christian Herald, 1918.

———. "The Great Divide or Christ and the Present Crisis." *School and Church*, July–September 1919.

———. "The Interchurch World Movement." *School and Church*, April–June 1920.

———. *The Menace of Modernism*. New York: Christian Alliance, 1917.

———. "The World Premillennial Conference vs. the Coming Confederacy." *School and Church*, January–March 1919.

"Riots and Continued Disturbances of the Peace." *United States' Telegraph*, July 14, 1834.

"Riots in New York." *Ohio Observer*, July 24, 1834.

Ritivoi, Andreea Deciu. *Paul Ricoeur: Tradition and Innovation in Rhetorical Theory*. Albany: State University of New York Press, 2006.

Ritter, Kurt W. "American Political Rhetoric and the Jeremiad Tradition: Presidential Nomination Acceptance Addresses, 1960–1976." *Central States Speech Journal* 31 (1980): 153–71.

Rodgers, Marion Elizabeth. *Mencken: The American Iconoclast*. New York: Oxford University Press, 2005.

"Row at the Chatham Street Chapel." *Providence Patriot, Columbian Phoenix*, July 12, 1834.

Ruotsila, Markku. *Origins of Christian Anti-Internationalism: Conservative Evangelicals and the League of Nations*. Washington, DC: Georgetown University Press, 2008.

"Sacred Music." *New-York Spectator*, April 29, 1833.

Sandeen, Ernest R. "The Princeton Theology: One Source of Biblical Literalism in American Protestantism." *Church History* 31 (1962): 307–21.

———. *The Roots of Fundamentalism: British and American Millenarianism: 1800–1930*. Chicago: University of Chicago Press, 1970.

Sargeant, Kimon Howland. *Seeker Churches: Promoting Traditional Religion in a Nontraditional Way*. New Brunswick, NJ: Rutgers University Press, 2000.

Schaller, Lyle. *The Seven-Day-a-Week Church*. Nashville, TN: Abingdon Press, 1992.

Scharf, John Thomas, and Thompson Westcott. *History of Philadelphia, 1609–1884*. Vol. 2. Philadelphia: L. H. Everts & Co., 1884.

Schneider, Robert A. "Voice of Many Waters: Church Federation in the Twentieth Century." In *Between the Times: The Travail of the Protestant Establishment in America, 1900–1960*, ed. William R. Hutchison. Cambridge: Cambridge University Press, 1989.

Schultze, Quentin J. *Christianity and the Mass Media in America: Toward a Democratic Accommodation*. East Lansing: Michigan State University Press, 2003.

Scofield, C. I. *The Scofield Reference Bible: The Holy Bible, Containing the Old and New Testaments: Authorized Version, with a New System of Connected Topical References to All the Greater Themes of Scripture, with Annotations, Revised Marginal Renderings, Summaries, Definitions, and Index: To Which Are Added Helps at Hard Places, Explanations of Seeming Discrepancies, and a New System of Paragraphs*. New York: Oxford University Press, 1909.

"Senator DeMint to Brody File: Tea Party Movement Will Bring On 'Spiritual Revival.'" *The Brody File: CBN News Blogs*, April 21, 2010. Http://blogs.cbn.com/thebrodyfile/archive/2010/04/21/senator-demint-to-brody-file-tea-party-movement-will-bring.aspx.

Shorris, Earl. *The Politics of Heaven: America in Fearful Times*. New York: Norton, 2007.

Shuck, Glenn W. *Marks of the Beast: The Left Behind Novels and the Struggle for Evangelical Identity*. New York: New York University Press, 2005.

Skocpol, Theda, and Vanessa Williamson. *The Tea Party and the Remaking of Republican Conservatism*. New York: Oxford University Press, 2012.

Smillie, Dirk. *Falwell Inc.: Inside a Religious, Political, Educational, and Business Empire*. New York: St. Martin's Press, 2008.

Smith, Oswald J. "Ecclesiastical Babylon." Editorial. *United Evangelical Action*, June 15, 1947.

"Southern Presbyterians and the Interchurch Movement." *Herald and Presbyter* 91 (1920): 4–5.

Stout, Harry S. *The New England Soul: Preaching and Religious Culture in Colonial New England*. New York: Oxford University Press, 1986.

Strobel, Lee. *Inside the Mind of Unchurched Harry and Mary: How to Reach Friends and Family Who Avoid God and the Church*. Grand Rapids, MI: Zondervan, 1993.

Strong, Josiah. *Our Country: Its Possible Future and Its Present Crisis*. New York: Baker and Taylor, 1891.

"Superchurch." *Time* magazine, December 1, 1975.

Szasz, Ferenc Morton. *The Divided Mind of Protestant America, 1880–1930*. Tuscaloosa: University of Alabama Press, 1982.

Tappan, Lewis. "History of the Free Churches in the City of New York." In *A Narrative of the Visit to the American Churches by the Deputation from the Congregational Union of England and Wales*, vol. 2, by Andrew Reed and James Matheson. London: Jackson and Walford, 1835.

———. "Riot at Chatham-Street Chapel." *The Liberator*, July 12, 1834.

Taylor, Charles. *Modern Social Imaginaries*. Durham, NC: Duke University Press, 2004.

———. *A Secular Age*. Cambridge, MA: Belknap Press, 2007.

A Thief in the Night. Directed by Donald W. Thompson. Des Moines, IA: Mark IV Pictures, 1972.

"Three Chapters on Religion: Chapter II: Class of the Fundamentalists." *Catholic Telegraph*, May 7, 1842.

"Three Chapters on Religion: Introduction, Chapter I: Class of Indifference." *Catholic Telegraph*, April 30, 1842.

Tippy, Worth. "Social Work of the Federal Council of Churches." *Journal of Social Forces* 1 (1922): 36–38.

Towns, Elmer L. *The Ten Largest Sunday Schools and What Makes Them Grow*. Grand Rapids, MI: Baker Book House, 1969.

Towns, Elmer, and Jerry Falwell. *Capturing a Town for Christ*. Old Tappan, NJ: Fleming H. Revell, 1973.

Trollinger Jr., William Vance. *God's Empire: William Bell Riley and Midwestern Fundamentalism*. Madison: University of Wisconsin Press, 1990.

Tucker, Ruth A. *Left Behind in a Megachurch World: How God Works through Ordinary Churches*. Grand Rapids, MI: Baker Books, 2006.

Twitchell, James B. *Branded Nation: The Marketing of Megachurch, College Inc., and Museumworld*. New York: Simon & Schuster, 2004.

Van Biema, David. "The Color of Faith." *Time* magazine, January 11, 2010.

VanderWerf, Nathan H. *The Times Were Very Full: A Perspective on the First 25 Years of the National Council of the Churches of Christ in the United States of America, 1950–1975*. New York: National Council of the Churches of Christ in the United States of America, 1976.

"Vanishing Fundamentalism," *Christian Century*, June 24, 1926.

Vásquez, Mark. *Authority and Reform: Religious and Educational Discourses in Nineteenth-Century New England Literature*. Knoxville: University of Tennessee Press, 2003.

Vaughan, John N. *The World's Twenty Largest Churches*. Grand Rapids, MI: Baker Book House, 1984.

Wadsworth, Nancy D. "Ambivalent Miracles: The Possibilities and Limits of Evangelical Racial Reconciliation Politics." In *Faith and Race in American Political Life*, ed. Robin Dale Jacobsen and Nancy D. Wadsworth. Charlottesville: University of Virginia Press, 2012.

Walzer, Michael. *The Revolution of the Saints: A Study in the Origins of Radical Politics*. Cambridge, MA: Harvard University Press, 1965.

Ward, Harry F. *The Social Creed of the Churches*. New York: Abingdon Press, 1914.

Ward, Susan Hayes. *The History of the Broadway Tabernacle Church, from Its Organization in 1840*. New York: Trow Print, 1901.

Warner, Michael. *Publics and Counterpublics*. New York: Zone Books, 2002.

Warner, R. Stephen. "Theoretical Barriers to the Understanding of Evangelical Christianity." *Sociological Analysis* 40 (1979): 1–9.

Weber, Max. *The Theory of Social and Economic Organization*, ed. Talcott Parsons. 1947. Reprint, New York: Free Press, 1964.

Weber, Timothy P. "The Two-Edged Sword: The Fundamentalist Use of the Bible." In *The Bible in America: Essays in Cultural History*, ed. Nathan O. Hatch and Mark A. Noll, 101–20. New York: Oxford University Press, 1982.

Whately, Richard. *Elements of Rhetoric: Comprising the Substance of the Article in the Encyclopaedia Metropolitana with Additions*. Boston: Munroe, 1852.

"What Willow Believes." *Willow Creek Community Church*. Http://www.willowcreek.org.

Wicker, Christine. *The Fall of the Evangelical Nation: The Surprising Crisis inside the Church*. New York: HarperOne, 2008.

Wilcox, Clyde. *God's Warriors: The Christian Right in Twentieth-Century America*. Baltimore, MD: Johns Hopkins University Press, 1992.

Wilson, Stephen G. *Leaving the Fold: Apostates and Defectors in Antiquity*. Minneapolis: Fortress Press, 2004.

Winkler, Carol K. *In the Name of Terrorism: Presidents on Political Violence in the Post–World War II Era*. New York: State University of New York Press, 2006.

Winter, Ralph D. "Polygamy: Rules and Practices." *Church Growth Bulletin*, March 1969.

Wolffe, John. *The Expansion of Evangelicalism: The Age of Wilberforce, More, Chalmers and Finney*. Downers Grove, IL: InterVarsity Press, 2007.

Wolterstorff, Nicholas. "The Role of Religion in Decision and Discussion of Political Issues." In *Religion in the Public Square: The Place of Religious*

Convictions in Political Debate, by Robert Audi and Nicholas Wolterstorff. Lanham, MD: Rowman and Littlefield, 1997.
Working Together through the National Council of Churches. New York: National Council of Churches, 1957.
Wright Jr., E. "Letter from Professor Wright." *The Liberator*, June 29, 1833.
Wright, J. Elwin. "The Federal Council Prepares the Way for Coming World Church." *United Evangelical Action*, March 1943.
Zarefsky, David. *President Johnson's War on Poverty: Rhetoric and History*. Tuscaloosa: University of Alabama Press, 1986.
———. "Rhetorical Interpretations of the American Civil War." *Quarterly Journal of Speech* 81 (1995): 108–38.
Zietsma, David. "Building the Kingdom of God: Religious Discourse, National Identity, and the Good Neighbor Policy, 1930–1938." *Rhetoric and Public Affairs* 11 (2008): 179–214.

Index

⌘

A

D

E

O

P

R

S